Environments and Livelihoods

Strategies for Sustainability

Koos Neefjes

Oxfam

First published by Oxfam GB in 2000   ISBN 0 85598 440 6 (paperback)
© Oxfam GB 2000   ISBN 0 85598 460 0 (hardback)

A catalogue record for this publication is available from the British Library.

Available from the following agents:

USA: Stylus Publishing LLC, PO Box 605, Herndon, VA 20172-0605, USA
tel: +1 (0)703 661 1581; fax: + 1(0)703 661 1547; email: styluspub@aol.com
Canada: Fernwood Books Ltd, PO Box 9409, Stn. 'A', Halifax, N.S. B3K 5S3, Canada
tel: +1 (0)902 422 3302; fax: +1 (0)902 422 3179; e-mail: fernwood@istar.ca
India: Maya Publishers Pvt Ltd, 113-B, Shapur Jat, New Delhi-110049, India
tel: +91 (0)11 649 4850; fax: +91 (0)11 649 1039; email: surit@del2.vsnl.net.in
K Krishnamurthy, 23 Thanikachalan Road, Madras 600017, India
tel: +91 (0)44 434 4519; fax: +91 (0)44 434 2009; email: ksm@md2.vsnl.net.in
South Africa, Zimbabwe, Botswana, Lesotho, Namibia, Swaziland: David Philip Publishers, PO Box 23408, Claremont 7735, South Africa
tel: +27 (0)21 674 4136; fax: +27(0)21 64 3358; email: dppsales@iafrica.com
Tanzania: Mkuki na Nyota Publishers, PO Box 4246, Dar es Salaam, Tanzania
tel/fax: +255 (0)51 180479, email: mkuki@ud.co.tz
Australia: Bush Books, PO Box 1958, Gosford, NSW 2250, Australia
tel: +61 (0)2 043 233 274; fax: +61 (0)2 092 122 468, email: bushbook@ozemail.com.au

Rest of the world: contact Oxfam Publishing, 274 Banbury Road, Oxford OX2 7DZ, UK.
tel. +44 (0)1865 311 311; fax +44 (0)1865 313 925; email publish@oxfam.org.uk

Printed by Redwood Books, Trowbridge

Oxfam GB is a registered charity, no. 202 918, and is a member of Oxfam International.

Contents

Acknowledgements v

Glossary ix

1   Introduction 1

2   Reflections on poverty, environment, and development 10
A short history of environment and environmentalism 10
Theories of people–environment relations 20
Questions of vulnerability 31
Questions of sustainability 41

3   Improving livelihoods 58
Sustaining livelihoods and environments: lessons from practice 59
The sustainable livelihoods framework 80
Negotiating change 98

4   Project management and environmental sustainability 113
Environmental Impact Assessment: large-scale projects 115
Environmental Impact Assessment of community development projects 124
Projects, participation, and the sustainability of livelihoods 140

5   Policies and strategies for sustainable development 160
Planning for sustainable development 161
National policies and campaigns for sustainable development 177
Global environmental policy and campaigning 196

Appendix 1
Selected international agreements on the environment 217

Appendix 2
Sources of information on environment and development 221

Notes 229

Bibliography 248

Index 264

Figures

3.1: The sustainable livelihoods framework 83

3.2: Basic aspects of participatory learning and action 105

4.1: The project cycle 114

4.2: The project cycle and Environmental Impact Assessment 116

4.3: Outline of the 'Leopold matrix' for the scoping of environmental impact 118

4.4: Participatory Environmental Assessment 143

5.1: Developing strategic, medium-term plans 169

Tables

2.1: A typology of disasters 32

3.1: Livelihood capitals and capital substitution 88

3.2: Practical methods of livelihoods analysis 96

4.1: Environmental measures in refugee responses (UNHCR) 136

4.2: Sectoral activities to reduce the negative environmental impact of refugees 137

4.3: Sphere Project: examples of agreed minimum standards for emergency relief 141

5.1: Environmental Profile: sample outline 164

5.2: A comparison of Strategic Environmental Assessment (SEA) and Environmental Impact Assessment (EIA) 166

5.3: The sustainable livelihoods framework and categories of indicators of sustainable development 175

5.4: Food security and the genetic modification of crops 186

Acknowledgements

This book is the result of many people's experiences and efforts to explore the importance of 'the environment' to poverty-related work. It is impossible to mention all those whose insights have made a contribution: colleagues, farmers, citizens of poor urban neighbourhoods, pastoralists, refugees, government officials, researchers, and development workers in national and international non-government organisations. I want to thank some of them individually, however, because of their particular contributions to the project that delivered this book.

The book draws on experience that has accumulated in Oxfam GB and its national partners, and also in the Intermediate Technology Development Group (ITDG), ActionAid, and Novib (based in The Netherlands). Some of the staff of the three UK-based NGOs took part in a workshop to discuss the book's outline and a workshop to discuss the first draft. Several years ago, Andrew Scott of ITDG initiated the idea of a guide for improving the environmental impact of small-scale and community-based development projects; he continued to support and advise the project as its objectives and structure evolved. Andrew gave us access to case material and documentation from ITDG, to which the book bears witness. Irene Dankelman (formerly of Novib) commented constructively, as ever, at several stages, and Harrie Oppenoorth (her successor) also read the first draft and shared his ideas. Laura Kelly of ActionAid took part in the first workshop and shared her knowledge of her agency's environmental policies. Her colleague Ros David had the idea of holding the workshops in the first place, and commented very helpfully on the draft in the second workshop. To work with Ros when she was still employed by Oxfam GB was always an inspiring experience.

Ian Scoones of IDS (University of Sussex) and Ross Hughes of IIED were also involved at the conceptual stage of the project, and Ian later became a key adviser in the two workshops. His knowledge, analysis, and creative suggestions were invaluable. Phil Woodhouse of IDPM (University of Manchester) commented extremely usefully on an article that prefigured part of the argument of this book, and also became a key adviser.

I thank the Environment Policy Department of the British government's Department for International Development (DFID) for funding an important part of the project. Dougie Brew made constructive comments at several stages of the project and shared useful materials. Julie Thomas participated in the workshops and made comments. Detailed and extremely helpful comments on the draft were also received from Arjan de Haan and Izabella Koziel (of both DFID and IIED). I was myself a member of the so-called Sustainable Rural Livelihoods Committee of DFID, which was chaired by Michael Scott and facilitated mainly by Diana Carney (formerly of ODI). The work of the committee, as written up by Diana, is clearly reflected in this book, although I have given it a personal flavour. Michael supported the book by enabling others to comment in detail, and Diana made comments on the draft.

Caroline Ashley (ODI), Karen Brock (IDS), and John Rowley (formerly of Oxfam GB) all made very valuable comments on the outline and led me towards useful materials. Naresh Singh of UNDP commented on the draft and, although I was unable to adopt all his suggestions for reasons of time, made me rethink and alter many parts of the book. Anne Grant of Green Cross UK commented on the parts that relate to environmental disasters and emergencies. Those sections are strongly based on materials and insights that I gathered through working with her and her colleagues.

At Oxfam, Sophie Bond's support was critical for the successful conclusion of this project. She edited case studies that were published in the fourth edition of Oxfam's internal publication 'Exchanging Livelihoods' and are cited in this book, wrote drafts of the appendices, helped to organise the workshops and the consultancy for one of the case studies, and brought together the overview of Oxfam's expenditure and breadth of involvement in the field of natural-resource management. She also did much of the literature search for this book. Abraham Woldegiorgis did most of the work on a survey of the impact — on Oxfam staff, some partners, officials, and members of deprived communities — of training in environmental impact assessment, sustainable livelihoods, and participatory methodologies. He also helped in other ways. It was a great pleasure to work closely with Sophie and Abraham for six months.

Oxfam Library staff, especially Joan Turner and Ros Buck, helped us to find books and buy books, and they allowed me to return some borrowed books long after they were due. Lynne Perry and Alison Farrell helped with the logistical arrangements for workshops and drafts. Other colleagues of

Oxfam's (former) Gender and Learning Team and the rest of the Policy Department helped with ideas and comments on sections of the text, and above all with moral support to continue. Margaret Newens, as my interim manager, encouraged me to set up the research and initiate the book, and Chris Roche challenged me as always to prioritise and focus when I got distracted by competing commitments. I have learned a great deal from his work on impact assessment, and he made extremely perceptive comments at the final stages of the writing. Fifa Stubbs, at that time the manager of the Oxfam programme in Central America and the Caribbean and formerly on the staff of the South-South Environment Linking Project, helped me to access materials and take part (several years ago) in two important meetings of Central American NGOs on environment and poverty. She commented on both the contents and the style of an early draft of the book. Richard Luff critically read the sections on disasters and emergencies in the first draft.

To complement Abraham's work on assessing the impact of training for programme staff, I interviewed a number of Oxfam managers in order to get a clearer idea about the importance of sustainable development in formulating programme strategies. That was extremely helpful and took the valuable time of Abhijit Bhattacharjee, Ian Leggett, Brenda Lipson, Paul Valentin, Tony Vaux, and Liz Gascoigne. Dan Mullins also provided his ideas and helped with references to materials on sustainable livelihoods. Working with him in Mozambique on several visits since 1994 was always a pleasure and a learning experience for me. The programme that he used to manage in Niassa, Mozambique, was selected for one of the special reviews that are highlighted as case studies in the book. In that programme it was Jowett Ndoro and Jenny Yates in particular who provided critical insights and practical support for the review, and also other staff, including Manel dos Santos Almeida, with whom I worked on all my visits since 1994. Thoko Fuyane was the main reporter for subsequent monitoring, and throughout I received support from the Oxfam Country Representative, Kate Horne.

A second programme review was done in Lung Vai, Vietnam, where the most important colleague with whom I worked was Do Thanh Lam; his critical analysis of the situation and also of the methodology that we used was extremely constructive. With Nguyen Quynh Trang and some specially contracted researchers, we interviewed numerous villagers and officials. This programme review was supported by other Oxfam colleagues in Vietnam also, including the Country Representative, Heather Grady.

The third case study was expertly conducted in Brazil by Silvio Caccia Bava, who interviewed many NGO staff in Recife. The case study was carried out through the facilitation of Edien Pantoja and Guillermo Rogel of the Oxfam Recife team.

I also want to thank my friends Elizabeth English, Koenraad Van Brabant, and Barry Coates for continuous encouragement and suggestions on some aspects of the text. And of course Catherine Robinson, of Oxfam Publishing, for her critical thinking, helpful suggestions, enthusiasm, and very professional editing.

I do not know how to thank Dung enough for her encouragement, support, critical reading, ideas, and endurance when I was locked away and working obsessively on my computer in Oxford, London, and Hanoi.

Finally, I must state the obvious: that mistakes made and opinions expressed in this book are mine alone.

Koos Neefjes

A note from the Department for International Development

This publication is an output from a research project part-funded by the United Kingdom Department for International Development (DFID) for the benefit of developing countries. The views expressed are not necessarily those of the UK Government.

Glossary and meanings of acronyms

ActionAid	British international development NGO
AoA	Agreement on Agriculture (of the WTO)
BCA	benefit–cost analysis
CARE	international development NGO, centrally based in the USA
CSD	Commission on Sustainable Development
DFID	Department for International Development (UK government department)
EIA	Environmental Impact Assessment
ENSO	El Niño Southern Oscillation effect
EOC	Environmental Overview of Country Programme (also EOP; of UNDP)
EU	European Union
FAO	United Nations Food and Agriculture Organisation
GATT	General Agreement on Tariffs and Trade (evolved into the WTO in 1995)
GED	gender, environment, and development
GIS	geographic information systems
GM crops	genetically modified crops
GNP	gross national product
HYV	high-yielding variety
IBRD	International Bank for Reconstruction and Development (World Bank)
IIED	International Institute for Environment and Development (London)

ITDG	Intermediate Technology Development Group (UK-based international development NGO)
IUCN	International Union for the Conservation of Nature (World Conservation Union)
LDCs	Least Developed Countries
LEISA	low-external-input sustainable agriculture
NCSs	national conservation strategies
NEAPs	National Environmental Management Action Plans (also known as NEMAPs)
NFIDCs	Net Food-Importing Developing Countries
NGO	non-government organisation
Novib	Dutch international development NGO, member of Oxfam International
NSSDs	National Strategies for Sustainable Development
Oxfam GB	(referred to as 'Oxfam' in this text) international development NGO, based in Great Britain, member of Oxfam International
PEC	Primary Environmental Care
PLA	Participatory Learning and Action (also known as PRA)
PRA	Participatory Rural Appraisal (also known as PLA or RRA)
RRA	Rapid Rural Appraisal (also known as PRA)
S&W	strengths and weaknesses
TRIPS	Trade Related Intellectual Property Rights
SEA	Strategic Environmental Assessment
WTO	World Trade Organisation
WWF	World Wide Fund for Nature (also known as World Wildlife Fund)
UNCED	UN Conference on Environment and Development (1992 in Rio de Janeiro; also known as the Earth Summit)
UNHCR	United Nations High Commissioner for Refugees
UNDP	United Nations Development Programme
UNEP	United Nations Environment Programme
WCED	World Commission on Environment and Development (also known as the Brundtland Commission)

1

Introduction

This book is based on the experience of a range of national and international non-government organisations (NGOs) that have spent several years exploring the interdependency between environmental change and poverty alleviation. It draws on a number of case-histories from Asia, Africa, and Latin America, and also on theoretical work by academics with strong links to development practice. It is a book for development professionals – for those engaged in helping to improve the plight of poor, deprived, excluded, or oppressed people. It aims to enhance their learning in the field of environment and development, or sustainable development in practice.

This first chapter explains briefly what the book is about. It defines environment and livelihoods, and highlights some of the main reasons why it was written.

People and environments

Environments are contested. Different people see them differently, have different interests in them, and have different relationships with them. In September 1992 a meeting in Managua of representatives of NGOs and grassroots groups from Central America discussed the meaning of environment, and produced the following:

Environment is both Nature and Society, which relate to each other and coexist. In the environment we find forests, human beings, land, mountains, water, air, animals, etc., which are mutually inter-relating. This relationship can be good or bad. It is good when human beings can make adequate use of other environmental components, like water, forest, and air. It is bad when humankind has destroyed them (for example with deforestation), or when a few people appropriate resources and thus endanger our survival and reproduction. That is why we need conservation, equity between human beings, and harmony between human beings and Nature. [1]

People depend on environmental resources – and deprived, excluded, or poor communities, both rural and urban, particularly so. The statement quoted above does not stress the exploitation of resources or (economic) growth: it emphasises equality instead. It talks of harmony between people and nature, and, significantly, of a whole entity and of connections between the parts that make up that whole: the definition incorporates connections between social development and natural-resource conservation.

It is striking that the participants at the meeting separated 'nature' from 'society': in other words, they saw people as different from their natural environments. That is not a universal view, for some belief systems hold that people are as 'natural' as plants or rocks. In fact, in some religious traditions the concept of 'nature' is similar to the notion of God in others. However, the participants stressed the interrelationship between nature and society and expressed a high level of concern for environmental resources, which suggests that they regarded environments as more than merely useful resources that might be controlled and exploited. They suggested that humanity has responsibilities for the relationship between society and nature, and (implicitly) responsibilities for the future of the natural environment and for future generations of people.

This definition of 'environment' includes people and their relationships and the natural world within one whole entity, called environment. For some, this concept is unhelpful or unnecessarily complicated. Dictionaries usually define environment as 'surroundings of human beings', and thus exclude people from environment. Indeed, many people who use the word 'environment' exclude themselves and others from that notion, consciously or subconsciously. The use of the word in development circles has, however, broadened its meaning, and it has now come very close to the definition agreed by the participants in the meeting in Managua.

This book argues that it is useful to think of environment broadly, and to include people and social relationships. 'Environment' thus becomes a vehicle for analysing and describing relationships between people and their surroundings, now and in the future. Nevertheless, the word is used in several places in its narrower meaning of 'surroundings', in particular when I speak of environments in the plural – and the context will make that clear. Nature can be seen as both broader and narrower than mere natural resources: it encompasses life (including human life) and thus could involve relationships between human beings too. In this text, 'nature' will be used to denote something separate from society and social relations, unless otherwise stated. Nature is something both rural and urban, contrary to popular perception: few people who 'seek communion with nature' expect to find it on the street corner of an inner city. However, air, water, and (for example) earthquakes are obviously important to the survival of human settlements, and none of those is created by people.

Poor, excluded, or deprived people often depend on their environments for survival, and sometimes they fall victim to environmental disasters. Some argue that poverty is an important cause of the global environmental crisis, and others argue that it is exactly the other way around: that environmental degradation, combined with a lack of environmental rights, is the main cause of poverty. True or untrue, much has been written on the relationships between poverty and environmental change, by development professionals, activists, and academics.[2]

The livelihood opportunities of poor, excluded, or deprived people are closely linked to questions of environmental sustainability, and looking at one without looking at the other does not make any sense. Different people have different interests, powers, and capabilities to improve their chances of survival and their livelihoods. Indeed, the concept of 'sustainable livelihoods' is central to this book, and is defined and explained in detail in chapter 3. 'Livelihoods' are also interpreted broadly, but are still primarily an expression of the material relationship between environments, people, and their social institutions.

A book about environments and livelihoods

Several lessons from NGO practice prompted the production of this book.

An unresolved question: why environment?

In the mandates of most development NGOs and national, bilateral, and multilateral development agencies, the eradication of poverty is central. Many also declare their support for 'sustainable development', and express their sympathy for environmental conservation of some sort. The debate about two-way links between poverty creation and environmental degradation has raged for some years now; it remains unresolved, even though academic work is progressing on theoretical frameworks, such as political ecology, that might help to settle it. The conviction that environmental change is important, no matter what the complexities or the precise nature of the relationship, has prompted agencies to develop appropriate policies. In particular from the late 1980s onwards, international donor agencies and thousands of their partners in low-income countries have searched for the positive links between poverty alleviation and environmental improvements or regeneration. They have developed policies and aims variously referred to as 'sustainable development', 'primary environmental care' (PEC),[3] 'sustainable livelihoods', and also 'sustainable land-use'.

These policies help to focus development programmes, and they support learning about the compatibility of the goals of poverty alleviation, (inter-generational) equality, and environmental care. However, internal assessments reveal that NGO staff have limited conceptual understanding of the complex links between poverty and environmental rights, degradation, and sustainability. These relationships require knowledge of climate change and trade relations, of socially differentiated resource use and resource degradation, of land-tenure relationships and demographic change, and much more. The question *Why is environment important in poverty alleviation?* remains, if only because these matters are complex.[4] Furthermore, evidence suggests that it is becoming more important than ever to understand and manage environmental change-processes in attempts to overcome poverty, for example because of the impacts on poor and vulnerable people of climatic changes that are enhanced by the 'greenhouse effect', and also because of the dependency of poor people on ever-degrading biodiversity.

Strategic directions

The strategic plans of development agencies nowadays demonstrate a reasonable degree of coherence in relating environmental change-processes to the agencies' core mandate of poverty alleviation.[5] Nevertheless, in-depth interviews with senior managers reveal the following strategic issues to which more detailed attention must be paid.[6]

- Environmental factors are centrally important in drylands and other fragile rural livelihood contexts, in particular in relation to food production. In urban areas and displaced people's camps, sanitation, water supply, and housing are of central importance. Environmental factors imply risks and often play a critical part in disaster creation, leading, for example, to flooding and drought.

- Macro-policies such as multilateral trade agreements often have an impact on livelihoods, and indeed on the environmental resources on which livelihoods depend. This happens mainly through globally connected markets that are influenced by those policies. For example, extractive industries are expanding rapidly, with economic liberalisation and the increase of foreign investment in developing countries. Their investments and profits are driven by the demand of rich consumers, but local people living near mines suffer the consequences of destruction and pollution. Similarly, trade and investment policies affect food prices and agriculture, transport, and the energy sector, all with obvious environmental aspects and impacts on the livelihoods of poor people.

- Control over natural resources, in particular water and land, is a central issue in (local) conflicts, survival, and livelihood sustainability, particularly for the poorest women and ethnic minorities. Policy work and campaigning on food security and land tenure is often national, as is environmentalists' lobbying on pollution, consumption, dam building, mining, shrimp farming, and deforestation. This public-policy work should take account of political risks that might be entailed for local communities, who must be involved in the process.

- National and international development NGOs are not usually well linked into environmental movements, at a national or international level. However, environmental debates offer opportunities to lobby on poverty-related issues.

- More and better impact assessment is important for learning, for communicating success, and for advocacy. Assessing impacts on livelihoods and health must include assessing impacts on various environmental factors.

- We need more institutional learning on sustainability, i.e. environmental, social, economic, and institutional/organisational sustainability.

- Development agencies must consider vulnerability, coping mechanisms, and survival, as much as the sustainability of livelihoods.

It is not controversial to interpret these survey results as strong evidence of the need for support with strategy development, research, and institutional learning on the subject of poor people's livelihoods and environments.

Limited knowledge of impacts on environments and livelihoods

NGOs do not systematically consider the environmental impact of their activities beyond a very general level. In Oxfam GB, for example, which has made on average about two thousand grants per year over the past decade, the administration system requires a statement of the expected environmental impact to be made on every individual grant-application form – but without specifying what that means. Snap surveys between 1994 and 1999 suggest limited understanding of what is meant by 'environmental impact', and reveal that the relevant section of the form is often not completed, even in cases where environmental impacts can clearly be expected. This is despite the provision of training and some written guidance for 'front-line' staff and partner organisations.[7]

The actual environmental impact of small-scale and community-based projects, some years after their initiation, is rarely assessed. The impact of individual community-based projects is often assumed to be insignificant and to be generally positive. This is, however, not always the case, and, whether impacts are negative or positive, their cumulative effects can be significant. Information on impact is thus not often available, and is complicated by a lack of clarity about what environmental impacts can be, and how they relate to local people's livelihoods and poverty.

There is also evidence that a very high proportion of grants and projects of development NGOs relate to natural resources, for example to water supply and sanitation, agriculture, and housing, and in urban programmes also to garbage collection.[8] An increasing number of such projects make explicit reference to environmental regeneration, for example through sustainable agriculture practices. Anecdotal evidence from evaluation of single projects or project partners, or groups of projects and partner organisations, is encouraging in the sense that many projects do consider environmental aspects in relation to livelihoods, health, social relations, and resource rights, as much as they consider physical environmental features. Many examples will be given in this book. Nevertheless, the difficulties in comparing the plans (given their diversity and lack of data, as pointed out above), let alone the data that are produced in reviews, evaluations, and impact assessments, make it extremely difficult to aggregate environmental change, changes in rights to environmental resources, and improvements in livelihood sustainability at a level higher than that of the project.

Guidelines and NGO staff capacities

Guidelines do exist for incorporating environmental concerns into small-scale and participatory development projects, and there are many guidelines available for larger projects. For emergency-relief operations, the UNHCR has published environmental guidelines, and most development agencies, including national and international NGOs, provide staff with internal guidance for ensuring at least some consideration of environmental sustainability. Most of these materials are project-oriented, focus on *how to* improve practice, and ignore the question that is of strategic importance: *why environment?* They also fail to consider some practical tools that might be used, while emerging evidence suggests that, in fact, existing checklists and other guidelines are not often used. Furthermore, strategic shifts of many national and international NGOs towards policy-influencing work and disasters-related work demand different and better analytical tools and, especially, strengthened information systems and institutional learning processes. The latter requires participatory research and indicator development, and not just the application of sterile checklists.

Training of NGO staff in practical approaches and tools to improve understanding of the impacts of development on poor people's environments and livelihoods intensified in national and international NGOs from 1992, the year of the UN Conference on Environment and Development in Rio de Janeiro (UNCED, also known as 'the Earth Summit'). Although limited evidence is available, it seems that the longer-term impacts of training on staff capacities, projects, environments, and livelihoods are mixed. In Oxfam GB and partner NGOs, the sustainable livelihoods framework has been promoted as an instrument to explain links between poverty and environmental change, together with tools to encourage the participation of deprived and excluded people. The adoption of the sustainable livelihoods framework was limited among all but the more senior staff, and checklists from environmental impact assessment (EIA) are still rarely used. More successful has been the adoption of participatory approaches to project management by staff and partner staff.[9]

The poor uptake of guidelines from training sessions by development professionals suggests the need for changes in direction and also for renewed efforts to apply the guidelines. NGOs and official development agencies too have reached a point where they have learned significantly about participation, local environmental change, and livelihood sustainability. Nevertheless, assumptions are often made that can no longer be sustained, and there are few handy tools by which theory and academic analysis can be linked clearly to development practice. The development of approaches and frameworks regarding sustainable livelihoods,[10] participatory monitoring and evaluation and impact assessment,[11] and lessons from attempts to improve the environmental impacts of NGOs in the 1990s are all important recent developments in this respect. This book builds on them, and aims to make a further contribution.

Overview of the book

This book is not a manual, but it does offer some practical advice, as well as introducing key theories and suggesting the strategically important questions that development professionals should ask – and it shows where answers may be found. Its relevance is to rural and urban communities in the developing world, but not exclusively. It can be used to help effective campaigning and lobbying, better formulation and implementation of development strategies, and participatory project planning, monitoring, and impact assessment. What makes the book different from most others is that it is firmly rooted in the experience of development NGOs, and responds to their needs for further learning.

The book first reflects on the relationships between poverty and environmental change, partly from a theoretical and historical perspective but also on the basis of lessons from development practice. Then it provides frameworks for action in development programmes, exploring power relationships and ideas of stakeholder participation, and in particular the notion of sustainable livelihoods. Thirdly, the book discusses practical tools and approaches in project management. Finally it looks at how strategies and policies can address the structural causes of environmental degradation and poverty. Each of these main themes is addressed in a separate chapter, as follows.

Chapter 2 provides a brief overview of the historical roots of thinking about 'the environment' and discusses contemporary forms of environmentalism. It continues with a summary of theories of environment and development, especially sustainable development. Much of this is centred on various means of valuing aspects of nature and the environment, and, indeed, on the question *what needs to be sustained?* – nature? natural resources? the physical environment constructed by people? social relationships and people's institutions? human capital? The book also considers situations where sustainability is far from reality as a result of wars and various environmental hazards: contexts where the concept of vulnerability is of central importance.

Chapter 3 begins with examples of participation in development processes and the resulting effects on livelihoods and environments in a city in Brazil and remote rural communities in Mozambique and Vietnam. There follows a detailed explanation of the concept of sustainable livelihoods and how it can be used by development agencies as an analytical tool for project assessment and policy formulation. The chapter concludes with a section on social interaction, power, and participation in development processes. It offers a range of ways to involve a variety of social actors in various processes, from project planning and project evaluation to strategic planning and campaigning. In fact, participation is seen here more as negotiation among various stakeholders, of which national and international development agencies and community-based organisations are just some.

Chapter 4 addresses project management and the integration of questions of environmental sustainability in the project cycle. It presents the idea of – and lessons from the use of – environmental impact assessment (EIA) in large projects funded by governments and private companies, and the importance of information generated by such processes for affected citizens and campaigning NGOs. The second section focuses on the application of similar formal processes in small-scale community development projects, which has met with some success. In this chapter the lessons and suggestions relating to project management are also applied to the more extreme conditions of disaster situations, where management is under enormous pressures from rising death rates, human displacement, and inadequate resources. In the third section a hybrid process is presented that integrates the concept of sustainable livelihoods, lessons from formal EIA, and participatory methodologies, including participatory rural appraisal (PRA). This chapter does not fully address the *how?* question in terms of prescribing guidelines for responding to disasters, ensuring the participation of various social actors, or assessing environmental impact, but it provides many leads.

Chapter 5 discusses some national and international environmental policies and strategies of governments and development agencies. It treats the idea of longer-term planning, i.e. strategic planning of development agencies, ranging from small, local activist NGOs to large international development agencies. The main question addressed is *how* ideas of sustainability, the realities of poor people's environments, and their livelihood needs can and should be integrated in policy processes. It refers to methodologies of strategic environmental assessment and also presents some general indicators for sustainable development. In this chapter important environmental issues of a global nature are explained in some detail, including climate change, biodiversity, and agriculture, and also industrialisation and urbanisation. It gives examples of campaigns in support of poor people's environmental rights, and campaigns for changes in national and international policies that condition local environments and livelihood opportunities.

Throughout the text, practical suggestions are provided. There is a long list of bibliographical resources, an appendix with details of some important websites, and another one that provides an overview of environmental treaties and historical events.

You are encouraged to pick and choose from these chapters and appendices, according to your particular interests. Indeed, I hope that the book will satisfy a range of needs, and above all that it will stimulate further exploration of the inter-relationships between environmental change and improvements in the lives and livelihoods of deprived people.

2

Reflections on poverty, environment, and development

This chapter addresses the ways in which nature and environments relate to poverty and development. The first section gives an historical and global overview of environmentalisms. Section 2.2 outlines theories that are useful for developing an understanding of environmental change and the relationship between people and environments, both local and global. History and theory underlie many of the actions and policies of development agencies, governments, and environmental organisations, but they are not always sufficiently understood and articulated. Section 2.3 discusses situations where human vulnerability is exposed by natural and human-made hazards, war, and displacement. Section 2.4 addresses the issue of sustainable development and wider questions of sustainability, and poses the question *What needs to be sustained?*. To be credible, answers must deal with various forms of valuing nature and the environment, and also social relationships, people's institutions, or other social and human capital. At the end of section 2.4, some 'environmental myths' are discussed.

2.1 A short history of environment and environmentalism

This section discusses the multiple historical and cultural roots of the interest in environmental issues, and highlights modern forms of global environmentalism.

2.1.1 Traditions of thought and the roots of environmentalism

Powerful expressions of environmental values and thought can be found in the huge wealth of spiritual and scientific systems that have developed over thousands of years. Modern science is dominated by Western thought, but there is much scientific thinking that predates this or has developed in parallel to it: ideas that find expression in opposition and alternatives to mainstream thought and politics. It is impossible to do justice to the diversity and depth of this thinking, but the following offers a brief introduction to it.

Very important for modern thinking and spiritual life among Hindus and many others is *The Bhagavadgita*. This book attributes the following words to Krishna, a human manifestation of the divine:

Earth, water, fire, air, ether, mind, intellect, and egoism – these make up Nature. This is the lower Nature, but different from this is the higher Nature – the principle of life which sustains the worlds.[1]

Mahatma Gandhi interpreted this work in 1926. His focus was on the non-violent message in the *Gita*, even though it is a part of an epic story about wars. His translation refers to 'My lower aspect' instead of 'lower Nature' in the same stanza,[2] demonstrating that people and their environments, the force of life, and the outward manifestation of it are seen as part of the same whole, whether called God or Nature.

Present-day ecological grassroots movements are still inspired by Gandhi's promotion of village life, simplicity, and self-sufficiency, and by his methods of non-violent protest against foreign domination. Examples are the 'Chipko movement', campaigning for access to and protection of forests, and the protests against a huge dam-building programme that affects the Narmada river, its watershed, and people. Gandhi argued against the rapid industrialisation that other political leaders promoted – indeed pursued – after India's Independence. There is evidence that Gandhi was aware that resources were simply not available for India to pursue the wasteful and exploitative growth model of its colonial masters. Gandhi and several of his associates promoted the use of organic fertilisers, recycling, measures against soil erosion, and improved (community-based) water management. However, Gandhi should not be portrayed as an environmentalist *avant la lettre* who foresaw the current ecological crises that affect India, or who had all the answers to present-day environmental problems.[3]

Buddhism expresses ideas about the relationship between human beings and the essence of life and nature in the doctrine of 'karma', which is a natural law pertaining to human behaviour. According to this law, the person who intentionally kills a spider out of cruelty incurs a distinctly different result (karma) than one who accidentally and unconsciously tramples on it – even though the spider dies in both cases. Buddhism holds that 'all sentient beings are intimately interrelated', and because it sees the struggle for liberation from rebirth as one that involves improving karma by cultivating compassion and wisdom, 'Buddhism endorses a spirit of toleration and co-operation with the natural world'.[4]

The major Chinese religions all seem to have in common an emphasis on practical benefits for human development and society, promoting modesty, work, honesty, and other moral values. When human desires predominate, the original harmony in nature that is expressed by balance between *yin* and *yang*[5] and the 'five elements' (metal, wood, water, fire, and earth) will be disturbed. Disharmony between these elements in individuals, society, and other parts of the world (i.e. what Westerners would call nature or 'the environment') will degenerate into chaos.[6]

For Muslims, natural phenomena should be seen as awe-inspiring signs of God's presence; similarly, scientific discovery of natural laws can be celebrated as revelations of God's wisdom and greatness. According to Islamic sources, God created animals in order to serve human beings, but Islam equally prescribes that animals should be treated well. Manuals of Islamic law also prescribe the nurture of land and water, and acknowledge the rights of private ownership – contingent upon good use of those resources.[7]

Many traditional belief systems can be characterised as the worship of nature. Their followers have a close relationship with nature and are often perceived as living in a balanced way with natural phenomena. They usually do not make a sharp distinction between society and nature, and they often worship particular natural forces and phenomena, such as thunder, rain, sun, moon, and earth. These systems of belief and their related social institutions rarely recognise the private ownership of land, but negotiate different uses of land by different peoples, and, for example, sanction the co-existence of herders and sedentary agriculturists in parts of Africa.

The domination of indigenous people by larger and more powerful groups has brought their different values into sharp focus, for example through the declaration of Chief Seattle, writing to the President of the United States of America in the nineteenth century:

Our dead never forget this beautiful earth, for it is the mother of the red man. We are part of the earth, and it is part of us. The perfumed flowers are our sisters; the deer, the horse, the great eagle: these are our brothers. The rocky crests, the juices of the meadow, the body heat of the pony, and man – all belong to the same family. The rivers are our brothers, they quench our thirst. The rivers carry our canoes, and feed our children. If we sell you our land, you must remember and teach your children that the rivers are our brothers, and yours, and you must henceforth give the rivers the kindness you would give any brother.[8]

Such words still inspire native Americans and some of their fellow citizens, as an implicit expression of an alternative to the mainstream paradigm of economic growth and human domination over nature.

Mainstream Western behaviour and views *vis à vis* nature can be traced back to ancient Greek and Roman thought, Judaism, and early Christianity. Of course there were and still are diversity and divergence from the mainstream, but if the dominant views in these traditions can be summed up with one phrase, it is 'man's superiority over nature'. According to the Christian Bible, which has absorbed Jewish texts, God created nature, man, and later woman, and nominated Adam, Noah, and their sons as caretakers, indeed masters and users of the earth and all plants and creatures on it. Equally, the ancient texts and ideas can be seen as endorsing the domination of 'man' over 'woman'. In this tradition God created nature for the use of people, and people are seen as separate from nature. Human interference with nature was (and sometimes still is) perceived as 'improving' upon nature, almost irrespective of what is done, and as conquering nature: nature is a resource for human use and also a threat, imbued with destructive forces.[9]

This mainstream view is of course not representative of all Christians and cannot explain all behaviour. Already in seventeenth- and eighteenth-century European philosophy, differences between thinkers such as Descartes and Kant were emerging. They differed over the perceived dualism between mind and body, spirit and matter, and the degree to which nature can be understood as the sum of its parts. The science of ecology developed, shaped by Linnaeus in the eighteenth century, Darwin in the nineteenth, and Frederic Clements in the twentieth. John Muir (1838-1914), an American 'nature lover', founded the National Park system in the USA. Indeed, in the late nineteenth and early twentieth centuries, romantic ideas about the beauty of nature started to emerge, contrasting with earlier mainstream notions of the harshness of nature and wilderness. In the USA in 1962, Rachel Carson published the best-seller *Silent Spring*, warning about the effects of chemicals like DDT on wildlife and people.

Thomas Malthus (1766-1834) argued the existence of a natural law dictating that population grows exponentially and that agricultural production, growing much more slowly, is based on limited natural resources. He thought that the limitations in growth of agricultural production would therefore act as a natural check on excessive population increase. Malthusian thinking is still debated, although in 1965 Ester Boserup challenged it very effectively. She showed that population growth affects agricultural development: when population increases, fallow periods decrease, which prompts the application and invention of new methods of cultivation and enhanced productivity. On the other hand, in a neo-Malthusian tradition, Garret Hardin argued in *The Tragedy of the Commons* that if people have the freedom to manage common natural resources, they will over-exploit and thus destroy these resources.

2.1.2 Global environmentalism: the past thirty years

Appendix 1 shows that from the early twentieth century a plethora of international environmental treaties and conventions has been agreed. They range from treaties to regulate the use of international rivers and access to Antarctica, through conventions regarding whaling, plant protection, nuclear accidents, and sea pollution, to protocols that regulate atmospheric pollution.

In 1972 at the United Nations Conference on the Human Environment (UNCHE, or 'the Stockholm Conference'), Indira Gandhi, then India's Prime Minister, set the tone for some of the differences of opinion and confrontations between industrialised countries and poorer States when she asked, *'Will the growing awareness of "one earth" and "one environment" guide us to the concept of "one humanity"? Will there be a more equitable sharing of environmental costs and a greater international interest in the accelerated progress of the less-developed world?*[10]

The conference agreed to set up the United Nations Environment Programme (UNEP), which was established in the same year in Nairobi, Kenya. Also in 1972 the so-called 'Club of Rome' published its report *Limits to Growth*.[11] This predicted global disaster for a world that could no longer sustain life at the current rates of growth, consumption, and pollution. In 1984 the UN set up the World Commission on Environment and Development (WCED), also known as the Brundtland Commission, which investigated environmental and developmental issues and proposed future management strategies. The commission produced the report *Our Common Future* (1987) and famously defined sustainable development (see section 2.2.4 of this book).[12] It recommended holding a world conference on environment and development,[13] the United Nations Conference on Environment and Development (UNCED), or Earth Summit, in Rio de Janeiro, Brazil in 1992. UNCED agreed the terms of Agenda 21, a programme for promoting sustainable development from 1992 through the twenty-first century.

Various further treaties were discussed at UNCED, and initiatives for global environmental management were taken. For example, the Framework Convention on Climate Change was produced, and the Convention on Biological Diversity was agreed in December 1993 as a legally binding treaty to halt the destruction of biological diversity. In Rio the Global Environment Facility (GEF) was reinforced, in order to provide funds for developing countries for environmental programmes. UNCED also initiated negotiations towards the ratification of the UN Convention to Combat Desertification, with particular relevance for Africa. This entered into force in December 1996. The Commission on Sustainable Development (CSD) was formed to ensure and monitor progress on Agenda 21.

The Earth Summit itself failed to raise the estimated US$600 billion needed to implement Agenda 21, and was perceived by a number of countries not to have fully addressed the environmental problems of developing countries.[14] An important sequel to the Earth Summit came in a Special Session of the United Nations General Assembly (UNGASS) in 1997 ('Earth Summit II'), to be taken further in 2002 ('Earth Summit III'). At the 1997 meeting, it was agreed that Agenda 21 had achieved only limited success. That meeting itself, and other initiatives such as the CSD, are not regarded as very effective or influential, even though they take place at ministerial level.

The organisers of UNCED made specific efforts to involve non-government organisation (NGOs), setting up the Global Forum with and for NGOs in parallel to the conference. However, authors like Finger (1993) have criticised the Global Forum as a public-relations exercise on the part of the UNCED organisers, and an instrument to co-opt the NGOs into endorsing a non-radical agenda promoted by governments and multilateral institutions. Preceding the Earth Summit II was 'Rio+5', a forum held in Rio de Janeiro by the Earth Council of NGOs, but it is widely agreed that Rio+5 did not make a significant impact on Earth Summit II.[15]

The main environmental issues of global significance that are currently being addressed, or urgently need to be addressed at the CSD and in other international forums, include the following:

- global warming and climate change;
- depletion of the atmospheric ozone layer;
- cross-boundary pollution, including 'acid rain', nuclear waste, and waste disposal in international seas;
- international co-operation on transport (to combat risks of pollution from oil tankers and to address the fact that airline fuel, being untaxed, fails to generate funds to mitigate the pollution caused by air transport);
- management and exploitation of international rivers;
- forest conservation policy (including 'Forest Principles');
- biodiversity issues, including the adoption of a Biosafety Protocol under the Convention on Biodiversity;
- rights to genetic resources, plant-breeders' rights, farmers' rights to save seeds, and the patenting of life forms, in particular in the context of international trade rules;
- over-fishing;
- extractive industries, including mining of the ocean floor, and particularly in areas where indigenous peoples' traditional land rights are violated;
- the environmental impacts of tourism.

Particularly important in all those discussions are the growing inequalities, between and within countries, in terms of access to resources, which can be offset only by a combination of reduced resource consumption by the better-off (people and nations), and rapid development and transfer of environmentally beneficial technologies to developing nations. The relationship between environmental resources and the human economy prompts the need to incorporate measures of pollution and resource consumption ('externalities') in economic indicators such as the gross national product (GNP), and the need to find other ways to resolve the failures in measuring development or human progress.

2.1.3 Modern environmentalisms

The different historical roots of human relationships with nature in the South, East, and West, and various theories of environmental change (elaborated in section 2.2) resulted in the diversity of present-day *environmentalisms*. An environmentalism can be seen as a set of ideas favoured by a particular group. Different forms are developed in different contexts. They are articulated in academic circles, among development professionals, and in the sphere of politics, be it by grassroots movements, international protest alliances, national party politics, or official international forums. Environmentalisms are often a reaction against mainstream views and are often borrowed from traditions of thought that are outside the mainstream.

'First World environmentalism' can be characterised by the irony of the widespread love-affair with the car 'which, more than anything else, opens up a new world, of the wild, which is refreshingly different from the worlds of the city and the factory'.[16] Many better-off urban people, mostly based in industrialised countries and with a world-view rooted in Western culture, have come to romanticise and admire nature and wilderness as something of which they are no longer part, something external to them and to be found in often remote areas. This sort of view can be traced back to the likes of John Muir and the dualism in Western and Judaeo-Christian mainstream thought.

More recently, Arne Naess, a Norwegian philosopher, introduced the idea of *deep ecology*, which was developed into an environmentalism in the USA and Europe.[17] The US variety has been described as having four characteristics:[18] (a) it takes a strongly bio-centric view (as opposed to anthropocentric 'shallow ecology'), which means that nature is awarded an intrinsic value, independent of its value to people; (b) it has a focus on pristine and unspoilt wilderness and is strongly preservationist, to the extent that it believes that people should be expelled from large areas of the earth; (c) it invokes Eastern traditions and belief systems to support its bio-centric views; and (d) it believes that it is at the forefront of the environmental movement. These characteristics of 'deep ecology' can be found to some degree in many forms of environmentalism and environmental organisations, mostly in developed countries.[19] Extreme views on the need to conserve nature, and also less radical views, are all based on the idea that there must be 'limits to economic growth'. People have started to articulate the down-sides of development in their own lives, and radicals and moderates have built temporary alliances, for example in local protests against road construction.

Many are sympathetic to deep ecology or similar forms of environmentalism, but criticise conservationism as harmful when applied to the Third World. For example, the separation of people from wilderness harms what are perceived as balanced relationships between rural people and nature. The expulsion of human communities from national parks has led to benefits for the rich at the expense of the poor. (For example, the Maasai people in Tanzania are no longer allowed to herd their cattle in what has become the Serengeti wildlife park, even though they have used it for hundreds of years. The park now serves tourists who enjoy the sight of wildebeest migrations and roaming elephants.) Western 'deep ecologists' are also accused of reading the main Eastern traditions selectively, to 'prove' that these are essentially biocentric, instead of anthropocentric. Equating environmental protection with wilderness preservation is a very American-European idea, and in some cases nature preservation in developing countries is perceived as an imperialist act, rather like the export of Coca-Cola and some forms of Christianity.

However, the debate is more complex and subtle than this. Many European and US environmentalists explain environmental devastation primarily in its social and historical context, in terms of social inequality, and argue for a reduction in the resource consumption of the global elites. These ideas would find a 'strong resonance in countries such as India, where a history of Western colonialism and industrial development has benefited only a tiny elite, while exacting tremendous social and environmental costs'.[20] In fact, Naess also argues the need for lifestyle changes combined with political changes.[21]

In parts of Africa, nature parks were created in the colonial era and are still maintained by national elites, foreign aid, and tourism. They still exclude local people and deny their historical rights to pastures, for example. Nevertheless, in some cases the interest of tourists and the presence of wildlife have been turned into an advantage for local people, who are increasingly recognised as the main wildlife managers, for example in the Zimbabwean Campfire programme. Conservationism also appeals to popular movements such as the ones led by Gandhi and his followers, and in the past few decades there have been some strong reactions against dominance by external forces (international companies and co-opted national governments) over both nature and peoples.

An example of the conflict between popular interests on the one hand and dominant business and State interests on the other is that of the plight of the rubber tappers in Brazil. Chico Mendes, a leader of a Brazilian rubber-collectors' union, 'discovered that he was also an ecologist only a couple of years before his death'.[22] His assassination in 1988 at the hands of a local landowner sent reverberations well beyond Brazil's borders, as by then he and the cause of his rural trade union were well known. His campaign against deforestation and expansion of ranching was not motivated merely by the urge to defend nature or to protect the environment for its own sake, but it was a protest against the ruthless intrusion of capital and global markets into the livelihoods of rubber tappers and indigenous people – livelihoods based on extracting resources from forests and streams, like nuts, rubber, and fish. Campaigning by Mendes and his union, with the support of national and international NGOs, has led the governments of various Brazilian States to map out 'extractive reserves', which are more or less protected from the expansion of (large-scale) ranching and deforestation.[23]

Ken Saro-Wiwa was killed by the Nigerian military regime in 1995. Saro-Wiwa, a writer and businessman turned politician, led protests of his Ogoni people against the failure of the Nigerian State and the Anglo-Dutch oil company Shell to channel benefits from oil drilling to local people. Very few schools, services, or jobs were generated to off-set the destruction of the local environment that was caused by drilling, oil spillage, air pollution from flaring gas, and the depletion of wildlife. This made agriculture and fishing virtually impossible for the people of Ogoniland – a small and very densely populated part of the Niger delta. In Saro-Wiwa's words:

The Ogoni people were being killed all right, but in an unconventional way ... The Ogoni country has been completely destroyed by the search for oil ... Oil blowouts, spillages, oil-slicks, and general pollution accompany the search for oil ... Oil companies have flared gas in Nigeria for the past thirty years, causing acid rain ... What used to be the bread basket of the delta has now become totally infertile. All one sees and feels around is death. [Petrolic] degradation has been a lethal weapon in the war against the indigenous Ogoni people.[24]

In the perception of the Ogoni people, the connectedness between humans and nature was being violated: 'petroleum was, in the local vernacular, being pumped from the veins of the Ogoni people'.[25] Saro-Wiwa saw MOSOP, the Movement for the Survival of the Ogoni People, as a movement that had political, economic, and environmental aims and set out to achieve an alternative, autonomous development path for the Ogoni people that integrated these aims. This should be seen as an attempt to bring the multiple, historic concerns and interests of different groups together – modernisation, but on the terms of the Ogoni people themselves.

Such protests challenge industrial, modern society, its insatiable demands for resources, and its devastating effects on the (mostly local) environment. However the issue is clearly much wider: it is about inequality, social oppression, and access to economic development as much as the more narrowly defined environmental changes. Furthermore, protests are just part of the story, because many activists also engage in the search for alternatives: ways of organising production, trade, and consumption that are more people-friendly and in tune with the natural environment than those that operate in mainstream, market-based regimes. The alternatives are usually about limiting resource consumption, about nurturing (local) environments, whether rural or urban, about stimulating local employment and local trade. They tend to be rooted in people's own initiatives and a high degree of voluntarism, led by enthusiastic activists, and supported by local governments or outsiders such as development agencies. Many alternative technologies, social arrangements, and livelihoods have potential for widespread adoption.[26]

Across the world, smallholder farmers are developing and adopting forms of sustainable agriculture which enable them to increase their productivity, reduce their dependency on external inputs such as chemical pesticides and fertilisers, improve the sustainability of their environments, and protect or even improve their own health and that of the consumers of their products.[27] Experience shows that participatory approaches to technology development and genuine partnerships between scientists and farmers are capable of providing alternatives, in sharp contrast to the failures of the Green Revolution of the 1970s and the claims of transnational companies that their genetically modified crops are the solution to world hunger.[28] Oxfam and other international agencies have long supported Philippine NGOs, scientists, and community groups in their campaign against destructive industrial fishing and their efforts to develop techniques that help to regenerate coral and fishing grounds.[29]

In urban areas, creative alternatives and solutions are sought by governments, citizens' groups, and NGOs alike. A much-quoted success story is the transport system in the Brazilian town of Curitiba, which has good infrastructure, based on privately supplied public transport, and green spaces for cyclists in the low-lying areas, doubling as flood canals in emergencies. Another positive example is the collection and recycling of urban waste by the Zabbaleen in Cairo.[30] Grassroots groups and NGOs such as PREDES near Lima in Peru take action against recurrent floods and mud slides that threaten the lives of city dwellers,[31] and initiate improvements to sewerage, transport, and housing systems, for example in the Orangi Pilot Project in Karachi.[32] Local Exchange and Trade Systems (LETS) are developing in the USA, UK, and other industrialised countries as ways to share resources, skills, and services among local people, and create new forms of community.

2.2 Theories of people–environment relations

This section discusses some theories of environmental change and the relationship between people and local and global environments. Different disciplines look very differently at the relationships between people and environmental change.

2.2.1 Eco-logical systems

Since the 1970s, the meaning of 'ecology' has been questioned. Scientists began to abandon earlier models based on systems theory, which describes ecosystems in terms of notions such as stability and carrying capacity. They now think in terms of uncertainty, disequilibria, and chaos, as in the fluctuations of populations of people, plants, and animals.[33] This shift first occurred in the study of local ecosystems, but is reflected in global approaches too. (See also section 2.4.4.)

Environmental theory and environmentalism are based on empirical data, in particular from the biological sciences, geography, soil science, hydrology, and climate studies. Data are compiled by UN agencies, private organisations, and various government services and universities.[34] In *The Gaia Atlas of Planet Management*, Myers (1994) and the many other contributors make good use of globally available data. The title refers to the concept of Gaia, as developed by James Lovelock in the 1970s. Gaia is the ancient Greek Goddess of the Earth, and Lovelock (1979) developed the Gaia-hypothesis to explore the idea of the Earth as a super-organism that comprises 'all life on Earth and its environment', with the atmosphere, oceans, the biosphere, and soil all part of the complex system. Disturbance of one part produces feedback to other sub-systems and can cause 'sustained oscillation between two or more undesirable states',[35] which means that the present relatively small differences between hot and cold years or dry and wet years could suddenly become far bigger.

Lovelock studied the impact of human activity on the global environment, and in particular on the atmosphere and biosphere, for example in its effects on the Earth's water and carbon cycles. His ideas, rooted in scientific analysis, lead to the conclusion that humanity needs to take great care, because of all the unknown factors that influence the Earth's sub-systems: the systems are too complex for the full results of any action to be predicted. Lovelock argues that it is not permissible to affect the Earth-system in any major way, because 'undesirable states' are likely to be harmful to people as much as to anything else. Nature must be given an intrinsic value that cannot be substituted for something else (such as financial capital or human activity). One of the most important sub-systems of 'planet Earth' is the atmosphere, and global warming is just one piece of evidence that humanity may have already gone too far in influencing it (see section 5.3).

This environmental theory, with its focus on the physical (eco)systems, has one important flaw: it does not describe *why* people change environments, and how that happens or can be stopped. Furthermore, it does not tell us how environmental changes have differing impacts on the poor and rich, women and men, the powerless and powerful.

2.2.2 Political ecology

Political ecology is an attempt to develop a theory of environmental change in its social, economic, and political context. It has been developed from research and experience in diverse settings in the rural, developing world. It is rooted in social-political science and geography, and its ideas are echoed in the analysis and policies of development organisations and social movements.

Blaikie and Brookfield (1987) are responsible for an important publication on political ecology. The main concern of their book is to try to understand why land degradation occurs, and why in some cases regeneration does not happen. This is for them a largely social question. They argue that '[land] degradation is ... a reduction in the capability of land to satisfy a particular use',[36] and they explain that different users of land will appreciate its capabilities differently. Land may be perceived as degraded from one perspective but as benefiting from increased capability from another. For example, hunters and gatherers may not value land that is converted from forest to cropland, and farmers may not share the satisfaction felt by industrialists when a factory is built on agricultural land.

These authors assert that degradation of land results from a combination of natural and human degrading forces, and it is off-set by natural improvement of land and 'restorative management': land degradation is not simply caused *either* by humans *or* by natural forces, and improvement is possible. Central to their concept of political ecology is the role of the *land manager*, i.e. the farmer, forest department, or herder who directly interacts with the land: 'fundamentally, the land manager's job is to manage natural processes by limiting their degrading consequences'.[37] Investments of capital and labour that improve the capability of the land are called *landesque capital*: for example, terracing or other erosion-prevention measures. Such an investment thus increases what others have called *natural capital*, and what happens is a substitution of *financial, human, and social capital* for *natural capital* (compare section 3.2). This takes them beyond Marx, who held that of the three production factors – labour, land, and capital – labour is the only source of a product's real value. Marx discussed the injustices of unequal ownership and control of capital and land, but saw land as an essentially free source: the owner can use it at will, and there is (theoretically) a virtually limitless supply. However, land can be mined and degraded in order to obtain a product, and the damage needs to be minimised or repaired if productive capacity is to be maintained over longer periods of time.

The phrase 'political ecology' is obviously drawn from political economy, and thus it is concerned with issues of class and power in society, and how they interact with land management and land degradation. Blaikie and Brookfield (1987) talk of *regional* political ecology, to express the fact that the theory takes account of the complex relationships between people and land-based resources over a fairly extensive and varied area. It incorporates processes and relationships on different scales and in different hierarchies, from individuals, families, and farms, to communities and local commons, nations and the world. Its language employs terms such as *resilience* and *sensitivity*, to express how land-based systems can withstand human interference, and ideas about *marginality* of resources and of people. With these concepts they relate closely to the study of, prevention of, and response to disasters, which, especially in semi-arid areas, often strike after a gradual process of social, ecological, and economic decline.[38]

An important theme in the book is the idea of single-factor explanations for degradation or improvement of natural resources, and in particular the population question. Blaikie and Brookfield reject the simplistic theories of Malthus and neo-Malthusians like the Club of Rome, mainly because the notion that land has a fixed carrying capacity (to maintain people's food production and supply) denies the potential of technological development. Technology is never equally accessible to all people, so the analysis must include socio-political differences. As we have already seen (in section 2.1), Boserup challenged Malthus by developing the hypothesis that population increases actually prompt the development of technology; but Blaikie and Brookfield (1987) qualify this claim by arguing that it is too simplistic to say that crisis prompts people to innovate and survive. Pressure on resources from increasing populations may equally result in a downward spiral. Which way the development goes depends on complex relationships, access to other resources, labour availability, market prices for produce, social organisation, and the role of the State.

Blaikie and Brookfield admit that there are severe limitations to scientific methods that attempt to quantify land degradation and to estimate the economic costs involved in degradation and restoration. They promote the improvement of quantitative and numerical methods of measurement and analysis, but argue also for a qualitative approach. By focusing on 'the land manager', they recommend the study of perceptions of degradation, which are different for different land managers; they support the need for case studies of degradation in different contexts, and for an analytical approach 'which allows for complexity, uncertainty and great variety'.[39]

Their conclusions reflect very much what development organisations, and NGOs in particular, preach and practise.

- First, they stress repeatedly that in analysis the land manager must be central and that the complexity of the land manager's reality must be respected. Local knowledge is important, and a 'bottom-up' approach, with a willingness to listen, is called for.

- Secondly, the analysis must reduce uncertainty about the causes of land degradation and find ways to avert it by making ever-better (quantitative) estimates of actual degradation, costs, and benefits.

- Pressure on resources can arise in different ways and for different reasons, which can include increasing population, but the pressure is usually enhanced or even caused by some 'surplus-extracting relationship' between the land manager and others, be they money lenders, local traders, or State bureaucracies that set low farm-gate prices. Thus relationships between land users and powerful groups in society must be studied, in order to understand the behaviour of the former.

- Analysis must also examine links with the State and the world economy. Blaikie and Brookfield stress the importance of assessing the land manager's access to, for example, land, capital, and State assistance. The role of the State is particularly important for strengthening local institutions, improving access to land and other resources for all, and ensuring pricing policies that enable surpluses to become investments in land. The State may also have to step in where local institutions are incapable of protecting or restoring marginal lands, in particular because soil conservation in marginal areas does not usually yield economic returns that can compete with alternative investments of capital (for example in 'high potential areas' or urban centres).

Not surprisingly, the work of Blaikie and Brookfield has been criticised, but political ecology has received much attention and is being developed further as a theoretical framework for the analysis of environmental change, for example by Peet and Watts (1996). They observe a number of shortcomings in the conceptualisation of political ecology, including (1) that not only poverty but also affluence can be a cause of environmental degradation; (2) that there is a bias towards rural and Third World agrarian situations; (3) that land is not the only (important) environmental resource; (4) that the concepts and language used sometimes obscure complexity, in particular of relationships between the land manager, (micro) environmental changes, and the external context; (5) that it still lacks theoretical underpinning and does not necessarily clarify causal links; and (6) that little attention is paid to politics and political processes, and the means by which groups and individuals actually access resources.

Research continues in these weaker areas, focusing for example on environmental movements, civil society, and environmental rights. Hayward (1994) takes political ecology beyond the rural and looks at more than just land-related environmental change processes. He calls for theoretical improvements in the science of political economy, which is strongly based on Marx's theories (i.e. what is known as Marx's critique of the political economy of his day). Hayward (1994) comments that Marx used the following concepts in his theory: the three factors of production (labour, capital, land); the forces of production (between humans and nature); and relations of production (property rights, labour; relations between people that regulate the relationship with nature). He observes that Marxist and neo-Marxist theories fail to accommodate reproductive activities, i.e the responsibility for maintaining health and family, which mostly falls on women. In the same way, these existing theories fail to appreciate the reproduction (of the productive capacity) of nature, land, or environmental resources. He writes: 'where political economy reveals the source of value to be labour, political ecology reveals the source of labour, and hence ultimately of value itself, to be nature'. It is social mediation that turns nature into value, and a theory of political ecology should 'extend [Marx's] critique to the exploitation of non-waged labour and the "labour" of nature itself'.[40]

2.2.3 Gender, environment, and development

The term 'ecofeminism' was coined by the French feminist Françoise d'Eaubonne in 1974 and promoted by Susan Griffin, Carolyn Merchant, Vandana Shiva, among others. Ecofeminists argue that women are closer to nature than men, and men are closer to culture (which is often seen as superior), and that there is a connection between male domination of nature and male domination of women. There are differing views on whether the 'special relationship' of women with nature is rooted in their biological role in reproduction, or whether it is purely ideologically constructed in order to maintain gender-based power differences.

Critics of mainstream development models that are promoted by Western-dominated institutions have argued that paternalistic, colonial, and neo-colonial values and forces have marginalised women's scientific knowledge. In more general terms they have introduced the dualism that so characterises Western thought, between nature and culture, nature and people, body and mind. These critics argue that indigenous people's knowledge – and in particular women's knowledge – of the natural world should be valued much more highly, and that their knowledge and experience are superior in promoting egalitarian societies and harmony with nature. Vandana Shiva claims that the values thus articulated as ecofeminist are also central to popular movements, such as the Chipko movement against deforestation in Garhwal in north-west India, in which local women played an important role through hugging trees in attempts to prevent loggers from felling them. Several analysts have, however, argued that movements like Chipko are based on a much broader coalition of people, ideas, and concerns.[41]

Critics of ecofeminism such as Bina Agarwal (1998) allege that ecofeminists (a) have failed to differentiate women by class, ethnicity, and caste; (b) have focused on ideological arguments and failed to address power and economic differences as important sources of dominance; (c) have failed to show how ideological differences are constructed (in social processes, by institutions, through history); (d) have failed to recognise that concepts of nature, culture, and gender vary across different cultures; and (e) have not really addressed the actual material relationship that women may have with nature. Further objections are that ecofeminism concerns rural people and environments only, and that the idea of harmonious, ecological, traditional societies should not be generalised.

Agarwal not only criticised ecofeminism, but also suggested an alternative concept, which she labelled 'feminist environmentalism'. This concept accepts ideological construction of terms like 'gender' and 'nature' and the relationship between them, but insists that the link between women and the environment should also be seen as 'structured by a given gender and class (/caste/race) organisation of production, reproduction and distribution'.[42] She sees feminist environmentalism as a struggle to transform notions about gender and nature, as well as the actual division of work and access to resources. Agarwal speaks of class–gender effects of environmental change, and in describing those for the rural Indian situation she highlights some of the core aspects of this relation: (a) the importance of shifts in land-control patterns (from common access to State control and privatisation); (b) land degradation; (c) population growth; and (d) technological choices in agriculture associated with the erosion of local knowledge systems. She describes poor households, and women and female children in particular, primarily (but not only) as victims of environmental change because of gender-related divisions in labour and unequal access to resources. The class–gender effects of environmental change are manifested as pressures on women's time, their income, their nutrition and health, their social support networks, and their (indigenous) knowledge. These manifestations and some of the underlying causes are echoed by experience from development practice, ranging from women's disproportionate suffering during floods in Bangladesh, the increased work burden and health risks for urban women in Senegal following economic crisis, and health risks in the workplace of women workers in plantations and micro-electronic assembly plants; all as a result of gender-related unequal rights and access to environmental resources and other resources.[43]

Agarwal's approach is similar to what Dianne Rocheleau (1995) has called 'feminist political ecology', and both have also been grouped under the concept of 'gender, environment, and development' (GED). All have in common an 'emphasis on material relations and on their structuring by gender relationships'.[44] This relationship finds particular expression in gendered knowledges of environments, sciences, and technologies. This knowledge should be seen as cumulative and dynamic, because it builds on the experience of the past, while adapting to the technological and socio-economic changes of the present. Appleton (1995) has shown that there are many examples of specific knowledges and technologies, held and developed by women within their specific gendered context.

Further to this, GED pays attention to issues like (a) the gendered division of labour and responsibility which influences women's particular relation to environmental change; (b) gendered property rights, as a mediator in gender–environment relationships; (c) gendered positioning in households, communities, and other institutions; (d) the influence on gender relationships and gender–environment relations of the wider political economy; and (e) ecological characteristics that determine the processes of gender and environmental change.[45] This is a brief list of what needs to be studied and analysed in any particular situation.

However, GED and ecofeminism remain strongly rooted in *rural* livelihoods, gender relations, and people–environment relations. Another criticism is that little attention has been paid to internalising the economic costs to environments of social and economic processes.

2.2.4 Environmental economics

In *Small is Beautiful: A Study of Economics as if People Mattered*, Schumacher (1973) argued that, in the 'modern' economic approach, labour and work are seen by employers as a cost factor that is to be minimised, and by workers as a sacrifice for which they need to be compensated. He contrasts that with Buddhist ideas about work, where it is ascribed three important functions: developing and utilising people's faculties; enabling people to overcome self-centredness by working with others on a common task; and producing goods and services for human existence. The former attitude leads to the replacement of labour by capital-intensive machines and extreme specialisation of people in mechanical tasks, for example in manufacturing industry. The latter, more idealistic view, would lead to the use of tools in creative and social production processes, employing 'intermediate' technology that is small in scale, manageable, and people-friendly. This Buddhist economics is not averse to increasing material well-being: 'the ownership and the consumption of goods is a means to an end, and Buddhist economics is the systematic study of how to attain given ends with the minimum means. Modern economics, however, considers consumption to be the sole end and purpose of all economic activity, taking the factors of production – land, labour and capital – as the means.'[46] Schumacher addressed problems that were taken up later by environmental economists.

Sustainable development was defined by the Brundtland Commission as 'development that meets the needs of the present without compromising the ability of future generations to meet their own needs'.[47] The concept originally emerged from a document of the International Union for the Conservation of Nature (IUCN, 1980), as an attempt to bring together concerns over the conservation of nature and development. Pearce *et al.* (1989) explain the term 'sustainable development' as made up of three core aspects: when compared with more classical approaches to economics, (a) it pays more attention to the value of the environment, (b) it extends the time horizon to include next generations, and (c) it addresses questions of equity among people now and also questions of intergenerational equity. The implications of this for how economics is seen and operationalised are vast.

Pearce *et al.* (1989) address the problem in classical and neo-classical economics that certain social and environmental costs remain external to actual prices as determined in markets. Gupta and Asher (1998) write that 'an externality occurs when action by an economic agent ... unintentionally affects the welfare of other economic agent(s) without being incorporated in the market price'.[48] This happens often to environmental resources, either when pollution occurs or when resources are mined. Besides capital wealth, locked up in infrastructure and productive goods, environmental economics looks at *natural capital*, for example stocks of water and forest, and then confronts the problem of valuing these environmental stocks. Such stocks are difficult to value until prices of environmental services from those stocks (such as logging or fishing) are revealed in the market place through buying and selling.

However, many doubt that markets can determine true values of environmental resources, for example because future values and generations of people are not represented in today's markets. There is no guarantee that an environmental good will not be damaged or depleted before demand is high enough to push up prices and limit consumption. Another complication discussed by Pearce *et al.* (1989) is risk and uncertainty, i.e. the risk of (environmental) damage, unrecognised in the present, that future generations must deal with. The authors conclude that 'anticipatory environmental policy' is to be preferred over 'reactive environmental policy', i.e. polluting and consuming at will, until the problems have grown so great that dealing with them can no longer be avoided. The latter approach is commonly associated with 'technological optimism', that is, the task of dealing with the problem is postponed in the hope that future generations will invent and mobilise technologies that can solve the problems caused in the past and present.

They also challenge earlier ideas that economic growth, usually measured as GNP growth, would necessarily suffer from an anticipatory environmental policy. They accept some trade-offs, but argue that economic growth can improve through the improved health of the workforce, jobs in environment-related tourism, and jobs in pollution control and clean-up campaigns. With many others, they criticise the use of the gross national product (GNP) as an indicator of wealth creation and economic growth. They argue that increased GNP suggests improved standards of living, even though it may be caused by an increase in pollution-related expenditure on health care, while a decrease in (i.e. depreciation of) environmental capital is not incorporated.

Pearce *et al.* (1989) argue that economic development (as distinct from economic growth) usually involves three sets of societal changes: (a) improved utility or well-being, made up in particular of income and environmental quality; (b) advances in skills, knowledge, capability, and choice; and (c) increased self-esteem and independence.[49] This echoes Schumacher's (1973) ideas about the function of work and employment in Buddhist economics. Pearce *et al.* (1989) equate sustainable development, however, with sustainable utility, meaning that 'well being of a defined population should be at least constant over time and preferably increasing'.[50]

They offer a choice between what others have called *weak and strong sustainability*: the former is about the next generation inheriting a total stock of wealth (natural and human-made assets) that is equal to or better than the current one; the latter is about the next generation inheriting an equal or better stock of natural assets. The central issue in choosing between these extremes is that natural and human-made assets need to be substitutable. For example, the loss of a species, of topsoil, or of a forest would be substituted for, say, a better habitat for people, high and sustained food production with non-natural inputs, and alternative livelihoods for forest dwellers. It is obvious that trying to compare the value of the existence of an animal species (that may or may not be used by people) or forest-dependent traditional livelihoods, with (say) the convenience and economic value of a motorway is an almost surreal endeavour, but that is what economists do, and must do for practical reasons. Spiritual values that people may attach to natural resources (for example ancestral domains, or certain animals) usually do not feature at all in economic assessment, other than indirectly through market prices and government regulation (governments can protect certain areas or restrict commercial use of natural assets on the basis of political preferences, which go beyond economics).

According to most thinkers in this field, including those who hold a 'weak sustainability' position, inheriting an equal or better stock of total wealth can happen only if, for example, the proceeds of logging natural forests are used to build up other assets, and not for direct consumption. It is also generally agreed that there are other – sometimes unknown – functions of the natural forest, besides the supply of timber, and there is the problem that some environmental changes – such as the extinction of an animal species –are irreversible, whatever the technology of future generations. If sustainable development is taken to mean no reduction in environmental or natural capital (i.e. the 'strong sustainability' view), one accepts the irreversibility and non-substitutability of some assets, the uncertainties and risks involved in environmental change, and the fact that technological development cannot be fully predicted nor be expected to solve all problems. Maintaining natural capital is particularly important for people who live on the edge of survival, and who depend for their livelihoods on resources in their immediate environments. Pearce *et al.* see this as an issue of intragenerational equity. However, poor people have little capacity to forgo consumption and substitute natural capital for other assets; in other words, they cannot easily aim to pass on similar natural wealth to the next generation and thus hand over an equal standard of consumption and survival potential.

Going further on the topic of sustainability, Pearce *et al.* borrow from agro-ecosystems analysis, seeing the sustainability of economic systems as their ability to maintain productivity under stress: the conservation of natural capital leads to increased resilience of economic systems, because it provides a flow of services to the economic system. They have come close to a 'strong sustainability' position as far as some environmental resources are concerned, which they have called 'critical capital'. They would like to see those resources conserved through (a) government regulation (for example standards for maximum pollution; exploitation permits); and (b) market-based instruments like taxation, subsidisation, and tradable permits for resource use and harmful emissions. However, they promote substitutability even for exhaustible resources. A third set of instruments of authorities is (c) those based on awareness and voluntary behaviour. Pearce *et al.* argue that practical economics cannot be conducted if a natural resource or 'the environment' is given an infinite price, which would mean that 'environmental assets somehow lie outside the realm of money values. ... [This] poses as many problems as it is supposed to solve since, quite clearly, people do have preferences for environmental services and do express them in money terms'.[51] We can conclude, then, that it should be possible to find environmentalists and economists who choose a more radical path to conserving environments and environmental capital.

So, as some criticism of environmental economics implies, what is the use of all this for developing countries and poor people? Are the latter not simply concerned with survival, and are developing countries not perfectly right in claiming that they need to substitute natural, environmental capital for consumption – in other words, is environmental economics an unaffordable luxury? Even the 'weak sustainability' argument leads to the conclusion that it is equally important for industrialised and developing countries to ensure that depletion of natural capital results in sustained economic activity, and that it is not merely consumed, unless survival is at stake. It is important to ensure that valuation of environmental resources happens in developing countries, because they too confront the future, and will want to avoid medical, infrastructural, and clean-up costs that may set them back after initial economic progress. Economic development is more important than unbridled economic growth.

Gupta and Asher (1998) argue that degradation of water, land, and air reduces the productivity of people and natural resources, with a potentially adverse effect on food security and the provision of other basic necessities – and that could lead to inflation. Ecological and economic linkages are multiple and complex, and many of the environmental change-processes are external to the market system, but not external to the economy, which is possibly even more true in developing countries than in the industrialised world. Governments of developing countries have an immediate interest in guaranteeing at least the survival of their populations and indeed of optimising the environment–economy links. In urban areas, human health is central to this, and therefore measures to reduce pollution and ensure good water supply, sanitation, and protection from mudslides should be seen as a basic right as well as a national economic necessity. In rural areas, maintaining the quality of natural resources on which primary producers depend for their livelihoods is vital, but unfortunately authorities do not always appreciate their value.

2.3 Questions of vulnerability

Before discussing sustainability (in section 2.4), we need to explore the role of nature and environments in the more extreme of situations – those where very little is or can be sustained. The first sub-section asks how natural or environmental disasters actually are caused. The environment can be the object of struggle and war, and the means of survival, as subsection 2.3.2 shows. The effects on the environment of disasters that involve large displacements of people are discussed in section 2.3.3.

In the situations discussed in this section, theories of environmental economics are less relevant in an operational sense, although it is obviously critical that economists should help to assess the human and material costs of failures to mitigate disasters. Political ecology has contributed to our understanding of some of the processes that lead to complex crisis, with a mix of environmental degradation, economic decline, and political violence. Ideas from the field of gender, environment, and development (GED) also remain important, both in order to understand the differing impacts of disasters on women, men, various castes, and social classes, and to assist in the targeting of mitigating responses. The physical causes and effects of environmental disasters are obviously the terrain of the natural sciences.

2.3.1 More or less natural disasters

Many have tried to define what makes a certain event, a catastrophe or natural disaster, into a human disaster. Most stress that a disaster needs to be seen as a socio-economic phenomenon that may be extreme but is not necessarily abnormal, and in which 'community structures and processes temporarily fail'.[52] Human disasters happen when some hazard or shock strikes and when the vulnerability of individuals and groups is so great that they cannot cope with it. They cannot withstand the shock (that is, they have limited *resistance*), and cannot easily recover from it (that is, they have limited *resilience*).[53] This explanation does not define disasters in a precise way and does not clarify exactly when some human crisis can be called a disaster, but it obviously relates to the more extreme of cases, when lives are at risk and indeed lost, and when the scale and extent are very significant.

Types of disaster

Section 5.3 considers the phenomenon of global climatic change and increasing concerns about the impact of human actions, in particular the use of fossil fuels. The increase in the frequency and severity of disasters is associated with people-induced climate change, in particular floods, cyclones,[54] and droughts. The severity and occurrence of other 'natural' hazards, in particular river floods, can also be influenced by people. Such floods are enhanced by deforestation and urbanisation of the upper reaches of river basins and also by canalisation, which reduces the natural flood plain and thus the water-storage capacity of rivers. Some disasters are entirely created by people, and others are not at all related to human activity, or in other words they are disasters that could be seen as totally natural.

A useful typology or overview of disasters should take a social perspective into account and must distinguish between different vulnerabilities of different groups of people. It also needs to be practical and embrace the possible range of mitigating responses, and not simply list the types of hazard that contribute to human disasters. Table 2.1 is an attempt to construct such a typology. It is evident from this exercise that nature or environment plays a central role in both enhancing vulnerabilities and generating actual hazards or shocks. The five main categories of disaster are distinguished mainly by the cause of the hazard: (a) natural disasters; (b) less natural disasters; (c) industrial disasters; (d) human displacement following war; and (e) slow-onset disasters. The box does not present the range of socio-political mediations that can increase vulnerability and translate a hazard or risk into an actual human disaster, a subject that is discussed in chapters 3, 4, and 5.

Table 2.1: A typology of disasters

Hazard: cause and symptoms	Vulnerability: who and why?	Response and immediate mitigation potential	Environmental impact and livelihood recovery
Natural disasters volcanic eruptions, earthquakes, and related tsunamis (flood waves)	• People living on/near to slopes of volcanoes • Poorer urban people in crowded and built-up inner cities • Fisher people and others living near the coast, especially poorer people outside sea-defence structures	• They strike unexpectedly but in known geographical regions. • Life-saving is always a first priority, and very few choices can be made or measures taken that reduce the immediate impact on livelihoods and environment. • Protection and preparedness are possible but costly.	• Impact on nature and environment is rarely irreversible (e.g. in terms of extinction of species or topsoil erosion). • Chemical installations may be damaged and cause long-term pollution. • Physical infrastructure can be rebuilt, depending on human and financial resources. • Market-based livelihoods may take a long time to recover. • Agricultural subsistence can recover comparatively easily.

Table 2.1: A typology of disasters (continued)

Hazard: cause and symptoms	Vulnerability: who and why?	Response and immediate mitigation potential	Environmental impact and livelihood recovery
Less natural disasters, enhanced by anthropogenic causes: floods, cyclones, droughts, forest fires	• People in coastal areas and valleys • People in poorly constructed houses and huts • People who are dependent on the informal economy • All those without insurance • People involved in subsistence agriculture and small-scale fishing	• They strike unexpectedly but in particular geographical regions, possibly more frequently in 'El Niño years', so that tentative warning is possible. • Life-saving is always the first priority, and some choices can be made and measures taken that reduce the immediate impact on livelihoods and environment. • Protection and preparedness are possible, and not all measures are costly.	• Impact on nature and environment can be irreversible, for example in terms of topsoil erosion. • Positive impacts of floods can occur (e.g. improved soil fertility[55]), and negative impacts on flora and fauna may be slow to become apparent. • Chemical installations may be damaged and cause long-term pollution.[56] • Physical infrastructure can be rebuilt, which depends on human and financial resources. • Market-based livelihoods may take a long time to recover. • Recovery of agricultural subsistence and market-oriented production may require very substantial support.
Industrial disasters: oil spills, nuclear-plant failure, chemical-plant failure, pollution from mining, etc.	• People in poor housing, living near industries, mines, and power plants • People with little political influence and financial insurance • Farmers and subsistence producers, e.g. those living along oil pipelines[57]	• They strike unexpectedly, but places and risks are known. • Life-saving may be a first priority, but in many cases measures to limit the environmental impact come first. • Protection and preparedness should happen and are normally enshrined in law; these costs should be internalised in industrial production.	• Much of the environmental impact is toxic pollution and either irreversible or extremely difficult, costly, and slow to repair. • Physical infrastructure can be rebuilt, which depends on human and financial resources. • Health impacts will limit people's ability to recover their livelihoods, urban and rural. • Agriculture and fisheries may have been made impossible, and relocation or alternative livelihood opportunities are needed.

Table 2.1: A typology of disasters (continued)

Hazard: cause and symptoms	Vulnerability: who and why?	Response and immediate mitigation potential	Environmental impact and livelihood recovery
Human displacement caused by war, and possibly compounded by environmental hazards	• Particular ethnic or political groupings • Especially the poorest; women, children, and the elderly	• Do not usually happen unexpectedly, although the scale may be a surprise. • Life-saving is often the first priority and is intrinsically linked to environmental health factors, which are in turn strongly influenced by site planning for refugee camps. • Protection and preparedness can be difficult and should involve host populations and authorities.	• Most environmental impact will be on renewable natural resources, in particular trees and forests. Minor irreversible environmental impacts are possible, such as depletion of confined groundwater aquifers or displacement into conservation areas. • It is vital to minimise environmental health risks: good water supply, sanitation, and waste disposal are priorities. • Livelihoods are usually limited to some local trade and employment and rarely subsistence production; people's basic needs need to be supplemented heavily over longer periods of time.
Slow-onset disasters that are triggered by minor hazards but caused by gradual degradation in resources and socio-political processes	• The lower classes or castes, or otherwise excluded people • Subsistence producers, often women-headed households and elderly people	• Slow build-up of crisis can be monitored and full crisis predicted. • Life-saving may become first priority once the full crisis is triggered, but before that a wide range of mitigation measures is possible, including those that limit degradation of local productive resources. • Protection and preparedness should be linked with efforts to reverse the gradual degradation and can be comparatively straightforward and affordable.	• Environmental degradation can be irreversible, including topsoil loss and chemical pollution. • People will normally explore a wide range of survival strategies, including going hungry, eating wild foods, petty trade, selling livestock and other productive assets, and (temporary) migration; these can be supported in many different ways, including employment programmes such as infrastructure development through food-for-work or cash-for-work schemes.

Development agencies in general and NGOs in particular respond in varying ways to human disasters, as suggested in Table 2.1. The actual response depends of course on the scale of the disaster, and on various contextual realities. For example, where local activists and NGOs are well established, it is possible to campaign for more safety and better adherence to environmental standards to prevent industrial and mining hazards, and in case of an industrial disaster to campaign for better compensation for victims. An example is the chemical disaster at the Union Carbide plant in Bhopal in India in 1984.[58] In the case of slow-onset disasters, development agencies tend to support forms of sustainable agriculture, community-level mediation and social development efforts, and/or employment programmes that support the poorest people and the local economy. These initiatives may be implemented by and through local agencies or by international development agencies themselves. Response to large-scale acute disasters usually comes from emergency specialists employed by governments and also by private companies and NGOs, from anywhere in the world. The United Nations has a special unit – the Joint UNEP/OCHA Environment Unit, based in Geneva – that aims to help to improve international response to environmental disasters, acts as a clearing house for information, and can mobilise some support. In the world of NGOs, Green Cross International, also based in Geneva, and its national affiliates have response to environmental disasters at the core of their mandate.[59]

The incidence of disaster: looking into the future
As population numbers increase, especially in hazard-prone areas, the impact of environmental disaster is also increasing, and, with deepening poverty and inequality in some parts of the world, the ground is becoming more fertile for slow-onset disasters involving large numbers of people. There is also a legacy from earlier days with a potentially lethal impact, in particular the threats to health and the natural environment that stem from very highly polluting industry, nuclear, chemical, and biological weapons manufacturing in the former Soviet Union, and also frequent oil spills.[60] The risks in that region are particularly enhanced by economic and political crises that make it almost impossible to address such problems effectively. Economic growth in other parts of the world involves externalities that are often ignored, including those related to pollution and to risks associated with mining and dam building.

Internal and international tensions (sometimes leading to war) that are linked to conflicts over environmental resources are impossible to predict; it depends on extremely complex socio-political mediation whether scarcity results in violent conflict or not. Nevertheless, the future will bring more population, scarcer resources, more inequality, and therefore more potential for conflicts. Conflicts of interests between North and South, as illustrated by greenhouse-gas emissions, and so-called solutions such as carbon trading, are unlikely to be settled through violent conflict, unlike the struggle for control over oil supplies, which was a key reason why the USA and its allies fought the Gulf War against Iraq. Regional conflicts over resources such as river water are more likely, although they will in many cases be settled through negotiation over long periods of time.[61] The biggest potential exists for internal conflicts over local and national resources such as land, minerals, water, forests, and fisheries – but these conflicts will be complex, with a range of causes. (Some examples are discussed in section 5.2.)

The coasts of poor countries in the Caribbean and Central America, of Bangladesh, India, Vietnam, and many others will continue to be hit by tropical cyclones, and possibly more frequently in future. The Andean region, Central America, and various countries in South-East Asia and elsewhere will continue to experience earthquakes and volcanic eruptions, and more and more people will be obliged to live in the critical zones. Drought and floods may worsen in parts of Africa, Indonesia, Brazil, the Andean Region, and elsewhere. Urbanisation and economic growth will increase the risks of industrial disaster all over the developing world.

The vulnerability of large groups of people depends on non-natural and non-environmental factors, although physical structures offer essential protection and means of escape in many instances. Income, general economic development, and reasonable levels of social equality and political influence are far more decisive in this respect. When compared with the situation 30 years ago, Bangladeshis are now far better informed of the risk of severe river floods or tidal waves associated with cyclones in the Bay of Bengal, and escape routes and structures are gradually improving. Over the next three decades, many millions of people will be affected by the power of extreme floods, and tens of thousands, if not more, are likely to perish. Even though the situation is improving in Bangladesh, the levels of suffering there for generations to come will remain out of all proportion to the problems experienced in rich-country (and also highly populated) flood plains and deltas such as The Netherlands. Alert systems to give warnings of tsunamis and earthquakes in Japan and hurricane warnings in the USA are far more effective than (for example) the preventative measures and early warning systems of which the governments of Central America and most Caribbean States are capable. Furthermore, the people in the latter States have generally no insurance cover to help with the cost of rebuilding infrastructure and homes.

Besides measures for mitigation, preparedness, and prevention, there are situations in which the impact of a hazard appears to differ according to the livelihood and land-use strategies that were in place before the disaster. There are livelihood strategies that reduce vulnerability, in particular in an environmental sense. Holt (1999), for example, reports that initial assessments in Honduras and Nicaragua following the devastation caused by Hurricane Mitch in 1998 suggest that farmers who followed a sustainable agriculture strategy with water-conservation measures and agro-forestry practices may have achieved higher agro-ecological resistance. However, in the most severely affected areas, the levels of destruction experienced by farmers who took part in the *campesino a campesino* (farmer to farmer) extension programme were not detectably less than those encountered by farmers not included in the scheme: beyond a certain threshold, differences in agricultural practices no longer matter in terms of the devastation caused by a cyclone.

Early warning refers to a range of systems for data collection, analysis, and communication. This range goes from elementary, community-based systems of observation and communication to highly sophisticated systems involving satellite observation and communication, computer simulation, and scores of specialists. They are particularly geared towards the advent of famine, tropical cyclones, and floods. Famine is not primarily a natural disaster, or even a less-natural disaster, but created by a complex web of factors that reduce the entitlements to food of particular groups of people.[62] Some of those factors are related to climate and agriculture, but the all-important political, market, and social factors make early warning by observation from satellites a perilous undertaking. Nevertheless, early warning of natural or less-natural hazards enables governments and aid agencies to act in a timely way, and tools are also available to spot signals from market behaviour and trends in nutritional status. The range of tools for obtaining early warning of famine includes systems put in place by NGOs and some governments to collect quantitative and qualitative information, with semi-participatory monitoring techniques (known as risk mapping, livelihood monitoring, or the livelihood-economy approach) to survey nutrition, markets, and agricultural production. Governments and international organisations such as the FAO and WFP also analyse satellite images and monitor rainfall to predict crop yields, and recently have begun work on drought prediction in relation to the so-called El Niño phenomenon (see also chapter 5). It is generally agreed that the latter is extremely useful, if complemented by detailed local information on nutrition and markets. Indicators of increasing vulnerability and the severity of hazards must be relevant for the authorities, the people directly affected, and the communications media alike.[63] Above all, the nature of disaster-risks needs to be understood in its local manifestation for any risk-management strategy to be effective.[64] These risks are clearly greater for the poorer, for the less powerful, often for women, and generally for excluded and deprived people.

2.3.2 Conflicts and natural resources

Links between violent conflict and environmental resources are several. War destroys people, livelihoods, and environmental resources, besides targeting the opponent's means of waging war. Struggle over scarce natural resources, such as land, diamond deposits, or water can lead to conflict. Natural resources can equally play a role in sustaining warring parties, and also in supplying the means of survival for victims. An important and immediate effect of war is often the displacement of people, with natural resources being degraded as an effect of the huge and sudden pressures, but at least supplying some means of sustenance in the form of fuelwood, building materials, and sometimes food.[65]

The environmental impacts of war

War can degrade the environment, besides killing and wounding people. Damage to infrastructure is an obvious effect, for example the destruction of bridges, airports, and factories. Destruction of chemical industries or, worse, nuclear installations or stores of biological and chemical weapons can also lead to unexpected and long-term health problems, as does the use of weapons containing depleted uranium. Several reports claim that such practices explain the high numbers of deformed babies born in Iraq following the Gulf War. Furthermore, smoke and carbon dioxide from burning oil wells during that war were emitted on a huge scale, with globally significant impact. Before this, in the 1960s and early 1970s, the USA used defoliants in the war against the Vietnamese: Agent Orange destroyed hundreds of thousands of hectares of forest. The forest cover in Vietnam has still not fully recovered, and the dioxins in the environment still cause deformities in newly born babies.[66] In the NATO war against Serbian domination and ethnic cleansing of Kosovo in 1999, petrochemical plants were bombed, and the resulting toxic pollution is expected to cause birth defects and cancer among people living in the vicinity of those plants for years to come.[67]

One cause of conflict among many

Environmental resources are often the objects of struggle and war, and competition for resources is seen as an (increasingly) important cause of war. Environmental causes are, however, always part of a far more complex set of factors, and of a historical process. New theories of war-related and drought-related famine and population movement look at the driving forces and internal rationale of the situation, employing the terminology of 'complex emergencies' and 'slow-onset emergencies' (or disasters). This analysis makes use of ideas from political economy and resembles political ecology (see section 2.2.2). The idea is that economic and environmental decline, increased competition for resources such as land, together with other factors (slowly) erode the resilience of certain groups of people. A relatively minor drought, ethnic or political confrontation, or other reason may then trigger violent conflict, displacement and/or famine. Such emergency situations are called complex because there is no single factor that is the cause of the crisis; causes include longer-term factors such as the breakdown of the State and a crisis in agriculture (deteriorating quality and availability of resources). What sustains a conflict and even a famine has been labelled the 'political economy of internal war'. It is essential when planning any kind of support for the losers to understand the interests of the winners, who institutionalise a political economy of war, and also to understand the wider economic and political forces that prevail. For example, the winners gain financially through (illegal) trade and accumulation of resources. People's survival strategies will include migration and the sale of assets (including land), so that the local situation changes drastically and permanently through the crisis, to someone's benefit.[68]

It is obvious that conflicts and their causes are complex and that contention over environmental resources or environmental degradation is a contributor to this complexity. The following is a suggested taxonomy of four aspects that are central to understanding causal links between environment and conflict:

- *trigger mechanisms* (as above), which include natural disasters, cumulative (environmental) change, accidents, and warfare;
- *political-geographical factors*, which show who and which levels of power and authority are affected by environmental change;
- *categories of environmental change*, including those affecting climate, land, water, fisheries, and forest;
- the *historical dimension* of society-induced environmental transformation.

All these aspects overlap, and a study of one can complement the study of others.[69] Nevertheless, workable hypotheses in the research of conflict-causation will have to focus on specifics in one or two of those groups. Research that follows does not need to make the case *that* environmental resources play a role in conflict (which is often evident); rather it needs to establish what their *relative importance* is. Furthermore, in the study of conflict one needs to take into account that parties involved are unlikely to understand the conflict fully themselves, and (false) images, 'conventional wisdom', and indeed fiction dominate. Such images can turn into unchallenged assumptions and may define the starting point of research into the causes of a conflict. For example, the idea of persistent drought in the Sahel in the 1980s was the unchallenged starting point in analysis of the border conflict between Senegal and Mauritania that broke out in 1989. This almost inevitably led to the conclusion that it was an environmental conflict. However, the story of that conflict can equally be told as an ethnic struggle, or one of struggle for Senegalese State power.

The causes of the extreme violence in Rwanda in the mid-1990s between extremist Hutus (who were guilty of genocide) and Tutsis and moderate Hutus (who retaliated against the crimes) included population pressure and competition for limited land among the predominantly rural population, according to many authors.[70] The land problem related (and possibly still relates) to the diminishing size of average family holdings, the fragmentation of plots, and the centralised control of land, combined with the effective existence of local land markets. Ethnicity is also an important factor in the history of Rwanda, and so are power struggles over control of the State and military. Control over the latter has for more than 100 years been in the hands of small, elite groups dominated by one or other of the two 'ethnic' groups (perceived as distinct, although Hutus and Tutsis share a common language, have intermarried a great deal, but were formally distinguished by colonial interests in the twentieth century). Nevertheless, the struggle for land and the lack of economic development are important causal factors too.

Sustaining conflict, guaranteeing survival
Natural resources are often important during conflict, sustaining warring parties and even fuelling the tension. An example of this is the mining of gemstones and logging of trees in Cambodia, and the trade in these resources that was conducted through Thailand, thus sustaining the Khmer Rouge guerrillas for many years. Natural resources can equally be the means of survival for those caught in the middle: environmental resources can thus offer alternative livelihood strategies (see the sustainable livelihoods framework presented in section 3.2). The following examples illustrate these roles of environmental resources in conflicts.[71]

The **civil war in Sierra Leone** in the early 1990s is a case where population growth and environmental degradation were *not* among the causes of war, but exploration and competition for natural resources like diamonds have contributed to social tensions and the recession of the State. Importantly, the ability to survive in rainforest (where much of the war took place) made an essential difference in the war. The rebel violence in Sierra Leone has been described as 'a mobilisation of youth on behalf of a small group of people angry at their exclusion from an opaque patrimonial system serving mineral extraction interests'.[72] Analysts assert that the key lesson to be drawn from this is that even during such a war, civil society must be supported and islands of peace must be built.

Also in West Africa, in Sinoe County in **Liberia**, an Oxfam project found in 1995 that insecurity and lack of production had forced people to eat palm cabbage, the tip of the growing tree. This constituted about 40 per cent of their diet, and this source was running out fast. Harvesting the palm cabbage means that the tree dies, and thus what is a key cash crop in normal years is lost. Palm oil and palm nuts are important foods and cash crops in this area. Such a bio-diverse environment thus helps survival, but people's survival strategies can have a negative impact on long-term livelihood opportunities.[73] In situations such as this, alternative food sources or food aid must be supplied, to safeguard long-term interests.

In the **Horn of Africa**, people adopt a wide range of livelihood and survival strategies that intricately link them to their environments in situations of human insecurity.[74] People have an intimate knowledge of their natural environment, which serves their needs for construction, tools, medicines, spices, herbs, food supplements, and forage. They need bio-diverse environments in times of food crisis and war, which has been a reality for decades, especially in Sudan. Livelihood and survival strategies also include migration for purposes of work, trade, and the grazing of cattle. Relief agencies tend to have very limited understanding of these local and resource-related survival strategies, do not tap into them, and do not strategise to support them. People's survival strategies are disturbed by gradual changes in markets and other institutions as well as natural environments, and by shocks that may occur in the form of livestock epidemics, political upheavals, or drought. These may be the triggers that turn a violent but localised conflict into a large-scale disaster. Wild foods often form an important means of survival, but in the north-east of Sudan the mesquite tree (*Prosopsis juliflora*), introduced by a forestry programme, invaded local environments and severely reduced biodiversity. War and political changes that restrict the movement of pastoralists, or government policies that promote forms of modern agriculture, are particular causes for reducing the resilience (i.e. increasing the vulnerability) of local people.[75] Development efforts must thus promote communication and mobility, and also land-tenure reform, sustainable agricultural techniques, and education in order to enable herders to develop alternative means of livelihood.

These examples and the associated recommendations suggest that supporting the (local) management of environmental resources, more or less equal access to and control over them, and support to improve the conditions for their sustainable use are of central importance, as they are also in situations of violent conflict. This should happen in particular through local people's participation, supporting their strategies and creating islands of peace through support for the elements of civil society that can deliver them. Education and support for the environmentally sustainable management of natural resources are also important, in order to improve prospects for both short-term survival and long-term livelihoods. These are not impossible dreams for outsiders to achieve, although it will be difficult: what is required first and foremost is a change in the mindset of relief agencies and a better understanding of local people's survival strategies.

2.3.3 Displaced people and environments

Crises that affect large numbers of people, in particular those associated with violent conflict, tend to cause displacement of populations, which can have significant effects on their own environment and that of their hosts. In such cases, survival mechanisms that exploit local natural resources may degrade the environment in various ways as a result. Agencies and governments responding to the needs of displaced people can make various choices that affect the quality of local environmental resources, and enable displaced people to achieve a minimum level of sustenance, as is explained in the rest of this section.

Civil war has raged in **Sudan** almost continuously since 1955. This has caused people to flee as refugees to neighbouring countries or to remain in the country as internally displaced people (IDPs). Many of the latter have migrated to the capital, Khartoum, making up about a quarter of its population of almost four million. The military government that came into power in 1989 has responded to the massive presence of IDPs with forced evictions and relocation of hundreds of thousands of people to new sites on the desert fringes of the city. In those sites no water supply and sanitation services exist, there are no employment opportunities, and traditional livelihoods (agriculture, livestock keeping) are virtually impossible. The scarce natural resources such as fuelwood that were available have long been depleted. The weakest people remain dependent on feeding programmes, food aid, and health services supplied by the international community, just as in refugee camps, and their plight has turned into a long-term reality. The international development agencies have to work in a very adverse political climate if they are to achieve anything at all.[76]

Refugees fled in extremely large numbers from Rwanda to Kagera in **Tanzania** and Kivu in the **Democratic Republic of Congo** (former Zaire) from April 1994 onwards. Refugee camps holding several hundreds of thousands of inhabitants were created overnight, and large numbers of people died in the first weeks after crossing the international borders. The international community and also local authorities responded with food distributions, the installation of water supply and sanitation systems, and the provision of various other supplies, including fuelwood. Several camps were located in places of water scarcity, and some were close to an internationally renowned World Heritage Site, the Virunga rainforest. There were camps on volcanic rock in North Kivu, rendering the digging of graves and pit latrines almost impossible, which caused major environmental health problems. There were also large numbers of refugees camped in local schools, parks, and churches. Thus, to save lives, the immediate environment of the refugees and also some of the host population was the concern of highest priority.

More generally, the environmental impact of this enormous flux of people was significant, and it was negative: deforestation, water depletion, soil erosion, and urban destruction were among the impacts. However, only in some cases could the changes be seen as irreversible or very difficult to restore, such as some soil erosion in South Kivu and damage to a research centre where particular genetic crop materials were held, and the depletion of confined aquifers of groundwater in Tanzania. All the other impacts were on renewable resources, forests in particular, and renewal started happening on a modest scale even before the refugees returned home. Some time after the exodus from Rwanda, it was possible to move the refugees to other areas, where more resources and better conditions were available and the environmental impact would be limited, but this proved to be extremely difficult and costly. Pressures to move refugees out of towns were very strong, however, in particular because their presence was highly resented by the host populations. The environmental destruction in the wake of the refugees' arrival played an important role in this. A few agencies did mitigate the impact by distributing fuelwood from other places, promoting the use of efficient wood stoves, and carrying out some 'beautification' in, for example, Bukavu town (in South Kivu) after refugees had been relocated. Most refugees have now returned to Rwanda, but there, in the DR Congo, and in Burundi, low-level conflict continues, preventing the repair of damage and regeneration of the local production base on any significant scale, and producing a very serious threat to one of the world's most famous gorilla populations. In Tanzania more environmental regeneration has been undertaken, through (for example) reforestation initiatives, compared with the other affected countries.[77]

Extensive analysis of the relationships between environmental change, refugee migration, and sustainable development in a number of cases confirms that environmental impacts are localised, and that dispersal of refugees should be an important strategy in limiting environmental degradation. This is in part because in the case of huge camps 'the environment' can provide so little that the whole burden of providing for refugees tends to fall on donor governments and NGOs. Resentment by host populations is common, because they are often equally poor and vulnerable, and their environments are rapidly deteriorating, but they are not assisted by aid agencies. More generally, refugee camps need to be considered as small or even large towns, with similar environmental problems. Their economic and also environmental sustainability depends strongly on its economic base – something that is rarely given a chance to develop.[78]

Furthermore, it can be argued that humanitarian emergencies are *not* fundamentally different from other development situations, and that therefore similar policy options, shaped by best practice in sustainable development and natural-resource management, should be applied.[79] However, this happens rarely in situations of forced migration, and initiatives of the UNHCR rarely refer to the notion of sustainable development. The explanation for this can be found in operational realities, which focus on logistics and outputs. The idea of encouraging participation by a range of actors in responses to disasters is often absent, because there is no economic incentive to do it, because local communities often lack social and political coherence, and because it challenges the professional status of agency staff. Analysis of the historical context of particular groups of people and geographical areas tends to be lacking for a range of reasons, and few development professionals acquire detailed environmental knowledge that would allow them to leave aside the blueprints that are often applied as standard responses (plant trees/promote improved stoves, etc.). Refugees rarely gain rights to employment or to use natural resources such as land in their host communities, which may be seen as a chance missed for the local economy and for local resource management. Despite the policies and efforts of governments and development agencies, whatever they are, local hosts and refugees are in fact doing the lion's share of natural-resource management. It is also important to note that in most cases the main burden of this management falls on women, with their central role in providing food, fuel, and water. This should be recognised by policy makers, who should respond in a supportive manner.

However, it cannot be expected that real participation and improved rights to environmental resources will automatically lead to good environmental management and social equity. Furthermore, ideas of 'strong sustainability' (see section 2.2.4) that put environmental resources and nature before human welfare and livelihoods should be rejected in circumstances of extreme human suffering, on ethical grounds, among other reasons.[80] Radical environmentalism stresses the interests of future generations of people and the 'non-use' values of nature, such as the mere existence of a community of monkeys in a remote forest. These are long-term concerns that cannot all be taken into account when short-term needs become so pressing (see also section 2.4.2).

2.4 Questions of sustainability

This section questions further the concept of sustainable development, which has become strongly associated with notions of 'environment' and 'environmentalism'. Both parts of the term, *sustainable* and *development*, as well as the meaning of the two combined, are problematic, and there are differing views in North and South on its practical translations into processes of human progress.

The book *Our Common Future* (WCED, 1987) defined sustainable development (as quoted in section 2.2) and explored the concept in some detail:

The concept of sustainable development does imply limits – not absolute limits but limitations imposed by the present state of technology and social organisation on environmental resources and by the ability of the biosphere to absorb the effects of human activities. But technology and social organisation can be both managed and improved to make way for a new era of economic growth. The Commission believes that widespread poverty is no longer inevitable. Poverty is not only an evil in itself, but sustainable development requires meeting the basic needs of all and extending to all the opportunity to fulfil their aspirations for a better life. A world in which poverty is endemic will always be prone to ecological and other catastrophes.[81]

This means that the concept of sustainable development expresses an overall aim and position, for example regarding the fulfilment of basic needs of the poor; that it must recognise limitations in technology, social organisation, and environmental resources; and that endemic poverty and ecological catastrophes are linked, in some way. There are fundamental questions to be answered, including (1) how poverty and environmental degradation are linked, (2) what needs to be sustained in order to reduce people's vulnerability, and (3) how patterns of consumption and technology development should help to achieve that. These questions are discussed in the following subsections.

2.4.1 Poverty and environmental degradation

Work on political ecology 'has affirmed the centrality of *poverty* as a major cause of ecological deterioration ... [although] ... at best only a *proximate* cause of environmental deterioration'.[82] Political ecology looks at the complexity of interactions between people and environmental resources and rejects single explanations, for example that the growth of (poor) populations would either cause severe environmental degradation to the point of self-destruction (cf. Malthus; see section 2.1.1) or would be the automatic engine for technology development and innovation (cf. Boserup).

Many argue that wealth is a greater threat to the environment than poverty, but that there are ways in which poverty causes local environmental degradation too. For example, when poor people cannot afford fossil fuels, they will use dung and trees, and are thus forfeiting the opportunity to improve soil quality and are causing land degradation, in particular in arid regions. However, this degradation mainly affects the poor themselves, and contributes less to global environmental change than the alternative, which is the use of fossil fuels. Comparatively poor people with the means to cut significant numbers of trees, who fish with dynamite that destroys coral, or who process leather (and pollute locally) may be blamed for local or regional degradation too. Large-scale deforestation, mining, and fishing are usually in the hands of big enterprises, controlled by the rich and often the more powerful from industrialised nations, but they can also involve large numbers of relatively poor entrepreneurs. This environmental decline does, however, happen in order to serve high-consumers who are reached through (international) markets.

Analysis of the causes of global warming and climate change and other global, international, or large-scale environmental degradation suggests that consumption by affluent peoples, in industrialised nations and increasingly in the developing world, is the main driving force behind environmental degradation. Air pollution and acid rain, ozone-layer depletion, climate change and sea-level rise, increased river flooding and the depletion of fish stocks, all such are caused by the very large 'ecological footprint' of high-consumption elites. Those consumers use the biggest share of the Earth's fossil fuels, consume much of its fish and forest resources, and most of the meat from livestock that is fed on high-quality fodder. All these resources usually come from far beyond the geographical boundaries of the countries where the consumers live. Better-off people and nations can afford not to be affected by environmental degradation. Pollution is transported to faraway areas, for example through good sanitation systems, and citizens of rich nations can afford to visit protected nature reserves. Their ecological footprint can be expressed graphically, for example as the forested surface areas that would be required to reproduce the fossil-energy that they consume or to operate as a sink to absorb the carbon dioxide that they produce by driving cars and running manufacturing industry: such notional surface areas are often many times bigger than the size of the countries or regions where the high-consumers live.[83]

As argued in section 2.3, the causes of environmental disasters are only in some cases entirely natural, and the potential impact of disasters has increased dramatically, because more and more people are obliged to live in volatile areas, ranging from flood plains to zones prone to earthquakes, on slopes of volcanoes and near to chemical factories and nuclear-power plants. Tokyo, Mexico City, Managua, and San Francisco are prone to earthquakes, yet they are all increasing in size. The people of Bangladesh are infinitely more vulnerable than those behind the dykes of The Netherlands. People in Florida can flee before hurricanes strike, insurance companies cover most material costs, and the US government can rebuild bridges. The impact of a similar hurricane in Central America is obviously different. Many more lives are lost, livelihoods devastated, and large-scale rebuilding funded by insurance money and government investment is not an option –

as was demonstrated by Hurricane Mitch, which hit Honduras and Nicaragua in 1998. Vulnerability to natural and other disasters thus depends strongly on levels of income.

In making generalisations about the poor and their relation to environmental change, it needs to be stressed that at all levels people are different, and have differing capabilities and access to resources. Bina Agarwal and other analysts (see also section 2.2) have argued the importance of differentiating relationships between people and environmental resources according to gender, class, caste, and age. This is important when considering whether poor people are victims or culprits of environmental degradation. Work on gender and environment and political ecology has also highlighted the need to uncover relationships between poor *urban* people and their environments. Unlike in rural areas, urban people depend less on their immediate environmental resources for their livelihoods, and they are less likely to degrade environments in attempts to survive in the face of severe stresses. In fact, poor people in large human settlements are often the ones who re-use and recycle, and thus limit the negative environmental impacts of cities as a whole.[84] However, their health is strongly influenced by pollution and bad living conditions, and their vulnerability to hazards such as earthquakes can be very high: in human settlements the notion of *environmental risk* must be central in analysis and policy.

2.4.2 Reducing vulnerability and sustaining environments

Vulnerability and its opposite – security – are concepts that are often invoked when 'sustainability' and 'resilience' do not seem to express the relative precariousness of livelihoods and environmental resources on which very poor people depend. When immediate survival has become more important than future prospects, sustainability may be dismissed as an irrelevant dream. Chambers sees vulnerability as one aspect of deprivation, associated with income-poverty, powerlessness, and isolation. Vulnerable people are those who 'are more exposed to risks, shocks and stresses; and with the loss of physical assets and fewer and weaker social supports, they have fewer means to cope without damaging loss'.[85] Ecological diversity gives security and offers survival possibilities, and high diversity of environmental resources enables multiple livelihood strategies. For example, in a drought certain foods may not be produced by a family nor be available on the local market, but a comparatively diverse set of wild plants in a local forest can be substituted and thus help people to survive. In normal times, the bio-diverse forest may offer many 'non-timber forest products' that can be processed and traded, or used as medicine.

UNDP, in the *Human Development Report 1994*, articulated *human security* as follows. 'It means, first, safety from such chronic threats as hunger, disease, and repression. It also means protection from sudden and hurtful disruptions in the patterns of daily life – whether in homes, in jobs or in communities'. Threats to human security are categorised as related to economic security, food security, health security, environmental security, personal security, community security, and political security.[86] UNDP has also outlined the concept of *sustainable human development*, which is a broader concept. It is compatible with most interpretations of sustainable development, for example in the fact that it addresses issues of intragenerational and intergenerational equity. It is supported in a practical way by indicators and data that provide the human development index (HDI), with offshoots, i.e. indexes that provide comparisons between countries in terms of the relative vulnerability and poverty of their peoples.[87]

If environmental resources and disasters are so important to livelihoods and human security, and sustainable development should capture that, then we must ask *what needs to be sustained?* Economists want utility to be sustained; health professionals want human health to be improved; social scientists want institutions to be reproduced and sustained; ecologists want species and ecosystems to be conserved. Critics like Sachs (1992) have argued that the concept of sustainable development is an attempt to incorporate environment in the otherwise unchanged goal of GNP growth: despite new rhetoric, it is mere growth that is being sustained. This required a process of 'blaming the victim': 'the poor were quickly identified as agents of destruction', and 'the environment could only be protected through a new era of growth'.[88] Worster (1993) finds it deeply problematic that the sustainable development concept does not provide a clear timeframe: *to sustain something until when?* Ten years from now, a thousand years, a million years? Furthermore, what needs to be sustained also depends on the level of aggregation: should the country sustain its total forest-stand, or should every village do so? In a constructive contribution to this debate, environmental economists write that sustainable development should imply 'that future generations should be compensated for reductions in the endowments of resources brought about by actions of present generations'[89] – this would be based on constant capital that can guarantee constant (or improving) welfare.

Most would agree that it is necessary to sustain health, utility (i.e. welfare), environmental resources, and more. Besides environmental sustainability, which implies sustaining some form of natural capital, it is possible to distinguish economic sustainability, and for example social sustainability, for which social capital would need to be sustained. *Social capital* has emerged as an important analytical concept in the past decade, and can be seen as something like the strength (or capital) that is made up of trust, norms, and more generally social cohesion, through the existence and functioning of social networks and civic participation in politics – high social capital brings benefits to all concerned. In this way it may be seen as essential for the management, reproduction, and evolution of a society.

Dobson (1998) analysed different interpretations of the need to sustain environments and nature. He developed a typology of three broad types of *environmental* sustainability, of which in fact only the first one is entirely anthropocentric, that is, primarily concerned with human welfare and therefore fully consistent with most notions of sustainable development. In summary, Dobson's three types of environmental sustainability are the following:

- **Type A**: This is the **'critical natural capital'** type of environmental sustainability, concerned with sustaining natural resources (capital) that are 'critical to the production and reproduction of human life'. Critical capital can be either renewable or non-renewable; if it is non-renewable, it can still be substituted, such as fossil fuels that can be substituted with energy sources from already existing technology. Critical capital can also be non-substitutable and non-renewable, in which case protection remains the only option for sustaining it.

- **Type B**: This is the **'irreversible nature'** type of environmental sustainability. Degradation of some parts of nature cannot be reversed, and adherents of this type hold that those parts cannot be substituted, even though they may not necessarily be critical for human beings. Compensation for this irreversible loss is impossible, and protection is an important strategy. Human welfare is central, but parts of nature are accorded an intrinsic value that goes beyond human utility. Attempts to price nature could still be acceptable, in other words: work by environmental economists is still seen as important.

- **Type C**: This is the **'natural value'** type, which values the non-human natural world in its own right; its objective is to sustain 'natural value'. It operates outside the realm of economics: there is no talk of capital, and thus no possibility of substituting for other capitals. Compensation for the loss of some natural aspect by another is not seen as possible either. Renewal of nature is possible only as far as it is renewal through the dynamics of ecosystems. This can be seen as 'absurdly strong sustainability' and is motivated by a sense of 'obligations to nature', mainly for protection. In this group we find many supporters of deep ecology (see section 2.1).

Chapter 3 on sustainable livelihoods discusses the use of five capitals in practical analysis: social capital, human capital, technological capital, physical capital, and natural capital. In this wider set of capitals, the question of substitution between them is discussed, because the main challenge is to sustain a good level of total capital.

2.4.3 Consumption and technology

So how can all these capitals be sustained, and poor people's vulnerability be reduced? Harrison (1992) proposes a model for assessing *environmental impact* as a result of changes in population, consumption, and technology, which are the main forces that affect environmental change and human vulnerability. Consumption is, in his view, extremely difficult to curb and must be minimised through changes in values and culture. He explains that population is very difficult to influence in a direct way too, and he argues that positive effects can be expected from guaranteeing women's rights, provision of good health care and family-planning facilities, poverty alleviation, more equal distribution of assets, and economic growth. He follows Boserup in seeing population growth as a driving force for technology development, particularly in times of (environmental) crisis (see also section 2.1). Environmental impact can and must thus be minimised, mainly through technological developments that reduce environmental stress.

However, from the analysis of Ekins (1993) it becomes clear that it is highly unlikely that technology development alone could solve current and future environmental problems. In line with proponents of the 'ecological footprints' approach, he has shown that the assumptions made in the Brundtland Report and subsequent discussions about the potential of technology development as a panacea for enabling the poor to consume at similar levels to the better-off are merely utopian unless the rich radically reduce their excessive consumption levels. His analysis is strongly based on the consumption of and pollution from fossil fuels.[90] That technology development would enable poorer populations to consume what industrial nations now consume is equally rejected by Ullrich (1992), but there are technological optimists, politicians and scientists alike, who are hoping for miracle technologies that could solve the problems of energy consumption and its pollutiing effects by means far less risky than nuclear energy.

Policies of governments and the international community to reduce the impact of consumption, develop ecologically less destructive technology, and make it more possible for poorer people to take part in more consumption can be categorised in three groups: (a) regulation, including tough (internationally agreed) standards for energy consumption and pollution; (b) market-based policies, including fiscal policies that provide incentives for reduced resource-consumption instead of taxing labour, and subsidisation to encourage the transfer of clean technologies from industrialised nations to developing countries.[91] Finally, (c) government policies can help to raise awareness and persuade industry and consumers to change their behaviour, including that related to environmental impact. However, such policies and the solutions that are implied by them do not necessarily help all poor people and all environments, nor help to recover the wider, social-cultural values of technology.

Technologies are 'bodies of skills, knowledge and procedures for making, using and doing useful things ... technologies are cultural traditions developed in human communities for dealing with the physical and biological environment, including human and biological organisms'.[92] In this sense technology is very much part of human creation and activity, but in modern industrial society a huge gap has appeared between the creator-inventors and the users of technology. Technology has often lost its (local) cultural value and has internationalised with the economy: it has been reduced to a matter of production and consumption only, and can be seen as the main driving force in modern economic development. The strongest expression of this is, of course, in manufacturing industry. That this is also very dependent on fossil fuel has provoked the comment that 'the essential lie of the industrial system [is] the pretence that the material prosperity ... was "created" by industrial production, by science and technology'.[93] Fossil fuels are the main engine for almost all material prosperity, including food production. They were created over hundreds of millions of years and are being depleted in no more than a few centuries. They are also the main source of waste generation (plastics), atmospheric pollution, and climate change.

Development agencies often work *with* deprived and marginalised people (i.e. they pursue participation) in order to develop and adapt technologies that are relevant for them. They do not, however, always appreciate the importance and the implications of technological development: the 'impact [of NGOs] on the development of technological capability can be contradictory'.[94] Nevertheless, there are increasing numbers of (grassroots) successes in the North, South, and East in the search for technologies and organisational structures that go halfway between a total absence of technological innovation and the adoption of alienating, wasteful, and unsustainable technologies.[95] Increasing productivity in a people-friendly and environment-friendly way is, however, often criticised, in particular by political leaders in developing countries, as an attempt to allow industrialised countries to continue with high levels of consumption, dominate markets as producers, and deprive Third World populations of the chance to modernise and 'catch up'.

2.4.4 Environmental myths

The existence of historical overviews and theoretical frameworks, and the wealth of experience in addressing human vulnerability and attempting to improve the sustainability of development, as summarised in the previous sections, does not mean that all those lessons have been learned by everybody. A number of environmental myths persist among development professionals and others, including the following.

Myth 1: Poverty and population growth cause environmental degradation

In fact, a minority of high-consumers are mainly responsible for global environmental degradation and, through markets, also for much local environmental degradation in areas where poor producers try to make a living (see also section 2.4.1 on ecological footprints). There is a large and growing body of evidence that some of the poorer people of the world, in particular in developing countries, actually restore degraded environments, and even create what was earlier perceived as purely natural capital. Increased densities of trees are associated with increased densities of people in parts of Kenya.[96] Comparatively poor people traditionally created patches of forest in the savannah of Guinée in West Africa, which challenges the orthodox view that the reverse would have been happening in the twentieth century, i.e. that the desert was entering the forests as a result of (poor) people's activities.[97] Moreover, the poorest may not be the ones to suffer environmental degradation, nor the ones from whom environmental regeneration should be expected. In a rural community in Vietnam, for example, 'the very poorest families, women and men, in Lung Vai commune did not take much part in the environmental change, whether negative or positive, and whether as culprit, victim or restorer of degraded environments'.[98] The relationship between numbers of people and degrees of environmental degradation is thus not at all as simple as Malthus would have had it (see also section 2.1.1): with more people, new and different ways of using and managing resources may be developed, and population growth does not need to be a problem at all.

Myth 2: Equity, participation, and environmental sustainability go hand in hand

In 1992, in connection with the Earth Summit, some development agencies promoted the strategy of Primary Environmental Care (PEC). This consisted of three core aspects: (1) popular empowerment, (2) securing basic rights and needs, and (3) caring for the environment. PEC stressed also the 'vital role for women' and the need for 'a supportive national and international framework and the political will to tackle the obstacles to sustainable development'.[99] Unintentionally, the presentation of PEC came close to feeding the myth of automatic synergy between more equity, more popular participation, and more environmental sustainability. Caring for the environment might result in strict forest conservation without any popular empowerment; basic needs can be met without empowerment and by means of environmental exploitation; and empowerment of some can lead to resource-exploitation, growing inequalities, and the deepening poverty of others.

Dobson (1998) asserts that 'systematic studies which show that poverty relief, rather than greater material equality is functional for environmental sustainability have not been made (nor, indeed, have studies which might show the opposite)', and 'despite sustainable developers' belief that distributive questions are key to sustainability, research to establish the precise nature of the functional relationship between such questions and environmental sustainability has not been carried out'.[100] We thus have little basis to argue that synergy does or does not exist between meeting basic needs (i.e. levels of equity) and environmental sustainability.

Participation and empowerment are discussed further in chapter 3, but it may be observed here that certain forms of empowerment *are* likely at least to help to improve local environmental quality. The Brundtland Report calls for securing property rights (in particular land rights) as a key issue on the road to sustainable development, which is possibly one of the least criticised recommendations that it made. The theories of political ecology and gender, environment, and development (GED) call for analysis of essentially complex situations, for participation of deprived and excluded people in political processes, and for continuous alertness to differences in impact on women and men, and people of different classes and castes (see section 2.2). The land manager of Blaikie and Brookfield can be expected to manage land better only if she is enabled by good policies and sees benefits now and in the future from doing things differently.

Myth 3: Nature seeks balance

The science of ecology, inspired by Linnaeus and Darwin, grew out of biology. In the twentieth century Frederick Clements and his successors developed the so-called 'climax' theory of vegetation (see also section 2.1). This theory proposes a process of succession of plant populations until harmony, balance, and a climax vegetation are reached. This will remain, in the absence of large shocks to the system from nature (for example volcanic eruptions, or climatic shocks) or interference of people beyond some critical point. An example of the latter was agricultural cultivation of the Great Plains in the USA without any measures to prevent soil erosion, which resulted in the Dust Bowl and economic devastation among the farming community in the 1930s.[101] The language of 'carrying capacity' and 'optimum yield' also fits in this context, i.e. the capacity of a particular ecosystem to sustain a certain extraction by people or livestock.

In recent decades the science of ecology has gone through major changes. Notions of balance, order, climax vegetation, and carrying capacity have been replaced with ideas of dynamism, chaos, and uncertainty (see also section 2.2.1). There is now also talk of 'permissive ecology', whereby ecologists do not just accept that ecosystems are affected by human use, but assume that shaping them by human interference is a right, if not a need – nature no longer sets the standard for what is good.[102] It has also led to a new way of looking at the interaction between pastoralists and their cattle and pastures in, for example, Africa. Pastoralists are no longer simply accused of irrationally degrading environments (i.e. causing desertification) by maximising herd sizes in times of water and vegetation availability. It is now accepted that pastoralists are acting rationally when they maximise herd sizes, respond to environmental changes in their herding patterns, and accept losses in times of crisis. Wide variations in vegetation-cover from year to year are actually more dependent on rainfall than on grazing. Indeed the whole idea of dryland degradation is being reassessed: it is not a clear-cut fact in, for example, non-equilibrium rangeland dynamics, where a high degree of variability requires flexibility and mobility of herders.[103] The upshot of ecological science based on dynamic, chaotic, and uncertainty principles is that it can no longer provide society with simple and clear answers to what would be the most sustainable use of trees, plants, fish, or wildlife. Equally, new insights have helped to explain the lack of success of pastoralist projects, since they were based on assumptions derived from equilibrium-based ecological analysis, which were wrong.

Myth 4: High-input farming is the only way to avoid a global food crisis

The so-called Green Revolution of the 1960s and 1970s (although it started earlier and lasted longer) is widely seen as having made a major contribution to increased food production, for example in Asian countries such as India and Indonesia. It promoted improved seed varieties (High Yielding Varieties, HYVs, which are normally hybrid seeds produced by in-breeding), widespread uses of fertilisers and chemical pesticides, increased irrigation, and some mechanisation. The Green Revolution has however become almost more famous for its failures and shortcomings. The agricultural practices that were promoted were strongly based on external inputs; natural soil fertility and organic-matter content have been depleted; soil erosion enhanced; and health risks (indeed, incidences of death from poisoning) increased with the use of pesticides. The technological package that was promoted was mainly relevant for land of higher potential, which led to geographical inequality because such land tends to be in the hands of the better-off farmers. Dependency of farmers on external inputs (provided by the State or markets) sharply increased, and the medium to large farms benefited, while smallholders and subsistence farmers either did not benefit at all or actually became worse off. Total, national production increased in several countries, but inequality sharply increased, and in some countries landlessness increased in its wake. Productivity per hectare increased, but the share of income from agriculture that went to (wage) labour decreased, which is in part attributed to mechanisation. The Green Revolution's main failure is that it has not managed to eliminate rural poverty and food insecurity; in fact, the FAO estimates that the total number of undernourished people has only very gradually declined over the past decades and was still 790 million people in 1999.[104]

Despite these lessons, and despite the fact that the world's food markets are currently well supplied, neo-Malthusian arguments are continuing to be used in order to promote rapid bio-technological progress and increased mechanisation and chemical inputs into agriculture (which are strongly based on the use of non-renewable fossil fuels and for that reason alone already environmentally unsustainable). In the late 1990s, those calls became substantially louder through the forceful business-led lobby for genetically modified (GM) crop varieties. Biotechnological developments could make crops more productive and more resistant to drought and pests, and they could increase the nutritional value of foods, which on the face of it could only be a good thing. However, the health and environmental risks of genetic modification are not yet well understood, and the companies that modify and patent the genetic materials spend much of their energy on developing herbicide-resistant or pesticide-resistant varieties, varieties that themselves produce pesticides (upsetting ecological diversity, as other pesticides do), and varieties that require high inputs of fertiliser and water. This seems a direction that is, once again, interesting for the better-off farmers in so-called high-potential areas, although they too will become ever more dependent on big business. As a result of new patenting legislation, seeds must be bought annually and cannot be saved legally by farmers (if they would viably germinate at all). GM seeds are developed to respond only to particular brands of pesticide or herbicide, produced by the same international companies. The environmental and social effects of the Green Revolution were nothing compared with the devastation that could follow from the spread to other plants of so-called terminator genes,[105] from pollution, soil deterioration, and, in particular, from the social inequalities that are associated with high levels of external inputs. In India, farmers have started protesting against the prospect of genetically engineered varieties by burning experimental fields, in Brazil activists and people's movements are in opposition, and governments in Europe are trying to accommodate public anxiety with the pressures for new international trade agreements that would allow international firms to bring genetically modified seeds and foods on to European markets.

Alternatives are available and spreading rapidly, and some believe that their spread is already so substantial that high-tech genetic engineering is not going to be as dominant as the Green Revolution technology was, whatever the attempts of big business. Sustainable agriculture[106] comprises a range of techniques and approaches that are being promoted by the FAO and others, both in the agriculture establishment and in progressive development organisations (see also section 5.2.2).

Food can be produced for the needs and wants of the (future) global population, and that does not have to entail the side-effects of social deprivation and environmental devastation imposed by the Green Revolution or its successor, the biotechnological revolution.[107] The successes of the alternatives are well documented and promising, but they need much better acceptance in the mainstream of agricultural development and food-policy making.[108]

Myth 5: Urbanisation and urban consumption are the biggest environmental threat

Earlier discussion concluded that 'strong sustainability' is impossible to achieve, locally or globally, without forgoing resource consumption by the better-off, i.e. the high-consumers (see sections 2.2.4 and 2.4.2). These people live in cities mainly, North and South, and contribute therefore to the notion that urban settlements are the most unsustainable part of civilisation. It is thus possible to argue that cities and urbanisation are an important – if not the main – environmental threat in the twenty-first century.

However, rural populations in industrialised countries are equally high consumers of petrol for their cars, or tropical hardwood for their garden furniture, and they have a very similar *per capita* impact on the global and local environments. It is estimated that 50 per cent of the poor of developing countries are living in cities at the start of the new millennium,[109] and indeed consumption and pollution are increasing, but urban population growth happens mainly among the low-consuming poor. They suffer from local environmental problems and are exposed to high environmental risks, but contribute hardly at all to global environmental degradation. This trend towards urbanisation is unstoppable and should be seen as an *opportunity,* according to many analysts, and not as a problem.

Rabinovitch (1998) acknowledges that, on the whole, urban settlements are deeply unsustainable because of their energy consumption, waste production, air and water pollution, and overcrowding, not to mention the problems of under-employment, social disruption, and poor housing and sanitation infrastructure. However, he also points to the fact that cities are the main engines for economic growth, all over the world, and that advantages of scale from having a large number of people in a small space are among the factors that can explain that. Using the example of the Brazilian city of Curitiba, with almost 2.5 million inhabitants, he points to the enormous potential for limiting waste production, for recycling, and for the creation of cleaner and more habitable cities. Central to Curitiba's environmental and economic success is the city's (environmental) planning processes, particularly in relation to roads and public transport, and also land-use legislation that dictates population densities. Curitiba has a cheap and highly efficient public-transport system that is largely run by the private sector, it has green areas and cycle paths in areas that should remain open for drainage of flood water, and it has a garbage-collection system based on the sorting of recyclable materials by households (70 per cent of which participate). Planners and politicians consult NGOs and neighbourhood groups, the poorer and the better-off. Curitiba has developed an efficient and transparent information system, in particular regarding property, which is seen to have curbed commercial speculation.

The city as an environmental opportunity instead of a threat seems indeed a real prospect, and not a dream. Success does however depend strongly on the influence of people over their own environments, on power relations and policy processes, on capacities to manage environments, and on the ability to analyse and articulate what exactly is the most critical thing to do in a particular situation. These more practical aspects are addressed in chapters 3, 4, and 5.

3

Improving livelihoods

This chapter outlines an approach to improving the livelihoods of poor, excluded, and deprived people, and improving local environments. The approach presented here has no generally recognised name, although it has been dubbed 'participatory environmental assessment' and also 'the sustainable livelihoods approach'. However, neither captures fully what is presented here, and indeed what is already being used by some development practitioners. The chapter's focus is on improving livelihoods and environments through a good understanding of power relations and environmental change, with help from the sustainable livelihoods framework, and through the use of participatory approaches.

Development agencies make choices based on ethics, political analysis, or other factors, and virtually all development agencies aim to alleviate poverty, to reduce human suffering, and to reach better levels of social justice (see chapter 5 for a detailed account of the policies of some development agencies). What is presented here works towards those aims, and is rooted in practical attempts to achieve them, as well as in theories of people–environment relationships and sustainability (see chapter 2). The chapter begins with some case histories of projects in which Oxfam staff and counterpart organisations worked with deprived people, with the ultimate aim of enhancing both local environments and livelihoods.

In section 3.2 the sustainable livelihoods framework is presented. This is an aid to asking the right questions about poverty reduction, livelihood sustainability, and environmental change.

Particularly important in any approach to improving livelihoods and environments is the principle of *participation*. Section 3.3 discusses lessons from social theory and development practice about power relations and interactions between various stakeholders in the development arena, including groups of deprived people, development agencies, government departments, and many other social actors.

3.1 Sustaining livelihoods and environments: lessons from practice

3.1.1 Urban environments and livelihoods

There are important differences between rural and urban contexts that need to be understood for the development of effective urban anti-poverty programmes. For example, in towns and cities people depend more on markets; housing security is more central to people's lives and livelihoods; there are higher levels of environmental and health risks that are at least partly preventable; there is more social diversity and change; and bad government has a bigger impact.[1] Residents' needs for improved livelihoods thus differ from those in rural areas, but the differences are gradual and not fundamental.

In large human settlements, environmental health (water supply, sewerage systems, etc.), housing rights, and public services are of greatest concern to excluded and poor people. For accessing services and improving (urban) lives and livelihoods, democratisation has become the central concern of citizens' groups and NGOs, as is shown in the following case history from Recife, Brazil.

Democratic space in Brazil

The democratisation process in Brazil in the second half of the 1980s, and in particular the adoption of a new constitution in 1988, created new opportunities for citizens' engagement with processes of decision making. SCJP (*Serviço Comunitário de Justiça e Paz* – Community Service for Justice and Peace) in Recife is an NGO with a long history of providing legal and practical support to citizens' groups struggling for the improvement of their *favelas* (slums).[2] About half the population of this city's 1.3 million inhabitants live in *favelas*. SCJP and its predecessor CJP were important from 1987 onwards in achieving new legislation that defined the terms for citizens' participation in municipal policy-making; but since the 1970s CJP had helped groups who occupied urban wastelands and claimed collective rights to construct houses.

A municipal law was approved in 1990 that formalised the rights of citizens to take part in local governance through referendums, councils, and sectoral committees and associations. Among the plethora of structures and processes that were created was a process of 'participatory budgeting' that takes place in six city-regions that are governed by hundreds of elected delegates. Also created was a municipal 'forum for zones of special social interest' (PREZEIS), with 'citizens' committees for urbanisation and legalisation' (COMULs), which concerned the urban neighbourhoods settled by squatters, i.e. neighbourhoods that were essentially illegal *favelas.*

Through PREZEIS and the COMULs, an important democratic space has been created where citizens from poor neighbourhoods can operate, with support from NGOs. This space is institutionalised and it is a legal space, in which (for example) land disputes are addressed. Its establishment is seen as a very important achievement for NGOs and citizens' groups. NGOs across the country played a key role in the formulation of the Brazilian Constitution during the 1980s. In Recife, NGOs had already been supporting citizens before these changes came, in particular NGOs with their roots in so-called liberation theology, as promoted by Dom Helder Camara, the former Archbishop of Olinda and Recife. NGOs also played a central role in setting up PREZEIS, and now they have an institutionalised role in the PREZEIS and COMULs. Their role now is that of advisers to citizens' groups and representatives in the many formal bodies. NGOs train residents and employ experts in legal matters and town planning.

SCJP works primarily to create and strengthen housing associations, in particular through legal aid. It accompanies urban communities once they have been legally recognised and the inhabitants can start participating in the many forums that are associated with their newly acquired status. SCJP is one of six NGOs with such a role in Recife, and a recent evaluation shows that its comparatively political approach makes it more successful in ensuring public investment in infrastructure in the communities, compared with other NGOs and associated *favela* communities. It is seen as a very significant achievement that *favelas* have been made legal, that citizens' participation has been institutionalised, that plans are being made for infrastructural improvements, that some public investment has been made, and that the authorities are now really listening to the representations made by marginalised people. Nevertheless, SCJP is also criticised for not making more efforts to overcome differences with the other NGOs and for failing to initiate collective, city-wide action for higher overall investment by the municipal government.

However, ten years of forums, legal processes, and the development of democratic space do not necessarily result in much actual influence for excluded and marginalised people. Their leaders go from one meeting to another, may have to give up their jobs in order to participate, and have little time left to consult their constituencies. Decisions take a long time to emerge, and power-brokering is conducted outside formal structures. Furthermore, NGO staff have in some cases become substitutes for the citizen-representatives, for example on technical committees; and NGOs have become partly financially dependent on the local authorities. The elaborate systems are now seen by some as a way for the government to legitimise its actions and deal with local tensions, but without much real improvement in poor people's environments, lives, and livelihoods.

Comparatively little is delivered in terms of practical outcomes and public infrastructure in *favelas*; the supply of decent housing and the environmental conditions have not improved much as a result of democratisation. The municipal government's budget for investments in what constitute the neighbourhoods of half its population is no more 1.4 per cent of the total municipal budget, and less then half of this tiny amount has actually been spent over the past five years. The evaluator of SCJP estimates that, at the present rate of investment, the implementation of the plans that are being made by the many committees or are waiting to be implemented would take 124 years to be completed.

Co-option by local politics and administrative systems is one hazard in what is essentially an important step towards the empowerment of *favela* dwellers. In this situation, participation is institutionalised, and politics is central. Behavioural change, participatory tools, and analytical processes facilitated by outsiders with some level of neutrality seem less relevant and do not really appear in the language of NGOs and citizens' groups in Recife, even though they do have the roles of facilitators and enablers. It could be argued that it is in exactly this kind of situation that the ones with power should be targeted for behavioural change. The way to achieve this goal might have to be equally political, and it requires more than just technical support for citizens' representatives.

Current experience suggests that many development agencies focus their support for excluded and deprived people in cities on services related to (environmental) health (including physical infrastructure) and also on housing, and less so on *direct* support for livelihoods.[3] Development agencies and poor people are concerned about people's capacities, social capital, and people's rights as enshrined in law and as affected by government policies or the behaviour of large-scale industries. Extensive NGO documentation of projects that give indirect support to livelihoods in the informal economy shows a focus on microfinance, technological support, and various types of training and capacity building, organisational development, and support for networks, and also on enabling (local) lobby work. There is a large body of practical experience from infrastructural projects, i.e. improvements to housing and water-supply and sanitation systems, and there is particular concern for the mitigation of environmental risks from pollution and (for example) mud slides.[4] In other words, urban livelihoods are supported mainly indirectly, and not with physical inputs into production processes.

For example, a workshop on environmental health and participatory research methodologies in Cairo, Egypt, addressed the progress of projects in response to the concerns of the *Zabbaleen*, a community of garbage collectors and recyclers. Their concerns were primarily about public health within their own community, and generally about the social and political conditions for livelihood strategies, rather than about physical production assets. They suffer various types of pollution and waste accumulation in their neighbourhood and they need improved sanitation and supplies of safe drinking water. Their main concerns are that they are denied support from the authorities and feel victimised by the national press, despite providing the city with an important service.[5]

A review of the environmental impact of 68 small engineering workshops in Bangladesh showed very limited impact on the wider environment, but uncovered important issues related to health and worker safety.[6] It was assumed that large numbers of small-scale informal production workshops would have some negative cumulative impact, and it was felt that this needed careful monitoring. That is still continuing, but initial findings do not suggest that there are particular grounds for worry, beyond the occupational hazards posed to the workers. Poor people's urban livelihoods are based on employment and informal trade, besides informal production and processing. The main respect in which they are 'informal' is that they tend to be too small and numerous for governments to be able to inspect and enforce health, safety, and environmental regulations: limited regulatory capacity is more usefully employed in large-scale industries. Improvements – or, rather, reduction of risks – should therefore come from awareness-raising and self-regulation, which is what NGOs such as ITDG attempt to support (see also section 4.2.2).[7]

Analysis of the experience of international and local development agencies related to *urban* livelihoods and environments has identified the following issues, among others.

Key questions for urban livelihood improvement[8]

1 What are the environmental health risks for a particular group of urban poor, or social actors, at work and at home?

2 Which physical infrastructure and technological capabilities are essential for poor people to access in order to ensure a safer environment?

3 What are the critical capabilities of poor and vulnerable urban people to enable them to make a living?

4 Which social policies, institutions, organisations, and networks play a critical role in enabling urban people to make a living, from petty trade, services, or small-scale manufacture?

5 Which policies, institutions, organisations, and networks are critical for achieving land and housing security for poor people?

3.1.2 Rural livelihoods: two case histories

Two rural case histories in which early forms of the sustainable livelihoods framework and a range of other analytical and development tools have been used are described below. The Niassa food-security programme in Mozambique focuses on a number of villages in three districts in the south of Niassa province; and in Vietnam there is a cluster of small projects in Lung Vai, a rural commune.[9] In both cases, agricultural production is of central importance to livelihoods and indeed to the programmes' activities. The presentations follow the structure of the most recent version of the sustainable livelihoods framework, which is discussed in detail in section 3.2. Each case history contains conclusions about project impacts, and in the sub-section following these two cases some common lessons are drawn out.

Food security in southern Niassa, Mozambique

The current Niassa Food Security Programme (NFSP) was formulated in 1996. It is rooted in Oxfam GB's earlier involvement in the south of Niassa province in Mozambique during and immediately after the civil war, in particular with distributions of seeds, tools, and clothes, and road rehabilitation. There are now an estimated 86,000 inhabitants in the three districts which comprise southern Niassa. After 1994 some staff training took place in participatory needs-assessment and monitoring, and also in the fundamentals of sustainable livelihoods. A review of programme impacts in 1998 focused particularly on the agricultural sector and has subsequently been updated.

Livelihood strategies

Agriculture is the main livelihood strategy of the majority of people in the districts. The better-off households have prepared sizable fields, on which foods for consumption and some cash-crops are grown. Maize and cassava are the most important staples, but many individual families in all three districts lack staples, are dependent on gifts and *ganho-ganho* (piece work), and eat forest foods in at least part of the year. Social-ranking exercises indicated that in 1996 50-80 per cent of households lacked staple food from their own fields; by 1998 this had declined to 10-20 per cent in some communities, while in others up to 50 per cent of families still suffered shortages. The improvements are largely attributed to the stability that has come with peace.

The rearing of small livestock is being stimulated, but the scale of these activities is still limited – keeping cattle is not possible, because of tsetse infestation. Cotton is the main cash-crop in the region (grown on contract for a large cotton enterprise), and other cash-crops such as groundnuts, maize, and tobacco are also sold in small quantities. Small markets and petty trade have started in the district towns. Some imported goods are coming from Malawi, and excess maize and other products are taken out of the region on bicycles over very large distances, in part to Malawi. Some micro enterprises have been set up, including sunflower-seed processing for cooking oil, for local consumption.

Human capital

In most villages in the district, children have access to basic primary education; but there is no secondary education at all, and boys are in the majority at school. The infrastructure is very basic, and teaching quality very low. Although schools have been established since 1959, most women have not been educated.

The main diseases are preventable, but there is a lack of capacity for the conduct of vaccination campaigns. There is a very rudimentary curative health service in each district, and in every village there are traditional healers and birth attendants. A few of those have received professional training in nutrition practices and attending births. The Mozambican Red Cross has health visitors who reach 15 small communities in Nipepe district with some basic drugs. Similar efforts are made in the other districts, and some new international aid is expected, but the health of the population remains very precarious.

In agriculture the main limiting factor is the availability of labour for opening new *machambas* (fields). The poorer families have less labour available; the least well-off in this respect are young couples who have not yet cleared fields, the recently arrived (who were earlier displaced by war), old and sick people, and single mothers. The poorer families also have limited time to prepare their fields, because they are earning money through *ganho-ganho*. There are three government agricultural extension workers in each district who conduct some very basic agricultural training courses and who manage demonstration plots and visit farmers. There is a lack of knowledge about the effects of pesticides among farmers who cultivate cotton, although the foreign-owned cotton enterprise does give some basic instruction when it delivers the chemicals.

Social capital

There is a strongly paternalistic culture, which is reflected in social networks, family structures, and local decision making. About 1700 people in the three districts are members of farmers' groups that were initiated by the NFSP. Of this membership, a minority are women, and women rarely participate actively in community meetings in the presence of men. They do talk and engage with problem issues when working in women's groups, for example on issues related to health. The older women with a traditional role as birth attendant or otherwise are the most prominent in such meetings. Participatory research in 1994 revealed that many of the women had control of part of their household money during the war, when many families were separated; however, research in 1996 suggests this situation has now reverted to normal, i.e. household money is the sole responsibility of men.

The social networks, determined by family ties and traditional structures of governance, do appear to be of critical importance in the redistribution of food produce to the infirm, old, and most needy in the communities. The Catholic Church and some Moslem groups are also important for welfare and service provision, and particularly for spiritual well-being.

Natural capital

The area is thinly populated, tropical humid savannah and dry forest. It is widely agreed that maize harvests in the early 1990s failed or almost failed in two consecutive years, but in 1996/7 yields were good, and the 1997/8 harvest slightly less so. Erratic rain with an average of almost 1000 mm/year is the main explanation for relative success or failure of staple crops; drought stress appears to occur roughly every other year.[10]

There are few fruit trees beyond old mango stands, and the poorest people harvest wild roots and fruits from the forest in times of crisis, especially in the so-called hungry season. Near some of the permanent streams and rivers, people cultivate vegetables and tobacco, but not all communities have access to an all-year water source. Local people clear forest and then cultivate for two or three years, but the less well-off are obliged to use depleted soils – land that has been cultivated for several years already.

Large wildlife, in particular elephants and monkeys, are considered a nuisance, because they occasionally raid fields of staple crops, especially those grown at some distance from settlements. Hunting is not an important activity.

Physical capital
The distances are huge and the road conditions bad, but road rehabilitation is being supported by some international development

agencies. Since 1994, vehicles have been able to enter the remotest district towns of southern Niassa, but some villages are still accessible only on foot. The cotton industry has been re-established in the region with the return of the João Ferreiro dos Santos (JFS) cotton-trading company. They engage with farmers through negotiating contracts, delivering seeds and pesticides, and buying the cotton against prices set by the government of Mozambique. They transport the produce out of the region and have made a very minor contribution to initial road repair.

In almost all communities, there are problems with drinking-water supply from badly protected traditional wells at the end of the dry season (August–November). Some concrete and brick buildings of low quality can be found, but only in the district towns. Electricity is hardly available.

Financial capital

The cotton industry is the most important source of cash income for local people. The Portuguese-owned JFS re-entered the area in 1994 and started discussions with elders and other members of the population about reviving cotton production, which had been an important cash-crop in the colonial era. Cotton production did not restart until the 1995/6 season, increased substantially in 1996/7, but levelled off after that. This is partly due to low prices and a stop in the supply of pesticides to the smallest farmers, who failed to grow sufficient cotton to pay for the costly inputs.

Surplus produce is still regularly exchanged for clothes or other necessities, instead of being sold for cash. Very few farmers have the means to invest in agricultural inputs such as pesticides or fertilisers. Most use cash to buy basic necessities like salt, cooking oil, clothes, shoes, medicines, and materials for schoolchildren. Single mothers have particular problems in obtaining cash. The local markets have been slowly reviving since peace arrived in 1993, but there is still a lack of information about market prices in the towns and the even remoter villages. Traders need information about excess production of tradable goods such as beans and maize (in some years and some villages).

Policies, processes, and structures

There is strong male dominance in the traditional and formal structures. The *regulos* (local chiefs) are the community leaders, *muenes* are local chiefs in charge of smaller units, and *pia muenes* are local women leaders. The government administration works with these traditional leaders. The extension services and development programmes are very male-dominated too.

The most important factor that has affected livelihoods in southern Niassa is the signing in 1993 of the peace accords between the government and RENAMO – the armed opposition. In 1994 national elections were held, soldiers were demobilised, and people started to return to the villages where they had lived before the war. This meant that people could start cultivating crops, traders could develop their businesses, and the State could start rebuilding its service provision. However, in 1999 politics between the two main political parties of Mozambique was played out at local level, which led to tensions with Oxfam staff. As a result of this, Oxfam had to close down its activities in one of the three districts.

The District Department of Agriculture and Fisheries (DDAP) has extremely limited resources in terms of transport, staffing, and techn-ological capabilities, and the departments of Health and Education and Public Works have also very limited capacity. This means that national, provincial, or district policies in these areas have limited impact. Besides the Mozambican Red Cross, there are several international NGOs and bilateral agencies working in the area, all with financial resources that surpass those of the local government; they therefore wield considerable influence.

The cotton-trading company JFS is the most significant private enterprise in the province. Cotton farming is regulated by the government through minimum farm-gate prices, but the government does not have the capacity for the effective monitoring and control of practices such as the use of chemical pesticides. An important operator in food trading is the parastatal trading organisation IMC, but private traders are gaining in strength.

In neighbouring areas, a significant group of white settler farmers from South Africa have established some very large farms, at the invitation of the Mozambican authorities. The area is as yet thinly populated, and problems related to private land titles and traditional cultivation rights have not (yet) been reported.

Impacts of the Oxfam programme on livelihoods and environments

Expenditure. Over the two years 1996/7 and 1997/8, the actual programme expenditure (including most overheads) was £309,784, or £182 per family of direct beneficiaries, as organised in groups in two years (i.e. an estimated £36 per benefiting family member). This cannot be described as cheap, in particular since the impact of the programme is still limited. This can at least in part be explained by the very high transport costs to reach the areas where the programme works, and because the starting point for the programme was a situation of extremely limited local capacity. The programme will have to continue for several more years before real benefits in terms of improved livelihoods and environmental quality can be expected.

Recovery from war. Over the years since the war, the most important impacts of the programme are perceived to be on transport (and indirectly on trade) and on the revival of agricultural production, both of which started as emergency rehabilitation efforts. Distributed seeds were usually open-pollinated varieties, purchased locally, which means that the local genetic stock was maintained and not unwittingly contaminated with inappropriate varieties. Agricultural tools were distributed at a time when markets were incapable of supplying them, and indeed people had no capacity to buy tools even if they had been available. Distributions of seeds and tools reached the majority of the population. Rehabilitation of roads and bridges was carried out with local technology and labour, and with payments in kind and also in money. Most of these impacts were attributable to activities and expenditures that pre-dated the NFSP and what has been mentioned above.

Farmers' groups and capacities. Since 1997, the NFSP's agricultural sector has worked through 26 locally recruited animators, of whom initially just three were women, working with the four Oxfam supervisors and staff of the District extension services. Later more women animators were recruited. The NFSP works with 104 farmers' groups in total, comprising an estimated 1700 members, of whom about 27 per cent are women. Within the farmers' groups there is as yet little management capacity, although traditional forms of collaborating do exist. Nevertheless, leader-farmers were expected to take over the role of the animators in the course of the year 2000. Some of the communities with farmers' groups are among the worst-off in terms of agricultural production and food security; others are among the better-off. Assuming a total estimated population of 86,000 people in the three districts, and an estimated family size of five people, it seemed that the NFSP was reaching 10 per cent of the population in 1998 through its agricultural work, and this percentage is rising.

Sunflower oil and micro-enterprises. The distribution of sunflower seeds by the NFSP has created some enthusiasm among farmers, partly because they see it as an alternative to cotton as a source of income. Sunflower production has become significant, and seeds are being processed into oil for local consumption. The micro-enterprise sector has, however, not been very successful, because of errors in project design and also because the potential for micro-enterprises is very limited. The programme supplied loans to about 25 people, mostly men, for oil presses and other micro-enterprises. Some oil presses and tools are under-used, because of problems with the supply of raw materials. Following repayment problems, a moratorium on loans was declared in September 1997, but new initiatives to support micro-enterprise and especially trade were launched in 1999, with the stimulation of markets and trade as a focus for the second phase of the programme (1999-2002).

Staple crops and production technology. There is so far not much impact on the productivity or sustainability of staple-crop production that can be attributed to the NFSP extension activities, although recent distribution of improved maize varieties (open-pollinated, short-duration) has been welcomed by farmers. The NFSP has also distributed sweet-potato vines, cow peas, groundnuts, sorghum, and millet seeds. These distributions have helped to revive or stimulate production of those crops, albeit on a limited scale.

Traditional practices include certain ways of inter-cropping, but it is doubtful that nitrogen fixed by the leguminous plants is actually benefiting other plants under current practice (due to late sowing of the beans). The NFSP has promoted alternative planting techniques and established some on-farm variety trials, but the results have not yet been analysed with and by farmers. There are very few small animals and no cattle in the area, which makes it difficult to maintain soil fertility with organic waste and dung.

Horticulture and livestock. Horticulture has not developed much beyond a few villages with a good water source, but since 1998 horticultural seeds have been distributed. A very small-scale initiative to distribute small livestock and rotate the offspring in 1994 was assessed and extended to a larger scale in 1998.

Institutional capacity. Oxfam supervisors, government extension staff, and animators have attended a number of workshops, covering group organisation, extension, and some technical issues. However, the staff's knowledge of both conventional and low-external-input farming techniques remains limited. Farmer-controlled trials and the introduction of new technologies are still at an early stage. In 1999 a national NGO partner began to participate in the work, which is a promising development.

Nutrition. The nutrition-awareness activities of the programme have had very limited impact on dietary habits. The NFSP has identified the need for support in the grinding of maize and other foodstuffs, and is undertaking initiatives in this respect.

The position of women. The activities in the agricultural sector have not had much impact on gender relationships. It is still difficult to ensure the active participation of women in community meetings in the presence of men. Anecdotal evidence suggests some changes, but as yet there is no firm evidence of improvements in women's position in the communities. There are significantly more girls attending school, compared with the pre-war years, but boys are still the majority, and anyway this change cannot be attributed to the programme. The NFSP has made a good effort to include women in the farmers' groups; they are still a minority, but women are clearly present in most groups – a change that is unlikely to have taken place without active encouragement.

Markets. The activities of Oxfam and its local counterparts before the start of the NFSP helped to revive trade through improved transport and agricultural production, which is demonstrated by government data. Markets have emerged in the district towns, but not elsewhere in the districts. Local people earn cash through selling small quantities of food crops, like maize and groundnuts, as well as cotton that is traded through a foreign company. There are problems with low crop prices, which are set by traders. There is also a lack of information about traders and prices among the local people, and traders lack information about surplus production. Over the past years, the programme has played a small role in stimulating trade through the communication of prices and product availability, which should improve in future.

Livelihood diversity and vulnerability. Many local households have recovered their former production levels, some have started to diversify crops and ventured into small-livestock keeping, and a few are involved in petty trade or micro-enterprises. Maize varieties that can produce under some drought stress have been introduced. Local capacities are being developed, and women's voices are slowly strengthening. The conclusion that vulnerability to adverse events has decreased for many people seems to be justified.

Improved livelihoods in Lung Vai

Oxfam GB has supported projects in the commune of Lung Vai in Muong Khuong district, Lao Cai province, in Vietnam since early 1994. This work was initiated after a request from the authorities for agricultural development support for a small group of displaced people. In response, Oxfam staff organised a training workshop on Participatory Rural Appraisal (PRA), combined with the use of the sustainable livelihoods framework. Oxfam works through a number of project partners, mostly departmental services of the province and district. In 1994 the Land Allocation Project was initiated, later followed by the Agroforestry Project. Both took a participatory approach. Teachers in the area were also supported, as was the construction of basic facilities for primary education in some hamlets. More recently a programme of support for agricultural extension services was launched. Other activities include a credit and savings scheme for women, support for a small irrigation system, the building of some small bridges, and a programme for building capacities throughout the province in participatory irrigation management.

Livelihood strategies

A large majority of the population are involved in agriculture in one way or another. Shifting cultivation has declined strongly in the past few years, but farming on steep slopes is widespread. All the households are involved in rice production for consumption, and some are able to sell their surplus. Rice is cultivated in the valleys, and dry-land rice is grown on the hillsides; but farmers prefer the lower fields, where irrigation and paddy cultivation are sometimes possible.

In the 'hungry periods', forest foods, root crops, cassava, and maize are eaten; the latter is also cultivated as fodder. Most households keep livestock (buffaloes, cows, pigs, and sometimes chickens).

Illegal logging from the forests benefits a few people from towns and some labourers from a State Farm which is located in the commune but managed separately and has a separate community of people. Local people are allowed to use timber, but beyond that they do very little forest exploitation or trade in forest products.

There is a marketplace in the commune centre where tradespeople from towns and other communes come, and there is some petty trading by locals (mainly the sale of chickens or wine). From some households young men have left to find work in occupations such as construction, and they send money back to their families.

Human capital

Overall school enrolment has improved gradually since 1993. There are now classrooms for primary-school Grades 1 and 2 in (for example) Bo Lung and Ta San hamlets, which means that the youngest children no longer depend on the school in the main settlement of Lung Vai, where a lower-secondary school was built in 1997.

Despite some adult literacy programmes, the literacy rates among adults remain low in comparison to other parts of the country, especially among women of the ethnic minorities, who often do not speak Vietnamese (i.e. *Kinh*) at all. Some men have undergone basic instruction courses at an agricultural college and have also benefited from technical briefings from the extension service. The provincial Department of Irrigation provides training for two people in each commune (including Lung Vai) to improve local management of irrigation systems, and those two are responsible for sharing what they learn with other irrigators in their commune.

The health infrastructure in the district has recently improved, and the health status of the communities is gradually improving: witnessed, for example, by a strongly reduced incidence of malaria since 1993. There is a 'culture centre' in Lung Vai with access to television, and some of the better-off households have TV sets, although rarely so in the remoter hamlets where various ethnic minorities live. In particular in these communities there is a general lack of understanding of laws and regulations, including the land-allocation process that was initiated in the late 1980s.

Social capital

The population of the commune is just over 2000 people. There are various formal and informal groups in the commune, for example a Water Users' Association, an Agricultural Extension Club, and savings and credit groups. The members are mostly men, but the local branch of the national Women's Union has played an important role in a credit and savings project.

Wives participate in decisions about family spending, and sometimes they market produce and procure necessities; however, in general husbands control household money. Women tend not to go out in the evening, but in the daytime some of the older ones do attend community meetings; only men attend the community meetings that are held in evenings.

Hamlets are represented in commune discussions by their leaders, who tend to be men elected from among themselves. The hamlets tend to be ethnically homogeneous, or dominated by one particular group. (There are in total seven distinct ethnic groups living together in the commune, of which one is the nationally dominant Vietnamese or *Kinh* group, most of whose members migrated into the area in the second half of the twentieth century.) The ethnic minorities have strong kinship ties beyond their hamlets and commune, but tend to be less influential in commune affairs and are generally among the poorer people.

Natural capital

The commune area is approximately 5500 ha, made up of 'barren hills' (usually covered with shrubs) and forest and some low-lying agricultural land, the latter of which is less than 300 ha. It also includes a large tea plantation (the State Farm).

Swidden agriculture on the higher and steeper slopes has caused soil erosion. Twenty families from a neighbouring commune were displaced to a lower-lying part of Lung Vai as a result of landslides caused by a combination of heavy rainfall and reduced soil cover. Swidden agriculture has now virtually stopped. Most families now have Land Use Certificates (LUCs) for low-lying agricultural land.

Some of the 'barren hills' and parts of the forest are now managed by small groups, the commune, or the District. Forest patches continue to be logged legally, and also illegally. Timber and fruit trees have been planted in small stands near homesteads and on fields; they show reasonable survival rates, but few are yielding as yet.

Water is tapped from some of the permanent streams for drinking and irrigation, but this does not benefit all hamlets or households of the commune.

The households in the medium-to-better-off range own two or three buffaloes each (mainly used for ploughing), cows, pigs, and/or chickens. The main crop is rice, but maize, soybean, cassava, and potatoes are also grown.

Physical capital

School-building, bridge-construction, and irrigation schemes have helped to improve some of the infrastructure in the commune. Most people live in wooden houses; those of the better-off have tiled roofs, and the others have thatched roofs. The poorest have 'temporary houses'. The better-off households have small machines such as threshers and huskers. Some own bicycles, and a very few have motorbikes.

The majority of households can afford to buy at least some improved seed varieties, (subsidised) fertilisers, and also pesticides and livestock drugs.

Financial capital

The average agricultural production was estimated by the authorities to be 310kg/person of 'rice equivalent' in 1993, rising to 360kg in 1997. This is more than twice what is internationally thought of as the consumption requirement, indicating a fair amount of marketed surplus for the commune as a whole.

The government provides loans and subsidies for seeds and fertilisers. Other sources of money are The Bank for the Poor and allowances from the Resettlement Programme. There is also a small credit and savings scheme for women, managed by the Women's Union, which increased from 33 to 49 million Dong over two-three years until July 1998. Some households receive small war-pensions from the government.

The better-off households are able to save every year, and sometimes benefit from remittances. There are some artisans and petty traders, and there is a fairly well-established regular market in the commune. Farmers sell produce to traders, who transport it to towns farther away – the commune is situated along the road between the provincial capital Lao Cai and Muong Khuong district town.

Policies, processes, and structures

The government introduced a classification system for the land and it issues land-use certificates (LUCs). If the land is not used, the State may reclaim it, but otherwise the arrangement is equivalent to a long-term lease, with the possibility of inheriting the title. The provincial Land Law and Land Management Department regulates and implements the issuing of LUCs, with guidance from the equivalent national ministry. Land-surveying for the purpose of issuing LUCs can now be replaced by consultation with local leaders and reference to sketch-maps. LUCs now feature the names of both husband and wife, whereas formerly only the head of household was mentioned.

The Province Department of Agriculture and Rural Development manages rural extension services and also the bigger irrigation schemes. There are similar structures at district level, but with considerably fewer resources. New national laws enable local farmers' groups to manage small irrigation systems.

The government effectively subsidises the provision of hybrid seeds (especially rice) and inputs such as fertilisers and pesticides. It has improved veterinary care through a better supply of drugs and free vaccinations of livestock. It has reinforced its policy of forbidding the practice of shifting cultivation in forests and the so-called barren hills. There is also strict regulation governing where cows and buffaloes can be kept, particularly at commune level.

Impacts on livelihoods and environments

Expenditure. Oxfam has spent about £28 per person in Lung Vai, over a period of about four years, on projects that are directly beneficial to the commune. Further expenditure has benefited staff of Oxfam's (government) partners and some advocacy activities. The total expenditure on Lung Vai and some wider activities was expected to be £123,504 by early in the year 2000, or £60 per capita over five years. This excludes some internal Oxfam overheads. Given the mostly encouraging impacts of the programme, the costs are considered acceptable.

Well-being and equity. Some of the poorest families in all the hamlets have progressed from a state of extreme poverty, while almost all of the very poorest have improved their livelihoods, although in some cases to only a very small degree. Many of the better-off have achieved greater improvements than the poorest, and there is now somewhat greater socio-economic inequality in Lung Vai than there was in 1993, both between individuals in the hamlets and between hamlets.

Production. Livelihood improvements are at least partly due to new hybrid seed varieties, the provision of loans, and the availability of subsidised fertilisers and livestock drugs (none of which was due to the specific projects, as all are part of general government policy), besides normal life-cycle events (for example children growing up and starting to help on the fields). The subsidised agricultural inputs have contributed to increased rice production, as have improvements in irrigation, which was partly supported by the projects. The Oxfam-supported credit scheme has had some impact on the lives of poor women.

The production improvements carry some environmental risks, and longer-term production and natural resources may be jeopardised. Mono-cultures increase the risk of pest occurrence, pesticides create resistance (a problem that increases over time), and hybrid varieties (i.e. the subsidised seeds) usually require more fertilisers and pesticides, which implies an increase in health risks. The farmers will become increasingly dependent on these external inputs. Risks of increased pests are greatest for the poorest farmers, who can least afford inputs – and there is a risk that subsidies may be reduced in future.

One positive aspect of agricultural intensification accompanied by improved veterinary care is the development of pig-keeping and the related production of dung, so that a potential for improved composting exists (the use of manure on fields is common practice).

Land policy. The government's approach to land allocation has changed dramatically, in Lao Cai province and now also elsewhere in Vietnam, partly on the basis of experience in Lung Vai, where consultation with farmers and the use of sketch-maps was pioneered. Land allocation now formally requires consultations with farmers and leaders, use can be made of sketch-maps, and two names must now be included in LUCs – those of wife and husband – which is seen as offering women a better chance of guaranteed access to land, in the case of divorce or death of the husband. The actual impact of this latter change can however not be substantiated yet. These policy changes were achieved in collaboration with other international agencies and government departments. Scope exists for policy dialogue in other fields, such as agricultural technology development, subsidisation of agricultural inputs and services, and building of capacities in participatory approaches and organisational development at the lowest levels.

Land. Several farmers who have benefited from the allocation of land have been stimulated to invest time, effort, and money in the cultivation of trees, and to implement some measures to conserve soil and water, with strong support from the projects.

Permanent cultivation of crops on established fields (on slopes) following a virtual halt to shifting cultivation is due to a combination of stronger policing and the provision of subsidised inputs for wet-land rice cultivation in particular. These changes imply reduced pressures on forest and 'barren hills', reduced risks of landslides, soil erosion, and improved water conservation. The agro-forestry project has supported these changes and made many tree seedlings available; however, the better-off families received more seedlings, for a number of reasons, which suggests that once the trees are mature, socio-economic inequality will increase.

Forests. Some forests have been allocated to particular hamlets, an initiative that is said to have reduced conflicts over these resources. Local management with strong restrictions on commercial felling may be expected to bring environmental benefits too, while local people benefit in terms of their own timber and fuelwood requirements.

The poorest. The very poorest people in Lung Vai commune do not take much part in the new production methods or environmental improvements. They were not (and are not) responsible for felling trees in the forests, and they were not pioneers in opening new fields on 'barren hills'. Some of them can afford some hybrid seeds and fertilisers, partly because of the subsidies; some have done some successful pig-keeping, but others, lacking access to the veterinary services, watched their animals die. Most managed to plant just a few trees; they have only a limited amount of registered land on which trees would be planted. They have very little land for paddy cultivation, usually insufficient for home consumption.

Voice. The research has not produced conclusive evidence that the poorest and most vulnerable families within hamlets now participate more in the affairs of the commune; in fact in this case there seems to have been no change and no impact. Nevertheless, there is some evidence that women participate more readily at commune level. Within households women may have stronger voices, in some cases, but it is doubtful whether credit for this can be claimed by the projects. More generally, people across the commune now communicate with some ease with outsiders; they openly articulate their problems, needs, and opinions. There is more interaction between the most marginalised ethnic minorities and outsiders as a result of the projects. More opportunities have been created for local leaders to voice their concerns to higher-level authorities.

Institutional capacities. There has been a significant impact on the attitudes of the staff of service departments. The projects have strongly promoted participatory approaches to extension, irrigation management, and land allocation in the various departments at district and province level. Extension staff now recognise the need for further collaboration with farmers, in order to achieve technological improvements and higher and more sustainable production. Operational/lower-level staff were trained in participatory approaches and some technologies, but they still lack skills in project monitoring and evaluation.

The commune leaders involved in the Management Board of the agroforestry project and the women's credit and savings scheme have learned some management skills. Ideas of farmer-to-farmer extension are being developed. Comparatively little capacity building and organisational development has happened in terms of farmers', women's, and youth groups or irrigation-management organisations at commune or hamlet levels, but this is being considered.

Livelihood diversity and vulnerability. Most local households have increased their productivity and production levels; many have planted at least some fruit and timber trees; risks of soil erosion have decreased; and some are doing well from keeping pigs. The government subsidises hybrid seeds, pesticides, and fertilisers, which may imply some risks. But institutional capacities are strengthening at all levels, and farmers are benefiting from various extension initiatives. The voice of women and ethnic minorities is gradually strengthening. Prospects of employment elsewhere and of small trade are improving. Socio-economic inequality is increasing, but even the poorest are getting a little more prosperous. Local livelihoods of the large majority are more secure now, compared with the situation five years ago.

3.1.3 Lessons from Niassa and Lung Vai

There are important similarities – and differences – between the situations in Niassa and Lung Vai. In southern Niassa, ethnicity is fairly homogeneous. This very remote area has strongly underdeveloped markets and a very low population density; literacy and health services and administrative structures are extremely weak; and the country is emerging from decades of war, which still resonate in local political controversies. Lung Vai is comparatively remote from major centres of population, and in fact the area was deeply affected by a border-war with China in 1979, which added to the devastation of the wars before 1975. However, recovery has gradually taken place: relations with China have improved; markets are much more developed; the political situation is very stable; services are present and getting stronger as a result of national economic growth; and administrative structures are highly developed. Unlike Niassa, the residents of Lung Vai belong to seven distinctly different ethnic groups, and there are strong discrepancies between them in, for example, access to education.

Participation and civil society

Oxfam has worked with local authorities, rather than through local NGOs, over a substantial period of time, but in both cases grassroots groups are emerging, and citizens are more involved in local decision making: a microfinance project operates through the Women's Union in Lung Vai, and in Niassa collaboration has started with a local NGO. Participatory approaches to project management have contributed to this gradual strengthening of civil society and have helped to change the behaviour of some local leaders and officials, in particular in the Vietnamese case. Nevertheless, for involvement of civil society in decision making more needs to be done, including conscious efforts to organise new structures and groups.

A very important interface exists in Niassa where local, traditional leadership structures in villages and districts interact with administrative structures and the political leaders of the two main political parties. In Lung Vai, the administrative structures and political leaders also interact with the leaders of hamlets, which are often dominated by just one ethnic group, with its own culture and rules of authority.

In the case of Lung Vai, there are indications that the voice of the ethnic-minority groups at the level of the commune is heard more clearly, but that gain is modest. The lesson here seems not so much that empowerment is impossible, or that the programmes were not well implemented, but that empowerment is a slow and difficult process, and it requires persistence on the part of the external agency to create forums in which minorities can voice their concerns and demonstrate their abilities. Significant change in the behaviour of project staff and officials is reported from both sites; skills were learned, and analysis of development processes improved. Perhaps the most important conclusion is that *'participation is difficult'*, in the words of an outsider-facilitator.

Women's participation and influence

The interfaces between local people, local political officials, and higher-level government administrators are strongly male-dominated in both cases. It is where most local power and decision-making are concentrated, and an outsider-initiative cannot and should not attempt to circumvent this fact. The participatory events, monitoring visits, and (participatory) impact assessment in both programmes suggest some progress in terms of the involvement of women in community decision making, but only on a very modest scale. One obvious lesson from this is that any positive change in the status of women, their incomes and food security can be expected only from real change in the behaviour of men (at these interfaces), and indeed from the participation of women in formal and informal decision-making processes. In both cases some success can be claimed in this regard, for example the inclusion of wives' names on Land Use Certificates in Vietnam; but there is largely unexplored potential for more work with *men* in which gender relationships, and gendered relationships between people and natural resources, would be addressed.

Politics and policy change

In both cases, the importance of politics is visible in the interfaces between local and higher authorities, district, province, and national government, and between national NGOs and international donors. In Niassa, political wrangling between local representatives of the two political parties (one dominates government) spilled over into criticism of Oxfam staff, and the programme had to withdraw from one of the districts. National and provincial policies, laws, and regulations are important, because they determine the democratic space and the rules of engagement between citizens and formal decision-making processes. However, these rules are not fixed. This was expressed in Lung Vai, where experience of the participatory allocation of land-use certificates (i.e. the implementation of a national policy) led to the acceptance of the use of sketch-maps in the absence of detailed topographical surveys. The lessons for external NGOs appear to be: don't get entangled in local politics, yet do assume that policies and laws can change on the basis of good development work and close engagement with policy processes.

Livelihoods and production

In both cases, the impacts of the projects on livelihoods and agricultural production were moderately positive. The greatest impacts were from very particular activities, such as seed distribution in Niassa, and in Vietnam through government subsidies on seeds and other inputs, and tree planting supported by Oxfam. Oxfam's most important contribution to improving the livelihoods and production of the poorest in Lung Vai (and indirectly elsewhere) may have been its support for land allocation. Thus the impact studies showed that a strategically chosen intervention, based on good analysis of needs and realities, is more important than aiming to support all the assets and capacities of local people and national livelihood policies.

In both cases, efforts by extension staff to change agricultural practices and enhance farmers' technological knowledge were geared towards reducing dependency on external inputs and improving both the size of yields and the sustainability of production. Obviously more time and very significant resources are required, if real impact on a substantial scale is to be achieved. In neither case did the projects manage to develop a fully effective system, which would have involved training selected farmers and facilitating farmer-to-farmer technology transfer in a comparatively short period; but both programmes have laid the foundations for such an approach (for example, farmers' groups were set up).

Environments

Natural resources are used by farmers in both cases, and in Vietnam efforts were made to protect and regenerate them, through strengthening local forest management, tree-planting initiatives, and some efforts to conserve soil and water and to discourage shifting cultivation on comparatively steep hills. In Niassa the dominant environmental risks relate to the provision of drinking water (which the project did not address), and the use of pesticides without proper protection and training (in cotton farming through contracts with a big company). In both cases the technological changes include improvements in soil fertility and pest resistance through 'sustainable' or 'low-external-input' techniques. The successes in this respect are modest, as argued above. These alternative techniques must be developed and spread much more widely, partly because the poorer farmers cannot afford agrochemicals, but also because of the risks to the health of farmers and consumers, and the potential damage to future productivity.

Analysis: towards strategic choices

Any positive changes and impacts arising from development projects are the result of very complex interactions between different social actors, and should not be seen to follow automatically from participation in project management, the empowerment of women and minorities, or farmers' increased capacities. Development agencies generally aim to improve the plight of the poorest and the excluded, improve social equity, and enhance environmental sustainability. They use their influence to persuade others to adopt policies and practices that serve those goals – they participate, as other stakeholders do. Although synergy from working towards these different objectives can certainly happen, it depends very much on whether the analysis of complex reality has indeed uncovered the most strategic type of intervention from a bewildering array of themes and approaches: work on health, education, farmers' technological knowledge, farm inputs, microfinance, the many government policies and processes that influence lives and environments, the operation of markets, etc. The next section elaborates on the so-called sustainable livelihoods framework, which systematises such themes and can be used as a tool for analysis.

3.2 The sustainable livelihoods framework

This section presents a detailed discussion of the sustainable livelihoods framework, which is referred to in many parts of this book. It can be seen as an analytical framework that structures when and why environmental issues are important in human lives and particularly in relation to livelihoods, but without ignoring the complexity of the human reality. The current shape of the sustainable livelihoods framework evolved during the 1990s, based on some theoretical work and practical experience, in particular in programmes of the UNDP, CARE, and Oxfam.[11] In earlier versions the framework has been used in the formulation of development programmes and (smaller) projects that were looking for ways to address both social and environmental concerns.[12] Attempts to improve environmental sustainability alone, divorced from the social and economic context, had met with limited success, and it became clear, as the first sub-section here concludes, that there is indeed a need to systematise relations between people and nature, and not just to list environmental categories. The framework is presented in detail in sub-sections 3.2.2–3.2.6. Sub-sections 3.2.7 and 3.2.8 discuss how it can be used in analytical processes, based on experience gained from actual use of the framework and from training staff in its use.

The framework is compatible with the participatory and rights-based approaches to development that are used in the case histories discussed in section 3.1, and which are explained in more detail in section 3.3. The sustainable livelihoods framework is thus part of a wider approach to development.

3.2.1 Checklists of environmental issues

Environmental issues that are important for poor people have been assigned to categories that can be found in the very diverse and sometimes contradictory literature on social and political sciences, geography, biology, or other natural sciences, and philosophy too. Categories usually include various *aspects of nature* (for example trees, forests, and wild plants, land and soil, oceans, rivers, fisheries, and wildlife); *human-made environmental resources* (such as physical infrastructure, factories, and housing); issues of *social relations* (including access to and control over environmental resources); *disasters* (flooding and drought, earthquakes and volcanic eruptions, cyclones, and industrial disasters); and environmental *quality* (water supply and sanitation, energy, and various types of pollution).[13]

People, their surroundings, and livelihoods are affected by global and national change processes in, for example, markets and by changes in environmental phenomena. The driving forces behind local environmental change are partly international: inequality in wealth and power, unregulated consumption of (natural) resources, and unregulated trade lead to wasteful patterns of consumption among the rich minority. Poor people or local decision makers do not necessarily perceive this to be important. Besides local environmental concerns, there are thus wider issues to consider:[14] global *climate change* (consequent on the production of greenhouse gases); reduction in *bio-diversity* and developments in *bio-technology* (with risks for global and local ecosystems); *atmospheric changes* (for example 'acid rain', or destruction of the ozone layer, with risks of skin cancer and also impacts on certain flora); *pollution* across borders (for example nuclear fall-out, pollution of seas, oceans, international rivers and aquifers); and *depletion of resources* (especially from the global commons, such as fish from oceans, rainforests that absorb carbon dioxide and act as 'sinks' for greenhouse gas, and also fossil fuels and ores).

Attempts to systematise environmental issues and present them in checklists for assessing the potential environmental impact of projects can be useful (see also chapter 4). However, they often result in unwieldy overviews, they lead to an undue focus on the physical aspects of environmental change, or they are incomplete. A synopsis of environmental categories can also be problematic, because classifying or grouping issues is an arbitrary business in the absence of some kind of reasoned relationship between people and their surroundings. Furthermore, any framework needs to be compatible with the analytical concepts of the people who are both the main target of the project and the ones who are expected to participate in – if not lead – the development processes that are assumed to produce improvements in their lives and surroundings. The sustainable livelihoods framework attempts to accommodate the complexity of real life and the entirety of the world-view of deprived people, and it provides an outline of the relationships between environments and social processes.

3.2.2 Sustainable livelihoods: definition and diagram

The concept of sustainable livelihoods has been defined as follows:

A livelihood depends on the capabilities, assets (including both material and social resources) and activities which are all required for a means of living. A person or family's livelihood is sustainable when they can cope with and recover from stresses and shocks and maintain or enhance their capabilities and assets both now and in the future, without undermining environmental resources.[15]

The sustainable livelihoods framework, as expressed in Figure 3.1, is essentially people-centred and aims to explain (in a necessarily abstract and simplified way) the relationships between people, their livelihoods, and their environments, (macro) policies, and all kinds of institutions.[16]

Obviously this framework is a simplification of real life. It contains some 'feedback' arrows that suggest flows between categories, and there is overlap between two of them, which suggests a strong interlinking; but not all possible links are shown. This picture of the framework should not be read in a 'linear' way, with a starting point and a finishing point, and not even necessarily from left to right, even though it draws attention to *outcomes* at the right-hand side. *Livelihood outcomes* will have a strong influence on both

Figure 3.1: The sustainable livelihoods framework

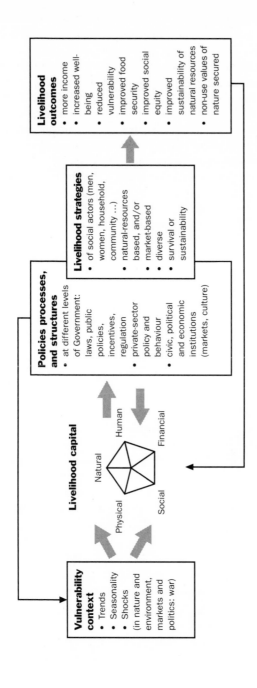

how *capitals* (i.e. assets, capabilities) are built up, and also on how they are substituted for one another, although the latter happens in particular in the process of pursuing livelihood strategies.

Livelihood strategies have been made to overlap with the *policies, processes, and structures*, which suggests an intimate and direct relationship between people's strategies, social institutions, and public policies. The feedback arrow from *policies, processes, and structures* to *vulnerability context* suggests that, whereas people cannot directly influence this context, some inroads can be made through policy change and the collective action of governments and others, in particular in respect of non-natural trends and shocks.

Participatory processes, as discussed in section 3.3, generate a range of perceptions of the different factors of the framework, even in one particular project or community. The framework sets out to provide a common language for development managers and officials, beneficiaries, and also activists, and a way of thinking about livelihoods that accommodates the approaches of economists and environmentalists alike. The framework should be seen as slightly more sophisticated than a conventional checklist of the factors that analysts need to consider before making overall judgements about environmental degradation or improvement in livelihoods and sustainabilities – but no more than that. The framework is generally compatible with the holistic, interrelated, and complex way in which poor people think about their own livelihoods.

As with every tool, it is necessary to keep in mind what it can be used for, and it should be stressed that not every stakeholder in a development process has to understand the full details and workings of it; some actually do not need it. Experience shows that the degree of abstractness and the level of sophistication of the framework make it hard for field-level staff and partners to understand and operationalise: some attempts to discuss it with local people have left them dumbfounded. However, if the design of the framework serves the purpose of broadening the analysis of higher-level development professionals, or specialists in natural-resource management, it will have done its job. In citizens' groups and community meetings, a basic list of general questions and semi-structured dialogues will normally suffice to identify local needs and problems, their causes, and opportunities for improvement: expert outsiders can keep the framework to themselves.

3.2.3 Livelihood outcomes and strategies

Livelihood outcomes are the most normative part of this framework. They can be seen as the overall aims of certain social actors. The more detailed or lower-level objectives of (for example) deprived people and development agencies can be found elsewhere in the diagram. Ultimately, most will agree that well-being, income, food security, resilience (or livelihood security), and social equity should improve, for both present and future generations. Improving resource ownership and maintaining the quality of the various capitals are one step before that: i.e. they are a means to those ends. However, the achievement of sustainability, perceived as the maintenance of welfare (i.e. maintaining total utility), is ultimately possible only if what cannot be substituted or created is protected: of the five capitals, four can be fully created by human beings, but natural capital (in all its forms and qualities) cannot be so created. Environmental-resource sustainability can thus be seen as essential for intergenerational equity, and as a genuine outcome.

For those who want to go further down the 'strong sustainability' track, another outcome may be the sustaining of aspects of the environment that cannot be considered as capital assets or as material resources for human utility – but which have a spiritual or political value. For example, people may choose to protect a sacred bush in Uganda and keep tourists away from it. 'Eco-warriors' in the UK chain themselves to concrete blocks and bury themselves several metres under a site destined to become an airport runway, in order to mobilise political support. (See also chapter 2.)

The desired outcomes of change processes depend strongly on the dominant group of stakeholders in the analysis or development intervention. For development agencies, gender equity and wider social equity may be a desired outcome of livelihood strategies, although they may be less important for some of the other social actors involved. Securing the symbolic value of a natural feature may be a religious necessity for local people, yet be seen as a waste of opportunity by entrepreneurs. There may also be differences of opinion about the desired income levels and degrees of food security and resilience to which a project should aspire.

The sustainable livelihoods framework has much in common with rights-based approaches to development that stress the importance of improving political, social, and economic rights, but it focuses on material improvements. Some local people, development agencies, or other stakeholders may also aim for outcomes that are not articulated as such in the framework: for example, freedom from violence, increased political participation, improved levels of education or social services, or a reduced incidence of disease and death. These aims (or: outcomes) are subsumed in the framework under other categories, and are thus portrayed as intermediary steps or means towards livelihood outcome. For example, good health and high and equitable educational achievements are essential in enhancing human capital. Other development aims, for example 'reduced risks of injury or death from natural hazards', and 'greater ability to pay school fees', can be seen to follow almost automatically from reduced vulnerability, as a result of improved physical infrastructure or increased income.

Outcomes represent the ultimate changes that people, citizens' groups, governments, and development organisations want to achieve, which prompts the word *impact*. Impact is the lasting and significant change[17] that is achieved and that can be attributed to the people themselves, and for example to a development project or to a campaign for a policy change. Opinions about desired changes differ between stakeholders, and the actual impacts of a project or a policy change are normally assessed by means of indicators that say something about them (i.e. outcome or impact indicators). However, actual impacts cannot be claimed to be fully objective either, because perceptions of the quality of change and value judgements about the contributions to change made by one or another stakeholder differ and need negotiating too. And impacts on differing communities, social groups, or household members are not always identical. (See sub-section 4.3.2 for more on the subject of outcomes.)

Individual women and men, households, and communities usually pursue multiple livelihood strategies. These strategies may or may not depend on environmental resources, and they depend more or less on markets and employment in the formal or the informal economy. People can use what is accessible in their immediate environments and they can migrate, for example between cities and rural areas. Their choices depend on their degrees of vulnerability and poverty, and on the assets or *capitals* that they can access. Their strategy may be one of survival, or it may be one of sustaining and improving what they already have and do.

The people who are central to the analysis and who generally also take part in the analysis can be seen (or see themselves) as individuals, households, groups of men and of women, as ethnic groups or age groups, and as communities. Most importantly, individuals and particular groupings are social actors, for example as members of a political party, religious society, or tribal clan. Analysis should combine and contrast the change observed and perceived by various social actors, because people live primarily in these realities, i.e. in families, communities, and peer groups (see section 3.3 for more on social actors and interfaces).

3.2.4 Livelihood capitals

Of primary importance for poor and marginalised people seeking to pursue their livelihood strategies are the necessary assets or *capitals,* including natural resources, infrastructure, money, social capital, and above all their own labour, skills, and knowledge – *human capital*. Different types of capital have been conceptualised by many analysts, with the aim of developing models and theories that enhance understanding of the interaction between social processes and environmental change. Different capitals are what people have at their immediate disposal, or not, for pursuing their livelihood strategies.[18] They include intangible assets, which can be expressed as *human* and *social capital*, and also *financial capital, physical capital,* and *natural capital.* The capitals thus include tangible resources as well as human capabilities to create, use, maintain, and improve them.

The concept of capital implies a valuation of a stock of tangible or intangible assets. A stock is a quantity, and a capital is a quantity with a certain unit-value. A smaller stock in future, compared with today's stock, can thus represent a larger amount of capital, if the unit value has increased. The science and practice of development struggle with quantifying all the values of (for example) human and social 'stocks', and of natural stocks. They are not as easy to count as money, or as easy to value in monetary terms as physical, human-made stocks. This is especially complex, because not all dimensions of human, social, and natural stocks actually contribute to material well-being or utility: it is possible to appreciate and value nature simply for its own sake and, for example, to demand education for spiritual development, which means that time, effort, and money are spent to achieve something non-material.

To make matters more complex: capitals flow. Money and other stocks change hands, and in this process the stocks are valued in some way or another. Furthermore, one capital can be substituted for another, which is what happens in human societies and economies, even though absolute values and quantities cannot easily be ascribed to all the capitals in the livelihoods framework. Nevertheless, societies seem to arrive at ever-changing balances of different capitals through political-economic processes. Aspects of nature are turned into resources (stocks) when they are seen to be useful for human beings, and natural capital is valued when the resources enter into markets (or hypothetical markets, as in 'willingness to pay' assessments – see also section 2.2.4 on environmental economics). Once sold, this natural capital turns into financial capital for the seller, and, once used by the buyer, into physical capital (for example, a tree is turned into a log and later into a bridge). It can also be consumed (for example, a wild plant or fish is eaten); basic consumption is essential for life and reproduction, and thus the consumed fish contributes to maintaining and building up human capital. It can be argued that there are just two 'ultimate' sources of all those capitals: human beings, their labour and ingenuity, and nature (interpreted as the world without human society). Table 3.1 explains the different capitals and gives further examples of how capitals are substituted for others.

Table 3.1: Livelihood capitals and capital substitution

Type of livelihood capital	Definition and explanation[19]	Examples of substitution
Human capital	*Skills, knowledge, ability and potential to labour, and good health, which together enable people to pursue different livelihood strategies[20]*	Human capital increases with good health services, education and training, which are normally enabled by a strong sense of community (social capital) and need to be paid for with money. Human capital (labour, technological knowledge) forms the core input in the process of (for example) turning steep forested slopes (natural capital) into terraced agricultural land or a human settlement (physical capital).
Social capital	*The social resources upon which people draw in pursuit of livelihood objectives, including networks, membership of groups, and relationships of trust.* Strong groups are beneficial for group members but may exclude other (possibly very poor and vulnerable) people.	Development agencies do much to develop organisations and institutional capacities. High levels of trust and collaboration (social capital) enable individuals and households to get help from peers and to be obliged to return the favour at a later date, which shows a direct interaction with human capital. Good collaboration between people (high social capital) often means that technologies and management processes develop which are essential for the creation of (for example) better water quality and more efficient use of fossil fuels, i.e. it is essential in the substitution processes between physical and natural capital.

Table 3.1: Livelihood capitals and capital substitution (continued)

Type of livelihood capital	Definition and explanation[19]	Examples of substitution
Natural capital	*Natural resource stocks from which resource flows are derived that are useful for livelihoods.* The quality of resources must be taken into consideration when assessing stocks, because (for example) land with depleted nutrients is of less value to livelihoods than high-quality, fertile land. In explaining natural capital, some make a distinction between environmental goods (i.e. stocks) and services (for example pollution sinks).[21]	Livestock is in essence natural capital, even though animals are domesticated. Indeed it can be kept solely for reasons of status or as a stock of (natural) capital, and only be substituted in times of crisis for something else, or consumed. By being sold or used as collateral, it is turned into financial capital (it can provide access to money). If the cow ploughs, it becomes a 'producer good' (physical capital), and when its dung is used to fertilise fields, it helps production too (this requires an input of human capital as well). Natural capital is also used up (i.e. substituted) through the manufacturing of (for example) machines or chemicals (creating physical capital) or the transport of people (contributing to social capital), which all require inputs of natural resources, result in air and water pollution, and use space for manufacturing plants and roads.
Physical capital	*The basic infrastructure and the producer goods used to support livelihoods;* this can also be called 'human-made capital'.[22]	Physical capital ranges from chemical inputs into production processes to infrastructure such as factories, roads, and water-supply systems. It also includes a pasture planted with mono-culture grass, supplied with a drainage system, and maintained by people (i.e. by inputs of human capital, social capital) and inputs like cow dung and fertilisers (also physical capital). The grassland is an area of land and possibly forest (natural capital) that was converted with all those inputs.[23]

Table 3.1: Livelihood capitals and capital substitution (continued)

Type of livelihood capital	Definition and explanation[19]	Examples of substitution
Financial capital	*The financial resources that are available to people in pursuit of their livelihoods, including savings and credit.* This includes flows as well as stocks, and it can contribute to consumption as well as production.	Financial capital basically represents other stocks, i.e. natural or human or other capital that has been converted: it is an intermediary in all kinds of substitutions (transactions) between the other capitals, and in that sense represents wealth and utility. It usually takes the form of money: paper, coins, or numbers on bank accounts that derive their value from trust in the markets, banks, and State institutions. Savings can also be accumulated in (for example) precious metals (on display around our necks or not), or in what is essentially one of the other capitals, like livestock. In that case, payments become 'in kind', and we talk of barter trade.

3.2.5 Policies, processes, and structures

The stocks or capitals represent an endowment, in other words a quality that is represented by them which, like a talent, may or may not be used. This endowment of the capitals, this promise of positive benefit can be turned into a real benefit for poor and vulnerable people only if they can *claim* it, i.e. if they can effect their right to make use of it. This means that the sheer existence of a capital, whether social, human, physical, financial, or natural capital, is not enough, even if its quality is high. Legal rights to capitals are important, but in themselves are not sufficient to ensure improved livelihood strategies either. Individual people, households, and certain groups or classes of poor and vulnerable women and men must actually access capitals in order to turn endowments into real livelihood and 'environmental entitlements', through their knowledge, skills, and in particular the social institutions that mediate their claims.[24]

Of central importance in claiming rights are local, national, and international institutions like markets, the system of governance and policies of a country, its laws, or the traditional rules and organisations that govern allocation of land in rural areas.[25] Governments generally make the policies, laws, and regulations that set the rules for such institutions, with some degree of participation by citizens in the process. All these things – the government structures, policies, laws, markets, cultural practices and institutions – are important in defining rights and responsibilities and also in defining the terms on which different capitals can be used and (re)generated, and be substituted for others. They are decisive in determining whether capitals can be used by poor and marginalised people. These policies and processes are thus of key importance for the creation of livelihood opportunities and strategies of poor and excluded people.

The policies, structures, and processes are obviously hugely diverse and complex, and they operate at several levels, from the social group and local community to agreements between governments. They can also be influenced by people in a more or less direct way at local, national, and also international levels. Citizens' groups, as part of 'civil society' (representing certain institutions and also certain 'social capital' in Figure 3.1), are in turn also influenced by the policies and behaviour of government and private businesses. The 'structures' here can be thought of as the organisations of government, citizens, and the business sector. Citizens' groups and NGOs often need support if they are to have an effective dialogue with the business sector and authorities – support that is called 'capacity building' or 'institutional development'.[26] In other words, they need strong social and human capital to influence the policies and structures that mediate between capitals and livelihood strategies. The interaction between social actors and policies and structures is highly dependent on knowledge and power, which are interrelated. In fact, policies and formal structures and processes are means to regulate the use of power and the dominance of one knowledge over another. However, power can also be used to violate rules and bypass structures.

Peet and Watts (1996) have written that they would like to see 'more politics in political ecology', and the same could be said about sustainable livelihoods, following the experience of a number of agencies over the last few years. As an analytical tool, the sustainable livelihoods framework pays direct attention to policies, and it should be emphasised that policy processes are all deeply political. However, the importance of power is not very obvious from the diagrammatic representations of the framework. Laws and also policies define rights, but power cannot be brokered as easily as that. Power cannot be expressed in straightforward capitals either, whether social or human or financial capital, yet it is an essential factor in the ability to pursue one livelihood strategy or another. Related to a more political approach is the idea of empowerment and participation, which is discussed in section 3.3.

The framework suggests that analysis needs to look at democracy, the role of the State, the private business sector, and the role of civil society. These are in some ways problematic divisions and they do indeed overlap (is a political party that is in parliamentary opposition to a government part of civil society or part of the State?), but they can help us to understand what is happening in a particular context. They are related both to the notion of *social capital* and to *policies, processes, and structures.* The question that can legitimately be asked by stakeholders in any situation is whether one accepts laws and policies as they operate, or whether they need to change. Also important is the question of how one can judge whether social capital is both high and good, or just high: crime syndicates often make strong networks and are based on high levels of trust.

3.2.6 Vulnerability context

Some factors are outside the immediate control or influence of people who pursue their livelihoods. Changes in this *vulnerability context* can happen in three different ways: trends, seasonality, and shocks.[27] *Trends* are gradual changes, partly predictable: examples are demographic trends, economic and technological developments, trends in resource use and degradation, and also gradual political changes, for example 'becoming more democratic' or 'becoming more authoritarian'. *Seasonality* occurs in the production of crops and food prices, in health (in particular because certain disease vectors are related to climatic factors), and also in employment opportunities, i.e. in labour markets. The latter are particularly seasonal in agriculture, but also in tourism, and trade is usually good in festival seasons such as the end-of-Ramadan celebration of Eidh, or the Chinese New Year. *Shocks* occur in market prices (a good coffee harvest in Brazil, for example, may cause a sudden slump in world market prices, and thus a shock for (say) small coffee producers in the Caribbean region), and in particular in nature. Drought, flood, volcanic eruptions, or earthquakes cannot be predicted with any certainty, although the regions where they are likely to occur are well known. In so-called 'complex emergencies', famine usually has a combination of causes, including war and the breakdown of parastatal food-trading organisations. In more general terms, famines occur as a result of a lack of 'exchange entitlements'.[28] Many processes of gradual change (i.e. trends) may have been happening, including soil degradation, reduced crop productivity, and a gradual concentration of land ownership in the hands of just a few. Crisis is then triggered by some event that may of itself be relatively minor, like a modest climatic drought. Other shocks include outbreaks of epidemics of human diseases, livestock diseases, and crop pests (see sections 2.3, 4.2.3, and 4.3.3 for more on vulnerability, shocks, and livelihood recovery).

Trends, shocks, and seasonality in contextual factors strongly define poor people's vulnerability. They may be anticipated in many cases, but are usually not in ordinary people's sphere of direct influence. Preparing for a decline in producer prices or a drought is often implicit in livelihood strategies: people build up capitals that reduce their vulnerability. Nevertheless, survival may be at stake, and responding to crisis situations is difficult: there is always a short-term cost and also a long-term cost. The context thus entails the risks and uncertainties that need to be lived with, and certain livelihood strategies will aim towards mitigation, without influencing them in a direct way. With regard to coping with shocks and stresses through improved resilience, the framework looks at environmental, economic, social, and institutional sustainability. Sustainabilities should be analysed at local, national, and also international levels. In sections 2.3 and 2.4 the notions of sustainability and also vulnerability, security, and resilience were discussed in some detail. A central question is: *what needs to be sustained?* Financial capital, the ability to herd cattle, or the education of children – or some sort of sum total of all capitals? Capital assets can be substituted for others, and that needs to be considered in an analysis that leads to value judgements: substitution (where at all possible) can be considered good or bad, depending on who is asked the question. Setting off against each other the trends in the five different capitals in the pentagon of Figure 3.1 is always a subjective exercise. Nevertheless it is useful at least to make a qualitative judgement of the trends in how the different capitals in the livelihoods of particular women or men, households, communities, or whole countries are changing. Maintaining some form of sustainability can also be seen as an aim in itself, and as such may be considered an important livelihood outcome.

3.2.7 Analysis of livelihoods

It is important that the sustainable livelihoods framework should not be used to define or structure the vastness of what *can* be researched, but it can be helpful in prioritising what *should* be researched and analysed. It is critical to ask questions about the most important livelihood strategies and outcomes in a particular situation; and in the case of particular people to consider the most important assets, policies, structures, and hazards that may uncover their vulnerability. It is pertinent that the critical social actors and social interfaces are identified and engaged with.

In fact, the use of the framework in conjunction with several existing analytical tools, at differing stages of development processes and in differing situations, has led some to regard the idea of sustainable livelihoods as an *approach*, not a methodology or tool in itself. Nevertheless, the framework discussed in the previous sub-sections should primarily be taken as a tool. 'Sustainable livelihoods' as an approach is broad, stresses popular participation, articulates reduced poverty as the main outcome, and encompasses a range of levels and approaches to improving livelihoods, from local micro-projects to international campaigning for policy changes. It combines several methodologies when used in long-term programme planning, project planning, and evaluation, or in campaigning.

Based on theories of political ecology, gender and environment, and environmental economics (section 2.2), a summary list of what an analysis should consider in development processes is given in sub-section 3.3.3. It is stressed there that consideration of social difference at every stage is essential, and an undifferentiated concept of community would severely limit the value of an analysis. Leach *et al.* (1997a,b) also stress the need for historical analysis of ecological and social change, in order to challenge accepted wisdom about the ideal or optimum ecological or social composition of a society. A good analysis ensures a dynamic analysis – to make sure that the static picture of today's situation of social difference, of landscape, and of resource use is not the core message, but how it became what it is, and whether there is potential for further change. For example, a landscape with forest patches in open savannah in semi-arid West Africa has conventionally been seen as a situation in which deserts encroach because people deforested the area. In this view, the forested patches would be the leftovers that are under threat – but historical analysis suggests the reverse, i.e. that people have created the forest patches in what has been open savannah for centuries.[29]

The sustainable livelihoods framework has been perceived as applying primarily to rural development. Although this may be suggested by its origins, there are no obvious ways in which the framework contradicts urban realities of poor and vulnerable people.[30] The framework does stress the significance of markets, which are increasingly important even in remote rural areas. Factors that are especially important in urban livelihoods appear to be included in the concept of social capital and physical capital, and the breadth of policies, processes, and structures is such that the relative weight of those in dense human settlements could easily be accommodated.

The language of *livelihood strategies* and *livelihood outcomes* articulates the dynamic nature of the framework, and it also helps to strengthen the notion of what all the processes of social and ecological change and mediation by institutions are for: women and men want to eat better, and to enjoy higher and more equal incomes and a sustained, healthier, and more productive environment. Scoones (1998) proposes that professionals and researchers should consider the following matters in order to ensure what he calls 'optimal ignorance', arguing that the right questions must be asked in livelihood analysis and that we should seek to find out only what it is necessary to know. This is an interpretation of his list:

- *Sequencing*: what capital, policy change, or action is the starting point for a particular person, social group, or social actor to establish a successful livelihood strategy?

- *Substitution*: Which combination of capitals is needed for the livelihood strategy, and can they be substituted for each other?

- *Clustering*: Do particular social groups or actors have access to particular clusters of capitals?

- *Access*: What access is available to social groups at differing levels (household, community, and region) to various resources or capitals?

- *Trade-offs*: What trade-offs confront particular social groups in deciding upon a certain livelihood strategy and the use of certain capitals, and by what rules, organisations, and power relations are they determined?

- *Trends*: What are the trends in the availability of resources (capitals), in terms of access and in terms of the external context?

There remains the question of how to prioritise specific topics to research in a project planning or review exercise, or in order to support long-term strategic planning of development programmes in countries or regions. Which part of the framework gets paid most attention will emerge from a gradual process of ever-increased understanding – see also chapters 4 (on projects) and 5 (on long-term strategies and policies).

Table 3.2 lists some practical methods for assessing various aspects of the livelihood framework – indeed, of people's livelihoods. These methods are based on research experience and will be of direct help in (for example) needs assessments or impact reviews. It should be noted that most of the methods concern certain social groups, women and/or men, and they should be used at household, community, regional, and/or country levels.

Some analytical tools stress quantitative and physical data, such as demographic statistics and aerial photographs, and others focus on qualitative and less objective data, including tools associated with (for example) PRA. (See also sub-sections 3.3.2 and 4.3.1.)

The next sub-section presents some lessons derived from the actual use of the framework.

Table 3.2: Practical methods of livelihoods analysis[31]

Livelihood outcomes	• Well-being ranking of social groups, communities, or populations in regions (at different moments in recent history) • Social mapping • Cause–effect diagrams • Study of historical aerial photographs and remote-sensing images and data, with a particular focus on environmental change
Livelihood strategies	• Ranking of income sources • Mapping of migration patterns • Inventory and ranking of income and expenditure • Seasonal calendars of production, employment, and income.
Policies, processes, and structures	• Venn diagrams • Actor network analysis and 'power network diagrams' • Cause–effect and flow diagrams • Market inventories and commodity-price tracking • Narratives or institutional histories from key informants (including traditional rules, tenure law and practice, and/or markets)
Livelihood assets (capitals)	• Livelihood diagrams • Asset surveys and resource mapping, including soil and vegetation surveys and inventories of the quality of housing stock, water supply, and sanitation systems • Seasonal calendars of asset availability and quality • Social network and Venn diagrams
Vulnerability context	• Study of meteorological and demographic data • Research in historical archives, with a particular focus on political conflict and market fluctuations

3.2.8 The sustainable livelihoods framework: lessons from practice

Staff in Oxfam GB and some Novib partners have been trained in the theory and use of the sustainable livelihoods framework. It was presented as part of a bigger 'package', with other tools for good management of development programmes, in particular participatory methodologies. Together they make up an approach to development that is expected to improve practice and outcomes. This is elaborated further in chapter 4 with particular relevance for project management, and also in chapter 5 regarding strategy formulation and campaigning.

In the two rural projects discussed in section 3.1 (in Niassa in Mozambique and Lung Vai in Vietnam), Oxfam staff, staff from various levels of government departments, and representatives of civil-society organisations were trained in participatory methodologies and behaviour, and in facilitating analytical processes. For the latter, the sustainable livelihoods framework was introduced as a means to ensure that the most important issues would be covered in participatory assessments, at the planning stages in 1993/1994 and several years later at review stages. This capacity development was reinforced by follow-up training in later years, which was combined with project reviews.

These 'participatory events' were thus facilitated by social actors who were mostly from outside the local communities, but were mixed groups made up of some of the key-stakeholders: the donor, partner organisation (government departments), and some local leaders. The assessments followed the pattern of engagement, data collection, and analysis that is described in chapter 4; they included meetings between various stakeholders, and dialogues with people from particular social groups (the poorest families, particular women, certain ethnic groups). Some of the events were more open-ended and participatory: that is, they allowed more space for the views of local women and men, in particular at the planning and appraisal stages, whereas the later reviews and evaluations followed a more extractive methodology. In both Niassa and Lung Vai, monitoring visits from Oxfam and higher-level authorities to the local project sites took place in between the assessments, which provided information on progress. These visits have influenced local actors' behaviour, but in neither case has monitoring (yet) become as structured and participatory as project managers wish; but good progress is being made.

There remains the question of whether the use of the sustainable livelihoods framework had a real impact. Initial assessment in the two cases and twelve others suggests that the actual use of the analytical framework remained weak. Nevertheless, the projects did adopt a broad or holistic approach, quite different from a 'rural integrated approach' that would attempt to 'do a bit of everything'. They began with workshops on participatory methodologies and sustainable livelihoods, and initiated participatory monitoring events, support for livelihood activities through training in sustainable agriculture, support for processes of land allocation, and various activities aimed at regenerating and protecting environmental resources. In more general terms, an assessment of the work of Oxfam and partners led to the following conclusions.[32]

- The sustainable livelihoods framework is too abstract for field-level, operational staff, even though much of their experience and practice seems to be neatly compatible with its holistic nature. Nevertheless, some learning resulted from the use of the framework.

- The sustainable livelihoods framework is used by higher-level staff in strategic planning processes, but very little in project appraisal or assessment.

- The idea of 'sustainable' was a message that appealed to many participants, but not the detailed idea of it in an environmental sense.

- Direct results from most of the field-based workshops on participatory methodologies and sustainable livelihoods were demonstrated in terms of new project initiatives; this includes initiatives that relate to environmental sustainability, and in particular to sustainable natural resource management (SNRM).

- Project management (planning, monitoring, evaluation) was supported through better data, improved skills in analysis (partly as a result of the stress on the analytical process, with the framework as the key tool), and improved participation by local people.

- However, the data are inconclusive about the attribution of programme impacts (on environment, livelihoods, etc.) to the use of the sustainable livelihoods framework in the workshops and thereafter.

These conclusions do suggest that the sustainable livelihoods framework, or more broadly an approach with popular participation and good analytical tools at its core, can help to achieve better impact on livelihoods, environmental sustainability, and social equity. It helps to improve development practice, but it is not a panacea, nor a substitute for common sense.

3.3 Negotiating change

The sustainable livelihoods framework can be applied to the analysis of the livelihood strategies of particular individuals or any social group. Whatever the particular focus of the analysis, livelihood strategies are influenced by other individuals, organisations, businesses, and authorities, who all have some stake in society, environmental resources, and other capitals. This section discusses processes of social interaction that determine changes in livelihoods and environments. It lays the groundwork for these processes to be influenced in order to achieve particular goals – through projects (see chapter 4) or campaigning to influence policy (see chapter 5).

Participation and the associated term *empowering* are words that express the idea that poor and excluded people get more influence over their lives and livelihoods; it implies a positive bias in development projects and policy processes towards excluded people. The first sub-section elaborates on the notion of participation and power, and interaction between various social actors. Sub-section 3.3.2 discusses some aspects of participatory approaches used by development professionals (particularly PRA). The final sub-section stresses the importance of negotiation in social interactions and gives examples of cases where social processes were geared towards improvements in the livelihoods and environments of deprived and excluded people.

3.3.1 Power and action

People power and people's participation in social-political processes and development activities have been analysed, and various typologies of 'participation' have been derived. The following typology is one of many, and expresses well the many interpretations of the word.

Typology of participation

Information Processes
1. Unilateral announcement
2. Listening
3. Consultation
4. Data collection

Project-Related Activities
5. Instrumental involvement
6. Functional involvement
7. Negotiation
8. Externally initiated organisation
9. Conflict resolution

People's Initiatives
10. Self-mobilisation
11. Empowerment

(extracted from Adnan et al., 1992)

Most of the forms of participation featured in the list are top-down or externally initiated, and only the latter two types could be classified as activism, where local people themselves take control of their resources, environments, and livelihood opportunities. Only 'empowerment' expresses the idea that disadvantaged and poor people increase their 'freedom of choice and bargaining power in relation to ... more powerful groups'.[33]

Development NGOs usually declare empowerment as an important aim, but they practise or achieve only some of the information-related or project-related forms of participation. Participation in the sense of activism is different. Local people set the agenda, and often charismatic individuals or small elite groups dominate social movements. The motivation for people to take part in them may be related to ecological conditions or to the need to find an alternative path of development. The latter does not necessarily mean that they oppose economic development. For example, concerning the well-known Chipko movement in India it has been said that 'Chipko's ecological successes resulted in new environmental regulations that compounded the lack of economic opportunities and development in the region ... I challenge some contemporary views that see new social movements in the Third World as grassroots agents seeking alternatives to development ... social movements in India are, contrary to these views, centrally concerned with access to development.'[34]

The question *who participates?* in a process of social change is critical, because at the heart of the process are aspects of power. Nelson and Wright (1995) present three ways of looking at power, as follows.

Three ways of looking at power[35]

'Power to'

Here power is seen as a personal attribute that can be increased through (for example) increased awareness, improved confidence, better negotiation skills, and stronger social networks. 'Human development' can increase the power to act and influence. Power is seen as something that can grow without necessarily having a negative effect on the power of others. The implication of this is that to some extent 'empowerment' is apolitical and non-confrontational. This view of power is held by many development professionals who declare the aim of empowerment.

'Power over'

In this approach there is a total amount of power in a given society; it can neither decrease nor grow, but groups of people and individuals fight, negotiate, and struggle over it. Power is exercised over social processes and social groups. Power is the object that everybody tries to get hold of, for example through participation in political decision-making processes. Power can be gained in particular from getting access to the formal institutions of society, for example through collective action.

'Decentred and subjectless power'

In this third way, power is considered not as a 'thing' that can be possessed; no institution or individual can claim to 'have' it. Power is seen as something that happens through a complex interaction of events, public discourse, and accepted ideology, institutions (especially those of the State), and social actors. This interaction leads to a particular outcome in terms of social relations – outcomes that are virtually impossible to plan and in fact are knowable only retrospectively. This notion of power challenges the idea of empowerment, by asking how power can be transferred if it is not 'held'. Real decentralisation of power, or empowerment of the weak and poor, requires a very high level of awareness and commitment of those who are embedded in the institutions that are influential in social processes.

Common reasons for groups of social actors to participate in social change processes, including development projects, are aspirations to material benefit, access to the development process, and more influence and control. External agencies may see participation *as a means* to achieve project goals efficiently, or *as an end* to enable local groups to take more control of their own situation.[36] The former can imply a stress on local people's knowledge of their own environments: they know about it, and can therefore manage it better than others. It tends to stress the tangible outcomes and impacts of development programmes. The idea of participation *as an end* usually implies some sort of positive bias towards including the poor and marginalised in the development process. It tends to be based on a political or ideological position: poor, subordinate people have the right to determine their own lives and livelihoods, and they must be supported in that.

The word 'stakeholder' has come to convey the idea of an 'interest group', i.e. a group (or person) with some stake in a policy, a project, a process, or organisation. The idea of multiple stakeholders, as in 'stakeholder analysis' or 'stakeholder society', suggests that projects, policies, or, for example, public services rarely have one homogeneous interest group. There are managers, politicians, donors, NGOs, and citizens of differing ages, ethnicities, genders, and social classes. Development organisations also talk of 'primary stakeholders', such as the poorest, or vulnerable women, or whomever they see as their target group – the ones towards whom the organisation has a positive bias. Interaction between stakeholders happens in complex and multiple ways. Development organisations are virtually always adding to this complexity, because they are stakeholders themselves, even in cases where they do no more than make a financial donation to essentially self-generated campaigns for social or political change. This interaction happens with a purpose and under certain conditions. Rules, laws, institutions, and customs influence the interaction, which is depicted in the sustainable livelihoods framework as *policies, processes, and structures*. Central to this interaction is power, however power is perceived, and people-power is generated in social groups, which is partly expressed in the framework as *social capital*.

Long (1992) does not use the language of stakeholders, but rather that of 'social actors', which seems essentially the same idea and is perhaps more clearly expressed. He writes: 'social actors are not simply seen as disembodied social categories (based on class or some other classificatory criteria) or passive recipients of intervention, but active participants who process information and strategize in their dealing with various local actors as well as with outside institutions and personnel'.[37] He also explains that social actors, such as political parties or church organisations, peasant associations, women's unions or other citizens' groups, are those who have some decision-making capacity and ability to implement decisions. In other words, social actors must have the quality of 'human agency', i.e. they must be both 'knowledgeable' and 'capable', so that they can influence social change processes. The notion of human agency is thus closely related to knowledge and also to power, and all depend to a large extent on the social networks in which the actor takes part.

Long's 'actor-oriented paradigm' is by no means limited to the powerful or dominant actors. It is important to stress that a social actor is not a natural given, a fixed entity, but rather it is a social construction that changes perpetually. All actors, including those who are subordinated to others, are seen to have some power and agency and are therefore able to influence social change, and all are part of (and shaped by) the same wider structures. He attempts to relate these wider structures (or 'macro' context) of (regional) political economies to the 'micro' particularities of what actors do, decide, and contribute to social and environmental changes. The 'macro' includes institutions such as markets, which mediate social-environmental change, i.e. how local people, agencies, and other actors negotiate and arrive at decisions that have an impact on poverty and environmental sustainability. The actor-oriented approach makes the assumption that there is room for choice and decision at the micro level, partly independent of these wider structural processes and trends, and that social transformation and change in environments is thus a result of human agency: even subordinate people have room for manoeuvre.

It then becomes essential to map or identify the strategies and rationales of particular actors in order to understand the changes within a certain (regional) political economy, and to be able to make a sensible guess at how external intervention might influence it. That is, influence it in such a way that oppressed and marginalised people improve their situation and the (environmental) sustainability of local livelihoods. The relationship between local grassroots groups on the one hand and national lobby groups or, for example, a local government project on the other can be seen to operate at several interfaces, where the exchange of experience and ideas happens, and where one social actor influences another. Studies of 'interface encounters', i.e. interaction between an individual or a group of actors with others, show how actors' values, knowledge, and perceptions are changed by the encounter itself.[38] That happens of course within a broader institutional context with differences in, for example, power and culture.

One particularly important and practical notion seems to arise from the concepts of *social actor* and *interface*: it is the need for focus in the research, analysis, and interaction of external development agencies. Not all social groups that appear homogeneous (for example 'the poorest women in the village') are social actors (because these women do not necessarily form a cohesive group); they may still be the main target group of an intervention. Not all interfaces are important encounters; not all actors' strategies need to be known; not all interactions are essential for understanding the main dynamics of a social-political arena; and not all social processes have a significant impact on poverty, deprivation, and exclusion. In participatory development programmes, it is often said that 'all important stakeholders' need to be included. However, 'all' is too many, and 'important' requires prioritisation.

A review of conservation farming projects in Kenya showed that the impacts of eight small NGOs and grassroots groups on local livelihoods, capacities, environments, and policies and structures were considerable. Various social actors participated in different ways in this review, in particular groups of women and men farmers, staff of local NGOs and national resource NGOs, staff of an international NGO, and members of national and international agricultural research organisations. The existing interface between some NGO staff and smallholder farmers was examined and new interfaces were created, in particular between the local NGOs and researchers. The review reached a good degree of consensus, despite obvious differences in power and interests. NGOs promote sustainable farming techniques and attempt to mobilise farmers to adopt these techniques and officials (including researchers) to support the development of the techniques. The review concluded that impacts of the NGOs on national research and agricultural policies had been minimal and needed to be strongly reinforced if greater impact on livelihoods and the sustainability of agricultural production was to be achieved. An update of the review a year and a half later showed that this agreement had been followed through at least in part,[39] which suggests that the review itself had generated action.

3.3.2 Participatory approaches

Development agencies operate at different interfaces, and most have the declared objective of stimulating the participation of excluded and poor people. Various approaches to achieve this have developed over recent decades. Ideas from adult learning and wider development practice, sociology, and geography produced what became known as PRA: *participatory rural appraisal*. This developed out of RRA, *rapid rural appraisal*, and later also became known as PLA, *participatory learning and action*. The shift from PRA to PLA expresses that the activity is not just rural and not just about appraisal, and that it aims at 'learning and action' – some kind of social change.

PLA is an approach, not a tool, and has been given many different meanings in different circles. There are those who tend towards a standardised method for project management through needs-assessments and baseline surveys, and who 'do a PRA'. Others see PRA or PLA as a term that indicates a certain type of behaviour, and as an expression of the radical empowerment of weaker groups in society and of social transformation, usually seen in terms of supporting and influencing change processes in favour of oppressed and vulnerable groups. Nevertheless, in essence it happens within the realms of 'development' with outsiders coming in, usually uninvited, and starting to play a role (i.e. becoming actors or stakeholders). The big challenge remains how to overcome the paradox of external intervention (of some kind) versus the ideal of vulnerable people's empowerment (see also 'decentred and subjectless power' in sub-section 3.3.1).

Figure 3.2 depicts the three core aspects of PLA:[40] tools, behaviour, and process.

Proponents of PLA promote shifts in behaviour and reversal of the conventional roles taken by development professionals and bureaucrats.[41] In processes of learning and action, meetings and interviews are set up where PLA tools are used to enable communication between 'outsiders' and 'insiders'. Insiders may include certain excluded and deprived people, but also a range of other social actors with whom researchers or staff of development agencies interact; but in fact each stakeholder can at some point be an insider and at other moments an outsider.

Of the three main aspects of PLA, 'analytical processes' (also called 'process of sharing') is possibly the most difficult one. Shared analysis between (for example) people with local knowledge and those with scientific and/or global perspectives, or between the weaker, less powerful, and poorer groups and the more influential and better-off, obviously cannot be resolved by bringing them together in a few public meetings. A process has to have a clear aim, it must have a beginning and an end, and it needs to be structured in the sense of the interfaces that it creates in meetings and forums. The framework of

Figure 3.2: Basic aspects of participatory learning and action

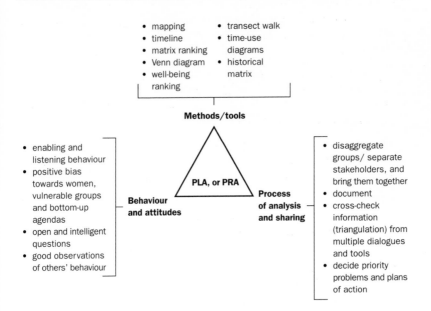

sustainable livelihoods provides a basis for dialogue and shared analysis.[42] It can be seen as a checklist for the outsider, but not necessarily as a useful dictionary for insiders who are being interviewed and enabled to take part in the analysis. For those who initiate and facilitate processes of learning and action with a range of social actors, the following considerations should be borne in mind. (See also section 4.3 on a learning and action process that is integrated with the sustainable livelihoods framework.)

Facilitating processes of analysis and action[43]

- A strengthened, renewed, or innovative process of progressive analysis and learning will react to or link in with existing processes of change. This enhanced activity can be structured, at least to some extent, and needs to be managed if it is to be successful. The initiative may come from 'insiders' and/or 'outsiders', and in all cases it is important that the lead or responsibility for co-ordination lies with a mix of stakeholders or actors, including (those close to) deprived and excluded women and men.

- This co-ordination group must give the enhanced process a clear aim, and set up a series of events that can be seen as interfaces between certain social actors.

- It is important to make explicit any expectations of positive biases towards particular social groups, such as 'the poorest women' or 'the most vulnerable ethnic group'. The choices in this respect relate directly to the aims of the project, policy, or development organisation concerned. This is also expressed in questions and hypotheses of 'action research'.[44]

- Important social actors among the target group and other social actors, i.e. individuals and groups with some human agency, need to be identified. These are *not* the same as presumed homogeneous groups of one gender, one social class, or one ethnic identity.

- The main strategies of these important actors that lead to social and environmental transformation need to be mapped and analysed, in particular if they are relevant to the livelihoods and environments of poor people.

- It is common practice to separate and (later) bring together stakeholder groups. Disaggregated social groups are sometimes called 'focus groups'; however, such groups should not be confused with social actors, because they may not act as one group. These groups cannot on their own decide the paths of change, and interfaces with others need to be created or used for arriving at decisions, and implementing them.

- Triangulating information and opinions from various actors and arriving at trustworthy conclusions that are acceptable for all is difficult, but the aim of facilitation should in all cases be to arrive at a good degree of consensus. This will involve negotiation, and sometimes conflict and mediation.

- Leaders or facilitators of change processes can be outsiders or insiders. In all cases they have, and need to make use of, levels of authority: they are social actors themselves, and need to address the apparent paradox of being comparatively powerful themselves and attempting to empower others. Key roles of facilitators include mediation between conflicting groups, enabling reporting and providing (secondary) information, interpreting positions, summarising and feeding back, and sometimes using authority, for example in order to break deadlocks and speed up decision making.

- Facilitators must also help to achieve, monitor, and report continuous progress in analysis. This progress is possibly the main motivation for participants to become involved in the process.

PLA tools contribute structure to dialogues and yet help to retain a fair amount of real-life complexity regarding the subject discussed. The tools avoid over-simplification and stimulate the discussion of inter-related problems and opportunities for change, which can be taken as 'holistic' analysis. The productive use of tools by outsider-facilitators depends on their behaviour and skills in guiding a step-by-step, 'semi-structured' dialogue from a very broad initial discussion to the specifics of comparing and challenging and changing what other participants in the dialogue assert. This is explained further as follows.

Dialogues at the interface

A 'semi-structured' interview or dialogue is often presented as a PRA tool, but wrongly: it happens all the time, in any encounter or 'interface'. A dialogue is a two-way (or multiple-way) process of communication and not simply an extractive exercise, which is the common understanding of what constitutes an interview. 'Semi-structured' usually refers to the idea that certain questions and topics have been prepared by outsider-facilitators, possibly with aids such as the sustainable livelihoods framework. A dialogue can also be 'semi-structured' as a step-by-step dialogue that is initiated by a facilitator, as follows:

1 Introduce people.

2 Introduce the main objective of the encounter: mutual learning/ engagement in a dialogue.

3 Present the general issue that you want to discuss: ask the first, general question.

4 Note or memorise the first answers.

5 Start structuring what has been said, for example with a diagram (a PRA tool) and by summarising (in different words) what has been said, and checking the correctness of the summary.

6 Ask more specific questions; register (and possibly summarise) answers.

7 Make further use of the diagram, if appropriate.

8 Observe participants' behaviour, and respond to that by 'handing over the stick', if appropriate, so that participants themselves develop the diagram and direct the dialogue.

9 Allow the discussion to evolve. Become a participant in the dialogue: raise new issues, contribute secondary information and 'external' ideas. Challenge, probe, rephrase, and summarise before moving the discussion on.

These dialogues constitute a very important part of the analytical, empowering process, in particular because they involve shifts in behaviour – unlike conventional interactions between officials and development professionals on the one hand, and excluded, poor people on the other. Shifts in behaviour can be summed up as follows.[45]

The facilitator (initiator, or 'outsider'), who by convention is dominant	*The facilitated (participants, or 'insiders'), who are usually subordinate*
Establishes rapport	Map, model, and draw
Converses, catalyses, facilitates, inquires	Rank, score, quantify
Suggests, adapts, improvises	Discuss, analyse
Watches, listens, learns	Inform, explain, and demonstrate
'Hands over the stick'	Identify and choose priorities
Probes	Plan, present, take action

The behaviour shifts promoted here are particularly geared to changing people who belong to the most influential institutions. (Compare the third way of looking at power: 'decentred and subjectless power' in sub-section 3.3.1; for more on behavioural skills, see also chapter 4.)

Chambers (1997) argues that power is in fact a disability: the realities of powerful people become dominant, but 'the realities of socially dominant professionals are often neither true or right'. He explores power relationships as a source of error, in particular error perpetrated by development professionals for whom interpersonal relationships are shaped by power differences.

Criticism of the practice of PLA/PRA and other participatory approaches used by development agencies includes the charge that real participation and empowerment of women and minority groups is not being achieved. It has been argued that participatory processes can in fact be exclusionary.[46] Guijt and Kaul Shah (1998) describe the origins of 'gender naivety' in development practice as partly the result of 'the myth of community': communities are difficult to delineate geographically and socially, communities are diverse, and above all communities are social arenas in which power and politics are as important as they are at any other level. In the case study from Niassa in Mozambique, presented earlier in this chapter, rural communities are defined by local people as 'pertaining' to particular leaders, which means that people of different communities are often geographically mixed: neighbours do not necessarily belong to the same community.[47]

Gender naivety in PLA-based processes can be further explained by the dominance of male development professionals with low levels of gender-awareness; by the dominance of poverty agendas; by the lack of sufficient time to build rapport with women; and by the failure of project documentation. Guijt and Kaul Shah also argue that feminist movements and gender studies have had limited impact on participatory approaches to development. They suggest practical reasons why gender analysis and efforts to include women in participatory processes have been comparatively unsuccessful, including a lack of appreciation of the constraints on women's time and space that make it hard for them to take part in dialogues.[48] They propose to address this *de facto* exclusion through methodological improvements and innovations, and in particular through ensuring more clarity on the meaning of the (local, contextual) concepts of gender, participation, community, and empowerment.

3.3.3 Negotiation to improve poor people's surroundings

Guijt and Kaul Shah (1998) also address the 'myth of consensus'. They stress that social change often involves forms of conflict, which may make it necessary for the outsider-facilitator to mediate between members of a community. Outsiders are influential in deciding which social actors are included, and they often exercise a certain influence over the outcome of participatory processes. This influence can of course be used positively if, as a result of their involvement, the most deprived are included. However, outsiders may misrepresent the knowledge and needs of poor local women or other social groups and actors, and may sometimes convey a false notion of consensus when communicating the outcome of the participatory processes.

Participatory approaches are essentially about power and change, and gender is an important dimension of this. Cornwall (1998) explains that there are several misconceptions regarding gender and gender relations, including the fact that gender is not necessarily the dominant source of difference and identity, that Western conceptions of gender difference and concerns have tended to dominate development efforts, and that power is not held by all men, nor by men exclusively. Participatory analysis must address complex gender relations, rooted in power differences; and the cultural values, particular identities, and the differing positions of individuals who move in different domains need to be recognised. She also warns the facilitators of participatory processes not to create 'notionally homogeneous interest groups according to wealth, age and so on [...] Creating artificial groupings according to presumed differences can produce misleading conclusions and, in addition, may offer little in the way of prospects for future work, as such groups would probably not exist otherwise'.[49] This is consistent with the assertions of Long (see 3.3.1).

Thus, on the one hand, participatory processes need to involve all significant social actors, who will negotiate their interests in different ways and at different interfaces. On the other hand, externally initiated processes must lead to benefits, especially for the most vulnerable and poor people in a particular community (and for the environments on which they depend).

In the case of the Food Security Programme in Niassa (see 3.1), several childless elderly couples and widows were ranked among the most vulnerable and food-insecure, yet they are not necessarily members of traditional structures of governance (which include a 'queen' from a different lineage than that of the male community leader), recipients of traditional health care or other social services, or members of the project-related farmers' extension groups. They are (and should be) interviewed regularly by development professionals, and invited to community or focus-group meetings, but they have very little power to act and change things. Other, less vulnerable women have more agency as members of groups that play a role in the community and wider society. Negotiation about programme initiatives, such as work with direct benefits for women, had to be conducted with the male traditional leaders, with some women leaders, and with several (almost exclusively male) government officials. There were also forms of negotiation taking place between officials and traditional leaders. Assessment in 1998 suggested that elderly couples and widows got little direct benefit from the programme, but were benefiting from social and environmental improvements through welfare mechanisms in the community. The programme has little influence on these mechanisms, but must understand something about them, if only to be sure that the most vulnerable in a society are gaining at least something – which appears to be happening.

The case of participation in formal democratic spaces in Recife, Brazil (see also section 3.1) demonstrates that formal democracy takes a long time to develop, and indeed to actually deliver material benefits to excluded people. Project-management methodologies such as PLA are less relevant than hard bargaining in political arenas, where consensus is often far away, and violence is just around the corner. Participation of local stakeholders in responses to the effects of armed conflict is even more obviously dependent upon a precarious set of negotiations, as has been demonstrated in the Ikafe refugee settlement in Uganda (see section 4.3.2).

Poor people usually value their environments positively, as something to improve and sustain. The main reason for this is obvious: they depend directly on their environments. This also means that in the social negotiation processes their positions tend to stress conservation and/or improvement of environments. Small farmers in marginal areas of Kenya, in particular women farmers, are adopting 'conservation farming' techniques to increase and sustain the productivity of their fields and increase their income (see also section 4.3.2 [50]) In mountainous Lung Vai in Vietnam, poor farmers equate 'environment' with tree planting, soil conservation, and integrated pest management. Their motivation to engage in these activities is also primarily an interest in (future, sustained) production and income.[51] In north-east Sudan, nomadic Beja men point knowledgeably to the multiple uses of wild plants in times of drought crisis, and to the risks for human survival of the spread of the exotic and invasive mesquite tree, *Prosopis juliflora*.[52] The Zabbaleen in Cairo, garbage collectors who recycle a large proportion of the city's waste, define as their main environmental concerns those related to their personal health, including a lack of safe drinking water and inadequate sewerage systems; the risks for girls and women of cutting their hands on sharp objects inside refuse liners (which they must open while sorting waste); and the hazards caused by smoke from self-igniting plastic bags (the main unrecyclable type of garbage) in the alleyways of their settlement.[53] Owners and employees of small engineering workshops in Faridpur, Bangladesh, do not perceive their activities to be particularly related to the wider environment at all, but they appreciate the critical importance of occupational risks to health and safety.[54]

This contrasts with much (Northern) alarmist environmentalism and also with regulations imposed by both Southern and Northern governments, which are predominantly concerned with minimising negative impacts of (for example) road building, airport extension, pollution from manufacturing plants, and the loss of wildlife habitats to the urban sprawl.[55] Poor and marginalised people depend on their environments, change them, and negotiate changes with others. To understand the reasons why people change their environments in particular ways, and how these changes affect social relations, theories of gender, environment and development, political ecology, and environmental economics are being developed (see section 2.2), and lessons from experience can be called upon. In summary, these theories and lessons show that it is important to consider the following.

Analysis of environmental and social changes

- Keep local environmental knowledge and perception central to the analysis.

- Ensure the best possible data to record physical environmental changes.

- Identify the social actors and interfaces that cause the main pressures on local environmental resources. The actors are linked through institutions such as markets, State regulatory systems, or local customs and traditional arrangements. Show how macro-policy relates to changes in local livelihoods and environments.

- Look for evidence of the (local) gender-determined division of labour, men's and women's knowledge of environmental resources, gendered control over technology, gendered property rights, etc.

- Analyse the changes in surroundings and livelihoods of specific social groups (defined by gender, class, caste, ethnicity, and age) and social actors, and relate environmental changes to gender and other social relations.

- Consider present and future economic values of environmental resources, in particular those externalities that are usually ignored (for example deforestation and the loss of non-timber products, and pollution), and also the non-use values of other aspects of nature.

- Identify the (potential) effects on the prospects for sustaining environmental resources that are implied by government regulations, market-based instruments such as taxation, and the behaviour of producers and consumers.

Development practitioners and researchers need such guidance to enable them to explore the complexity of social relationships and changes in livelihoods. The environmental problems that affect the livelihoods of very poor people and the (local) solutions that they explore are of course enormously diverse. Furthermore, it is important to realise that environments are not always a *problem* for poor people: in fact, in most cases environments (or, better, surroundings) are intrinsic aspects of their livelihoods and lives – they are lived in and lived with, cherished and regenerated. The sustainable livelihoods framework conceptualises the complexity of interactions and changes, but no more than that. Only specific case studies or project assessments can show the real richness of social interactions and changes in environments and livelihoods.

4

Project management and environmental sustainability

In this chapter, the management of projects is discussed from two particular perspectives: that of environmental sustainability and that of poor people's participation in development processes.

Projects are 'a scheme of something to be done', and essentially an instrument for organisations of people to reach a certain goal within a given time-frame.[1] Projects are an instrument for the management of people and resources, efficiently and effectively – to achieve agreed goals. They are a cornerstone of development as it is practised by NGOs, governments, and commercial enterprises alike. They may be what NGOs or grassroots groups 'do' in small villages or urban neighbourhoods, but they may also be popular campaigns or a series of lobby activities aimed at changing public policy.

The literature on project management distinguishes stages in what is generally known as a 'project cycle' and is sometimes described as a 'project spiral'. This upward or positive spiral might also be seen as a learning spiral. The project cycle can be divided into a number of stages, as Figure 4.1 illustrates. The stages in this cycle are essentially the same in all project management, whether in the private sector, the government sector, or the NGO sphere, although some of the language may be used slightly differently.[2]

At every stage of a project, it is critical that negotiation between stakeholders reaches some level of consensus. There is generally a marked difference in this sense between the small-scale, community-based projects of NGOs and grassroots organisations, and the large-scale development projects that are funded by governments and banks and often run by commercial enterprises. Section 4.1 touches upon such larger projects from the perspective of lobbying and campaigning. It asks what needs to be done to make large projects more accountable to affected people and prospective beneficiaries, and to make them more benign in environmental terms. To that end it discusses the Environmental Impact Assessment (EIA) of large projects, which is an important instrument in decision-making processes and

Figure 4.1: The project cycle

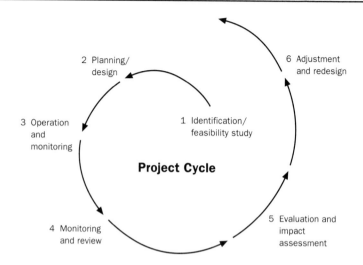

influential in policy making. EIA presents opportunities for NGOs and grassroots groups to access good information and influence what are often potentially harmful developments from both social and environmental perspectives.

EIA also offers some ideas for tools that are useful for NGO project management. In section 4.2 a practical perspective is taken, with a discussion of what to address in order to improve projects from social and environment perspectives. This section does not go as far as discussing in detail *how* to stimulate participation, facilitate negotiation, assess or measure environmental variables, but it gives a general picture and provides pointers for asking important questions in this regard. It thus gives an overview of EIA-type guidelines for small-scale, community-based projects. The special situation of humanitarian disasters and the (project) approach needed to assess and mitigate environmental impacts are discussed in sub-section 4.2.3.

Section 4.3 takes us back to the sustainable livelihoods framework by looking at the elements of the framework that are the most obviously influenced by projects. It identifies the critical questions that the framework helps us to ask, and the impacts that can be expected of projects. Following on from chapter 3, this section elaborates on aspects of stakeholder participation and consultation in various stages of projects, and discusses how participation determines project aims and indicators for success, and also the implications of popular participation for environmental sustainability. The section presents a 'hybrid' approach which makes use of learning about popular participation, the sustainable livelihoods framework as a tool for analysis, and some aspects of EIA also. In the final sub-section the recovery of livelihoods and rehabilitation of environmental resources is discussed, referring back to the more precarious of situations and more extreme forms of poverty and deprivation.

4.1 Environmental Impact Assessment: large-scale projects

In this section the common way of assessing potential environmental impact of big projects is discussed, and the implementation of environmental management plans. This is of particular interest for those who want to influence local policy processes, stimulate the participation of citizens in decision making, and claim their rights to information about often negative impacts on livelihoods and environments.

4.1.1 Screening, scoping, and full EIA

With the growth of concerns about the environmental impacts of large-scale developments such as dams, the expansion of manufacturing industry, the construction of whole new towns, irrigation schemes and highways, planners looked for ways to mitigate these impacts, but within certain financial and economic parameters. Environmental Impact Assessment (EIA) was developed for that purpose and has now been adopted by the majority of countries, in the North and South; and development banks and bilateral development agencies have adopted internal guidelines to this end.[3]

EIA can be seen as an add-on to the project-management cycle, and indeed steps or stages are usually distinguished in parallel to the stages of the project cycle. However, the focus of EIA is on the identification, planning, and design stages, early in the life of projects (see Figure 4.2). The first steps in this EIA-project cycle are the most critical ones, and they are what literature and practitioners focus on.[4] They are also the moments when many important decisions are made by technical experts without much (if any) public involvement.

Environmental screening
The earliest step in EIA is usually called environmental screening. It aims to assess proposed projects against some basic criteria, in order to decide whether further investigation of potential negative environmental impact is necessary at all. This stage makes use of checklists with types of projects that are likely to have significant adverse impacts on environments, as in the example from the Philippines overleaf.

Figure 4.2: The project cycle and Environmental Impact Assessment

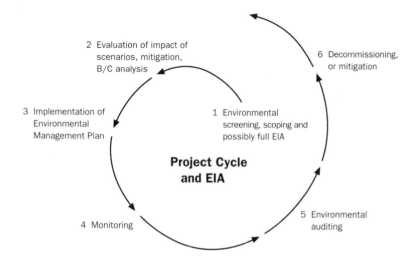

Environmental screening criteria in the Philippines[5]

Legislation about Environmental Impact Assessment was established in 1978. The following types of project are defined as environmentally critical and therefore in need of a full EIA:

- heavy industries
- resource-extractive industries
- infrastructure projects.

Projects in the following critical areas may also require a full EIA:

- national parks, watershed reserves, wildlife reserves, and sanctuaries
- potential tourist spots
- habitats for endangered and threatened species
- areas of unique historical, archaeological, or scientific interest
- areas traditionally occupied by ethnic minorities or tribes
- areas frequently affected by and/or hard hit by natural calamities
- areas with critical slopes
- prime agricultural lands
- recharge areas of aquifers
- water bodies.

Further criteria to determine whether some type of in-depth environmental analysis is actually necessary include project size and cost, and the level of uncertainty regarding potential impacts. Most (government, development) agencies require this early step to result in a brief screening note that is kept on file. The note would contain an explanation of the main environmental risks and set out what the next steps are, which could be to initiate a full EIA or to take an intermediary step: the commissioning of a less detailed study, usually called Environmental Analysis.

Scoping (or Environmental Analysis)

In the scoping stage, potential environmental impacts are identified in more detail, without embarking on an elaborate study. General and secondary data are collected (which will function as important baseline data), and the most significant potential environmental impacts are determined on the basis of expert experience and consultation with local people and other stakeholders. Qualitative statements dominate this assessment. Scoping should lead to terms of reference for a detailed assessment of environmental impact (if that proves to be necessary), but will already provide the basics. It makes use of checklists of the possible impacts of certain types of projects. It should also access data from Geographic Information Systems (GIS) that provide and overlay maps of various kinds, including maps of local demography, topography, hydrology, and soil quality, and maps displaying climate factors like rainfall. Scoping or Environmental Analysis tends to focus on a limited number of environmental issues.

In the scoping stage, an aid to visualising the potential environmental impacts of the proposal may be provided by diagrams of various kinds, including *network diagrams, problem trees,* and *systems diagrams,* all of which show relationships between (potential) environmental changes, their implications, and project activities. Particularly well known is the Leopold matrix, in which both the *magnitude* and the *importance* of possible impacts of proposed project components (on one axis) are scored in relation to particular aspects of the environment (on the other axis), as in Figure 4.3.

Full EIA

If projects are big and costly, and deemed to have significant impact on environments, a full Environmental Impact Assessment (EIA) needs to be initiated through the earlier stages of screening or scoping. EIA is usually a multidisciplinary study, making use of detailed field research that is specifically commissioned. In most countries, formal guidelines have been published by a specialist government agency, providing criteria for deciding whether an EIA needs to be initiated, and, if so, how it should be conducted.

Figure 4.3: Outline of the 'Leopold matrix' for the scoping of environmental impact

Proposed/possible project activities

M=magnitude I=importance of possible impact 1=low; 10=high	Road construction	Oil pipeline installation	Dam building	Etc.
Ground water quality	M / I	M / I		
Forest cover	M / I	M / I	M / I	
Local air quality	M / I			
Etc.				

Environmental characteristics

An EIA focuses on the most important potential impacts; detailed physical, biological, and chemical data will be collected, use may be made of simulation models, and experts dominate the process. Through the process of EIA, a number of scenarios with a range of potential environmental impacts are usually formulated. The negative environmental impacts of these scenarios are predicted, sometimes with the aid of 'risk analysis' that uses quantified potential impacts and statistical methods. Certain mitigation measures are normally evaluated as part of the formulation of alternative scenarios.

A detailed assessment of the potential environmental impacts of various scenarios needs to be accompanied by a statement of financial benefit-cost ratios, and usually some unquantifiable benefits and costs too. Benefit-cost

(B/C) projections include the environmental costs and benefits of the original proposal and of the range of possible mitigation measures (see also sub-section 2.2.4 on environmental economics). The actual EIA process involves costs that are generally below one per cent of total project cost (or below 0.5 per cent in very large projects, where economies of scale operate). Mitigation measures in response to negative impacts often involve costs too, and they may be well above one per cent of the total, for example the cost of equipment to reduce air pollution from factories, or the costs incurred by adopting longer trajectories for new roads in order to bypass sensitive wildlife habitats. Both the actual EIA and the mitigation measures often result in financial benefits too. Including environmental externalities and improving the quality of local people's environments and health, or protecting existing livelihoods, does in many cases make economic sense, even by conservative standards. Higher energy efficiency, reduced water contamination and soil pollution, less disturbance of landscapes, conservation of forests, and so on may imply reductions in immediate expenditure, savings in terms of future clean-up costs, and measures to safeguard the sources of livelihoods of people who do not benefit from the project. For example, highly polluting industries may cause diseases or even cost lives, destroy livelihoods of fisher people, and necessitate large repair or clean-up undertakings at some future date: EIA and mitigation costs should be off-set against the benefits that stem from preventing pollution and other environmental degradation.

A summary document that is sometimes called an Environmental Impact Statement then plays a central role in decision making (this is step 2 in Figure 4.2), usually carried out by government officials and financiers, and only sometimes with the direct involvement of local people (who are nevertheless in many cases the most negatively affected).

The use of EIA guidelines

Recent research has shown that the many EIA guidelines that are now available are not as effective as their authors will have hoped. Policy makers, advisers, field officers, and consultants appear to use them at best occasionally, or not at all when their use is not obligatory. Guidelines are perceived to be weak because they lack legal status, because they are often constrained by lack of time and inadequate financial support, they are too technical and/or bureaucratic, and because they focus almost entirely on negative (potential) impacts. They rarely convey 'best practice' and they do not respond to all the needs of the users, such as direct guidance on the formulation of terms of reference for EIA studies, assistance with training, and technical guidance. Furthermore, by their very nature, guidelines will appear inflexible, and sometimes they do not demonstrate the practical experience that should underlie their recommendations.

Obviously all guidelines can be criticised, and they cannot serve all the possible goals that different users may want them to serve. Research also suggests that there are important gaps in the guidelines that are currently available, for example a lack of customised guidelines for particular types of stakeholder and for specific contexts, such as small-scale and community-based development projects (see section 4.2). However, it has been argued that improvements in the practice of EIA might not come from rewriting guidelines or adding new ones, but from 'better institutional organisation and management'.[6] In addition to that conclusion, it seems obvious that ethnic-minority groups who are potentially affected by plans for mining of their lands, or urban slum dwellers who are threatened by industrial expansion, yet are well organised and articulate in their approaches to national or local authorities, can demand that, as a minimum, the national guidelines should be applied as the law or public regulation stipulates.

Statutory and organisational requirements

EIA was promoted in the 'Rio Declaration', one of the core outcomes of the UNCED in 1992 (see also section 2.1.2 and Appendix 1), and most countries have adopted national legislation in which the use of EIA or similar processes is made mandatory for projects with strong potentially negative impacts on the environment. Thailand and the Philippines were among the early adopters of such legislation in the late 1970s and early 1980s. However, countries vary widely in the demands made by their national laws, for example in terms of public consultation and information, and there is also great diversity in terms of national capacities to enforce legislation and regulation.

This diversity of legislation and mandatory procedures cannot be summed up here, but national procedures are usually summarised in literature and should be accessible to interested parties in a particular country. Studies of the effectiveness of legislation in developing countries show some common problems with EIA, besides enforcement difficulties. They include a lack of funding; very limited popular participation; a lack of guidance materials; excessively centralised EIA authorities; limited national capacity in terms of data availability, technical skills, and research facilities; and various ways in which authorities are co-opted by the business interests in large development proposals.

Most bilateral development organisations (governments of donor countries), UN agencies, and all the large development banks have produced and formalised internal EIA requirements in their procedures for project appraisal and implementation. These processes need to be matched, obviously, to national requirements, but that seems rarely to be a problem. In fact, where international funding is available for projects, the resource constraints and some of the other problems with EIA tend to be less pronounced. Nevertheless, internal World Bank studies and assessments of EIA effectiveness show that in these cases also there are many shortcomings.[7] These include a general lack of monitoring and auditing of actual environmental impact, which implies a missed opportunity for learning by all involved.

4.1.2 The Environmental Management Plan and its implementation

The scoping (i.e. Environmental Analysis) and/or a full EIA having been conducted, and a decision about the preferred project scenario having been made, an Environmental Management Plan (EMP; see step 3 in Figure 4.2) is written up and agreed. This plan articulates the agreed environmental aspects of project implementation, monitoring, evaluation (or audit), and – if relevant – decommissioning of infrastructure. It may articulate the following.[8]

- Mitigation measures that are to be taken to minimise negative environmental impacts.
- Measures that enhance environmental benefits.
- Environmental risks and uncertainties.
- Environmental legislation and standards that are relevant to the programme.
- Institutional support for and from agencies with regard to environmental management.
- A monitoring and auditing programme.
- Details of consultation and participation of various stakeholders.
- Resources and budgets that are required to implement the EMP.
- Contractual arrangements.

Monitoring

Monitoring of project implementation and operation should be done over the life of the project (see step 4 in Figure 4.2). Monitoring may be the responsibility of a sector Ministry, local authorities, or the national EIA authority, and will normally be led by the actual project-management structure or organisation. A good monitoring plan specifies locations for monitoring, and indicators and methods for assessing them. Monitoring needs to be both rigorous and feasible, and may include qualitative criteria that are informed by participatory research methodologies, in particular with regard to the social impacts of the project.

Auditing environmental impact

An environmental audit may be done at a later stage in a project, and is similar to or part of a review or evaluation (step 5 in Figure 4.2). The purpose of an audit is to establish the actual environmental impacts. EIA guidelines normally do not seek to support both planning and post-project impact assessment: rather, they concentrate on the former, while it is the latter that can be expected to contribute most to institutional learning and improving practice. Learning from audits towards the end of the project or after the project is phased out happens in only few cases.

An audit is most useful on industrial sites where pollution increases over time. It should be related to environmental standards, laws, and licences, and it will uncover liabilities. Further mitigation of environmental impact, such as the clean-up of polluted areas, may be proposed as a result of an audit. In countries where the particular liabilities are not clearly articulated in national legislation, environmental audits can serve as very important ammunition for campaigners, if the results are made public.

The term 'environmental audit' is also used by organisations and enterprises that operate in other contexts. Their performance may not threaten the environment, may not be big, and may not be of major concern to the government or activists. Nevertheless, an audit tends to uncover ways in which environmental impacts and often costs can be reduced, and sometimes it leads to net savings. For example, analysis of energy use in an office block can lead to investments in energy-saving bulbs; the existence of a market for waste paper can make separate collection and paper recycling cheap or lead to modest gains; and fairly traded products can strengthen their appeal to consumers with guarantees that products, production methods, and packaging materials are 'environment-friendly', organic, or sourced from recycled materials. These kinds of audit tend to be voluntary and may be regulated by parastatal organisations or business associations.

4.1.3 Participation in EIA and citizens' rights to information

The discussion of EIA has so far focused exclusively on environmental impacts, and on processes and decision makers that virtually exclude local people and the social impacts of developments. There is, however, a clear trend to widen EIA to encompass social-impact assessments, and to promote the active involvement of various stakeholders.[9] EIA legislation and regulation usually does stipulate that the public has certain rights to information and consultation, even though that may not be widely known or recognised by all civil servants and private enterprises involved.

There are thus legal and also moral rights that entitle affected people and others to be involved in decision making regarding potentially harmful developments. More pragmatically, it has also been argued that a range of practical benefits may be produced by participation. Such benefits may include (a) improved data arising from local knowledge, (b) improved focus on relevant issues, (c) better response to the needs of the stakeholders involved in the EIA, and (d) a reduction in costs, contingent upon reduced incidences of conflict and communication failure. Stakeholders in EIAs include the local people in whose environments proposed development projects take place, the enterprises that propose the projects, various levels of government, and beneficiaries such as the users of electricity that is generated from power stations or from water reservoirs behind dams in rivers. Development NGOs, business associations, and academics are often important, as are national associations for the protection of wildlife.

EIA is usually not really participatory, but it is consultative to some degree. Agencies conducting EIAs seek advice, organise public hearings, interview people, and in some cases invite representatives of stakeholder groups to serve on some form of panel or commission that oversees the process. Nevertheless, analysis of EIA practice suggests a number of constraints that inhibit the substantial involvement of stakeholders in EIAs, including the following.

1 Stakeholders are all too often short of time and money.

2 Low literacy levels and language differences may cause problems, because EIA results are often presented in complex reports and are not expressed in the local vernacular.

3 Insensitivity to gender-related matters during consultation processes and women's weak participation in decision making often mean that their voices are unheard during EIA.

4 Cultural differences and communication problems are particularly pronounced between indigenous people and non-indigenous experts.

5 Political and institutional cultures of decision making are often authoritarian, and officials may perceive citizens' groups and NGOs as threats.

6 Mistrust between other stakeholders, in particular between private-sector developers and citizens' groups, may limit popular participation.

7 Ineffective project management may cause EIAs to start too late in the project cycle and cause a lack of co-ordination between departments or sectors of the organisations involved.

8 Conflicting rights to manage natural resources, leading, for example, to land disputes, may enhance controversies between modernisers and those who want to maintain local and/or traditional livelihoods.

9 Ambiguity in legislation and guidelines complicates attempts to encourage better consultation.

10 The scale and complexity of projects, such as the Flood Action Plan in Bangladesh, may be so huge that citizens can no longer confidently engage with them.[10]

These constraints are hard to overcome, in particular by the most marginalised stakeholders, such as people who are displaced by dam building. They are, however, not unique to the EIA-aspects of large projects, and local action, supported by national and international networks and funds, has in some cases achieved much change. Polo Petrolândia, for example, a Brazilian NGO, has campaigned since 1979 for mitigation of the devastating social and environmental effects of the Itaparica dam in the São Francisco River. This huge dam displaced tens of thousands of people from the area of the reservoir upstream of the dam. The displaced people were given empty promises of compensation of various kinds for the loss of their land and livelihoods, following the completion of the dam in 1986. However, so far full compensation has not been paid. The lobby work of Polo Petrolândia has nevertheless led to important concessions from the government and the World Bank (which was the main financier of the dam), and a regional investment plan of US$290m in compensation was pledged a few years ago. The work of Polo Petrolândia was strongly informed by EIA studies that were done under the guidelines of both the national government and the World Bank. Further lobbying will have to ensure actual investment in accordance with the promises, but the coalition of Polo Petrolândia, local groups, and national groups with some international support may do just that.

4.2 Environmental Impact Assessment of community development projects

The effectiveness of conventional EIA in small-scale, community-based projects has been questioned, in part because it is difficult for rigid government-led or business-led processes to involve local people.[11] Other criticism regarding its application in NGO-type projects is also unsurprising, namely that EIA tends to fail to identify socially differentiated impacts and that it is usually meant to minimise negative environmental impact, instead of enhancing positive impacts on both people and their environments. NGO projects often target the poorest and most vulnerable women and men, and in many cases they are concerned with regenerating and sustaining environmental resources in order to improve health and increase livelihood opportunities. EIA costs may also be prohibitively high in the context of low-budget projects. Nevertheless, there are cases where the methodology is useful, for example where very limited negative impacts of many individual community-based projects add up to significant impact when put together.

This section gives a flavour of internal environmental assessment processes and guidelines of and for NGOs. It presents an overview of the potential environmental impact of small enterprises, which is accompanied by an example of the environmental impact of small engineering workshops in Bangladesh. In the final sub-section, project responses to mass displacement are discussed, and the question of how negative environmental impacts can be mitigated.

4.2.1 EIA guidelines for community development projects

Some bilateral agencies have produced or are preparing EIA guidance for NGOs, in part in order to enable them to comply with the planning procedures of donors,[12] but this guidance often concentrates on minimising harmful impacts. Existing guides or manuals on EIA (or, better, *environmental screening* or *scoping*) for low-budget projects are not necessarily participatory in their approach, may cover just a few of the great diversity of sectors addressed by NGOs, and are not usually incorporated in NGOs' mandatory planning and evaluation procedures. There are also indications that where guidelines exist they are not used often. In short, guidelines for small-scale projects appear to suffer from many of the same shortcomings as their counterparts for large projects. Nevertheless, EIA, and in particular environmental screening, does offer checklists that have proved to be useful in situations where experts are not available and development workers need to be confident that a full range of questions about environmental resources is being asked.[13]

Guidelines for screening and scoping
Below there is an example of generic practical guidelines for rural community-based projects, produced by the Canadian Council for International Co-operation (CCIC).

CCIC guidelines for environmental screening of NGO projects[14]

This 'kit' presents the very basics of potential environmental problems and solutions, and checklists with key questions related to (a) domestic water supply and sanitation, (b) irrigation, (c) small dams and reservoirs, (d) pesticides and integrated pest management, (e) coastal ecosystems, and (f) dryland agriculture. It is thus geared to address rural problems.

It explains how to incorporate environmental aspects into the project cycle:
(a) define the goals and objectives of the project;
(b) identify alternative methods to achieve those goals and to minimise negative impact on the environment;
(c) evaluate the costs and benefits of the alternatives;

(d) select the best project design (maximise benefits for the people, minimise costs to the environment); and

(e) incorporate a monitoring programme.

This is not fundamentally different from conventional EIA, albeit that costs are here not expected to be simply expressed in monetary units. The underlying assumption still seems to be that environmental impact is always negative and must therefore be minimised. However, the guidelines do provide ideas for alternatives, like the use of non-chemical pest-control measures.

The kit mentions eight 'sources of information', including local villagers, farmers and residents, and suggests for this the use of Rapid Rural Appraisal (RRA) methods – in other words, it promotes a consultative approach (compare this with other forms of participation in the typology in section 3.3.1). It provides many annotated references and addresses of organisations in Southern and Northern countries that work in the field of environment and development.

There are also cases where guidelines for small-scale projects were developed for specific contexts. An example of this is guidelines produced for the Independent Development Trust in South Africa, which deals with urban and rural community projects that range from the building of health clinics and schools, the construction of urban housing and water and sanitation systems, to rural energy supply and agricultural development. These guidelines consider social and economic impacts too, give some technical support, and provide pointers to relevant laws and organisations in South Africa. They are surprisingly brief on the issue of *whom to involve*, and they do not offer suggestions for *how to involve* beneficiaries or other stakeholders.[15]

Sector-specific guidelines, or guidelines for certain ecological and social realities, have also been developed, with increasingly strong notions of the need for participation by local people. Good examples come from the World Conservation Union (IUCN) and the International Institute for Environment and Development (IIED).[16] IUCN focuses on nature conservation in relation to community development, and IIED on gender, participation, and environment, and, with collaborators, on soil-fertility management, all with a strong rural bias. These guidelines provide many practical tools for assessing local ecosystem properties, social relations, people's needs, and environmental change; they are often based on PLA (RRA/PRA) diagrammatic tools[17] and earlier ideas from so-called agro-ecosystems analysis.[18]

Internal guidelines for NGO project appraisal

Most NGOs have long assumed that the negative environmental impact of their projects is negligible, but some anecdotal analysis in the early 1990s suggested that appropriate guidelines could be useful.[19] In 1991 Oxfam incorporated a question about environmental impact in its grant-appraisal procedure. The question is '... *what will the environmental impact of this project be (where relevant)?*'. Policy aims related to sustainable livelihoods were reflected in a one-page set of guidelines for the staff responsible for answering this question.[20] These guidelines are not a checklist, but they propose six fundamental questions, which reflect the sustainable livelihoods framework. In fact, these questions can be asked in any situation of appraisal, in the project-identification stage, during planning, grant assessment, monitoring, or evaluation. The questions are reproduced below.

Initial questions for sustainable livelihoods analysis

When thinking about **natural resources** (*such as water, agricultural land, rangeland, urban land, air, forest, flora and fauna*), and **human-created resources** (*such as shelter, water supply, sanitation, health-care systems, schools*), you could ask yourself ...

- What resources are important in local livelihoods?
- What is the quality of those resources? *(e.g. soil fertility, drainage potential, pasture quality, accessibility and quality of hospitals/schools, congestion, sanitary conditions, etc.)*
- Who uses which resources? *(women, men, children, disabled, ethnic groups, social classes, etc.)*
- Who controls decisions about how these resources are used?
- Who is helping to sustain local resources, and who benefits from this?
- And how will the situation be affected by the project?

These suggested questions were distributed widely among Oxfam staff, but brief surveys suggested that four years later they were not being used extensively, even though almost half of all Oxfam grants have some direct bearing on environmental resources.[21] The relevance of these questions in relation to the sustainable livelihoods framework and the implications of 'merging' EIA with participatory approaches to appraisal and learning (in several stages of the project cycle) are discussed in section 4.3.

Partly for reasons of cost, few NGOs appear to have adopted more than very basic internal procedures for pursuing environmental sustainability in their development programmes. NGOs may learn from bilateral development agencies and UNDP, who published a brief and accessible *Handbook and Guidelines for Environmental Management and Sustainable Development*. This publication outlines basic criteria for project screening and makes suggestions for preparing 'environmental management strategies' (see also chapter 5).[22] See below for a summary of what the guidelines propose with regard to project management. They reflect a structure very similar to what was outlined in section 4.1 on conventional EIA for larger projects.

Summary of UNDP project management (environmental guidance)

Step 1. Project identification

Check against environmental criteria that come from the Environment Overview of the Country programme (EOC).

Step 2. Project formulation

At this stage an Environment Overview of the Project (EOP) must be prepared, which (a) describes the natural environment of the project area; (b) gives details of the three most important environmental issues; (c) describes economics and the environment in the project area and how the project will affect this; (d) highlights environmental management capacities and laws in the area; (e) describes potential impacts on the environment and socio-economic impacts; and (f) proposes alternative project designs to mitigate environmental degradation and to take opportunity of environmental potential.

Step 3. Screening proposed projects

A checklist of project types helps to decide whether additional information is required, or changes to the proposal are necessary, or a detailed Environmental Management Strategy (EMS) is needed.

Step 4. Improvement following project appraisal

If necessary, the EMS is prepared at this stage.

Step 5. Project approval

Approval happens if the steps of this process have been taken satisfactorily. Some questions that help this consideration are (a) Has the EOP been prepared? (b) Does the project document include actions to protect and conserve the environment? (c) Have sources of positive or negative environmental impact been properly identified? (d) Have those who will be affected by the environmental impact been properly identified? (e) Does the project include environmental mitigation measures? (f) Have potential conflicts of interest been properly addressed?

Step 6. Project implementation

Environmental criteria should be considered when selecting project advisers and implementing agencies.

Step 7. Project monitoring and evaluation

In annual reviews and monitoring efforts, reference must be made to the EOP and EMS, and unanticipated negative and positive environmental impacts should be noted.

There appear to be no standards to determine what environmental impact is acceptable or desirable in UNDP project proposals, or in EIA guidelines produced by larger agencies and national governments, or in the little that is formalised by NGOs on the subject of environmental impact. In as far as standards or criteria exist, they amount to standards of procedure – of good practice – and not standards of actual environmental impact. This is probably a very good thing: it is important to agree *how to* improve environmental sustainability, and it is impossible to generalise what environmental changes are 'good' in all contexts and according to all key stakeholders. Nevertheless, governments around the world have set standards for maximum permissible pollution and for tree planting following commercial logging. These standards are important, and commercial undertakings as well as NGO projects should respect them.

NGOs and environmental data

A lack of access to environmental data is a key problem for small NGOs and grassroots organisations, and also for many of the larger international NGOs that embark on environmental assessment with the help of the above key questions or checklists and technical manuals. NGOs are rarely well linked to meteorological services, they do not usually know where to get aerial photographs, and they have few if any means to make technical assessments of pollution. Nevertheless, data are often available; satellite images may be captured from simple receivers; and the internet provides more and more geographical data (see Appendix 2 for several data sources and websites). Data are often available 'somewhere', in Ministries or larger development programmes, and accessing them may be just a matter of exercising some persuasion. Generating data is likely to be prohibitively costly, but basic assistance may be all that is needed for interpreting existing data, and that can prove invaluable.

During a review of a food-security programme in Niassa, Mozambique, five-day rainfall totals were obtained from a local meteorological station that had been functioning for the greater part of the previous three decades, despite war. The data were used for basic assessment of relative drought-stress for crops; they correlated directly with farmers' explanations of (recent) droughts and good agricultural years. This was important information for assessing project impact, because it expressed the comparative importance of climatic factors to project innovations with regard to crop yields.[23]

For the participatory assessment of land-tenure and ownership disputes in northern Tanzania, aerial photographs were photocopied and enlarged from a scale of 1:60,000 to about 1:45,000. The original photographs dated from the early 1970s – and thus pre-dated major resettlements of rural people in Tanzania. The photocopies were collated with tape. The resulting quality was obviously extremely low, but some villagers still managed to interpret them. They were used as an aid in an attempt to make a large sketch-map of the community (including pastures and forest), which served as a basis for discussion. Cross-checking the photographs with the map and with statements by local Maasai people about land claims and claims to hunting rights in the buffer zone of a national wildlife park greatly enhanced understanding of the problems by NGO staff from outside the area. NGOs support the local people in campaigns and legal cases to reclaim what are rightfully their pastures.[24] Some of those legal cases have now been successfully concluded.

4.2.2 Environmental impact of small enterprises

Small enterprises are increasingly important for generating employment in both urban and rural areas of developing countries.[25] They are crucial suppliers of consumer goods to local markets, and increasingly to foreign markets too. They also provide essential capital goods for infrastructure development and other production, for example the output from brick-making and metal-engineering workshops. It is often assumed that 'small scale' equals 'no environmental problem', but there are many grounds on which that could be challenged, in particular in the manufacturing sector. Nevertheless, small-scale and NGO-supported projects are rarely considered for a full EIA or an elaborate scoping exercise, either at the planning stage or later, retrospectively. Consider the case study below, which is one of few examples of such an exercise (see also section 3.1.1).

EIA of 'informal' engineering workshops[26]

A rare example of the use of a conventional approach to EIA in an NGO project is ITDG's support for small-scale engineering workshops in Bangladesh, known as the Dholai Khal project. In fact, this EIA is more like an audit of existing enterprises, and a means to provide baseline data for a three-year project aimed at improving the workshops.

The impact on the environment of 68 existing workshops, most of them with between five and ten employees, was assessed at the outset of the project in 1998. The EIA methodology was mostly that of a normal scoping exercise. It included mapping of land use with the aid of GIS (geographical information systems), the collection and analysis of soil, air, and water samples, and measurement of noise levels. The EIA team also held extensive consultations with several stakeholders, and through observations and discussions assessed waste production and waste re-use. The study found that the aggregated impact on wider environments is not negligible but extremely hard to quantify, spread thinly over a larger area, and not a cause for particular concern. There is some waste production and pollution, but that is not significant when set against 'background pollution' of the densely populated area and the traffic on the roads where the workshops are located. Still, all the workshops combined do have cumulative effects on the environment, probably comparable to the water contamination and air pollution and waste production of one larger enterprise with the same total production.

However, important health and safety issues must be addressed. Workers have eye problems from unprotected welding, respiratory problems from exposure to metal dust and heat, eye and respiratory problems associated with paint aerosols, and skin diseases associated with the use of oil and toxic chemicals. Workers are exposed to electrical and fire hazards, which are in part related to space constraints, and fire hazards are also important for others in this densely populated area. Workers' appreciation of all these hazards is very limited. The environmental management plan – that is, the recommendations emerging from the study – included various mitigation measures related to the occupational risks and also to the environmental impacts. Central to the improvements is the inclusion of messages regarding health and safety risks in skill-training programmes.

This case study confirms some of the objections against EIA in community development projects, for example the fact that it was expensive in the context of the overall project, and that, despite interviews and consultation, it remained difficult to engage workers and workshop owners in thinking about the notion of 'environment' at all. Nevertheless, in this case the methodology does not appear to be wholly inappropriate, because it has identified important issues that need to be addressed, in particular in connection with health and safety, and as a result waste production and pollution are likely to be reduced as well. Workshops may also make financial savings from such changes, following only minor investments. The study has played an important role in the early stages of the project and has helped to determine strategies for the training of workers and other project activities.

A known limitation in transplanting EIA to NGO-type projects is that EIA guidelines normally do not seek to support both planning and post-project impact assessment: they concentrate on the former. It is the latter that can be expected to contribute most to institutional learning and improving practice. NGOs need to learn from practice, in particular because of their limited financial resources available for training staff, hiring consultants, and contracting out planning exercises.

The ITDG project in Bangladesh has planned to assess the environmental impact of the workshops (including the occupational hazards) again after a project period of three years. The study has not been set in a wider framework, like 'sustainable livelihoods', but the overall project does consider a broad context. Gender-related factors were identified (most owners and workers are men, but not all), and further gender study has been initiated. The main aim of the project concerns improvement of human, financial, and social capital – the latter in terms of support for an association of the workshop owners.

In general terms, the environmental impact of small (manufacturing/ processing) enterprises should be considered in relation to the following factors:

- resource use (water, fossil fuels, and other sources of renewable energy, agricultural products, capital goods, chemicals);
- space use (and noise pollution);
- occupational environment (health and safety);
- pollution (of air, water, land; with (for example) dye effluent, oil, or fumes from welding);
- waste production (and waste re-using and recycling).

In most cases, the latter three are of central importance for the environment and for the employees and enterprises, as we saw in the case history from Bangladesh. They are also usually the ones where most can be done to reduce environmental and occupational risks without negatively affecting financial returns.

The small-scale, informal (i.e. unregulated, often unregistered, or even illegal) manufacturing sector might actually be seen as large, because in many countries it forms a very important part of the manufacturing sector, if not the larger part. Environmental impacts of many small enterprises could thus be compared with the aggregate impact of the few large enterprises in the same sector. In manufacturing or, for example, food processing, it cannot be assumed that 'many times small' is better for environmental quality than 'one-time large', but comparisons entail practical and methodological problems. Production processes on different scales usually make use of different technologies, and measuring the impacts of small units can be prohibitively expensive and time-consuming. Different production processes (leading to the same product) can also affect the environment in different ways. Research by ITDG found, for example, that brick-making in Zimbabwe in large enterprises produced more carbon dioxide (CO_2) per unit product than such activity in small and medium-sized enterprises, but large enterprises contribute less to land degradation. The latter is the case because large enterprises do not use fuel-wood and thus do not contribute to deforestation. Instead they use coal, which pollutes the air with sulphur dioxide (SO_2).

Small enterprises are often unregulated and even unauthorised, which makes accessing them and assessing their impact a sometimes controversial process. Fragile, small, and emerging businesses often perceive regulation as inhibiting their chances of developing successfully. Government standards that aim to limit pollution, regulate risks to health and safety, and set down rules for resource-use will often be perceived negatively as uneconomic hindrances, rather than as offering positive support to small entrepreneurs. Implementation of standards is also generally ineffective where authorities would need to deal with a large number of small enterprises, yet have very limited capacity. Indeed, exemption from all sorts of standards is often made official for enterprises with a small number of employees. Nevertheless, impact on the health of workers, on environments, and (indirectly) on the health of neighbours and future generations, impacts on flora and fauna, the quality of life, and other people's livelihoods can be significant. At the same time, a lot can be done with increased awareness and knowledge to limit impacts without affecting productivity and the immediate financial returns of the enterprises.

Criteria or indicators to judge progress in this sense should thus be mainly related to trends and processes, rather than to externally set standards and limits. For example, when introducing new skills to metal workers, attention can be paid to health and safety and to simple ways to limit pollution and re-use waste materials. Financial incentives can also be used in order to improve working conditions and reduce pollution and waste production. A further important way of reducing negative environmental impact is through 'voluntary compliance'. This could be the result of peer pressure from similar enterprises (united in industrial associations or artisans' organisations) and pressure from consumers, neighbours, and authorities: a 'stakeholder' approach to enforcement. Following a training programme or other support activities, it may be possible to establish a trend among workshops in a particular sector to adopt those practices and indeed to reduce negative environmental and occupational effects. This can be done through a number of in-depth interviews, simple observations, and perhaps a brief questionnaire survey. Success or failure can often be assessed without elaborate soil sampling, air testing, or other physical measurements.

4.2.3 Mass displacement and environmental quality

We have been considering well-planned development projects, but a wholly different situation arises when large groups of people are displaced as a result of war or some other catastrophe. In these cases, the very highest priority must be accorded to human safety and survival. That has environmental aspects too; 'the environment for survival' and human vulnerability are briefly discussed in section 2.3. Furthermore, the responses in aid of displaced people are projects themselves, even though planned and implemented in haste.

International NGOs such as CARE and the German bilateral development agency GTZ have made attempts to assess the environmental impacts of refugee movements and also the effectiveness of mitigation responses by relief agencies. Some NGOs have developed very basic guidelines for their internal appraisal processes, aiming to ensure at least a minimum of consideration for environmental resources, but few initiatives have achieved much. In 1994 the UNHCR produced draft environmental guidelines for use in work with refugees and also host populations and environments.[27]

EIA in crisis?

The UNHCR does not present a version of Environmental Impact Assessment (EIA) for refugee settlements, but the guidelines do display some EIA characteristics. In fact, EIA is not fully relevant for refugee situations in its original form as a project-planning and decision-making tool. This is in part because refugee movements are largely unplanned, so that responses cannot be easily planned either, although preparedness and precautionary measures are taken in most cases. A more important problem is that the EIA methodology was designed for project planning, whereas in situations involving refugees (and camps) the need to assess the impact of the actual arrival of the refugees is more important than assessing the impact of the project, i.e. the response effort. EIA was also designed to do cost-benefit analysis of environmental changes and mitigation efforts, which is extremely difficult in refugee situations and immediately encounters controversial questions about the price of human life.[28] The UNHCR guidelines do, however, promote the assessment of costs and benefits of measures that mitigate negative environmental change, but primarily from a perspective of financial efficiency.

The four best-known tools of EIA still have some useful application in assessing impacts on the environment, to inform programme adjustment and the formulation of mitigation measures at later stages of the emergency.[29] These are (a) checklists to identify possible environmental impacts; (b) matrixes that show project activities and potential impacts (the 'Leopold matrix', see section 4.1); (c) network diagrams that show causal relationships and/or spatial distributions of environmental change; and (d) maps that combine factors such as demographic, rainfall, soil, and topographical data. A problem with the latter in particular is that the availability and quality of data are often very limited, despite advances in the use of aerial photographs, satellite imagery, GIS, computerised databases, and access to the internet (by the UNHCR in collaboration with others).

UNHCR guidelines on environmental impact

The UNHCR guidelines were finalised in 1996 and complemented by specific guidelines on domestic-energy use, forestry, and livestock keeping in refugee situations. UNHCR has also appointed special officers in important operations. Humanitarian agencies (that is, mostly international NGOs) with a focus on refugees normally work under UNHCR co-ordination at field level and may thus be expected to take note of those guidelines. National and also international agencies that work with 'internally displaced' people will find some relevant material in these guidelines too, whether or not the UNHCR is present.

The UNHCR guidelines describe a number of 'principles of environmental activities' that are worth mentioning: (1) differentiate the 'emergency' phase, 'care and maintenance' phase, and 'durable-solutions' phase in deciding environmental activities; (2) follow an integrated approach with other sectoral activities in refugee assistance; (3) stress prevention and mitigation over 'curing' environmental problems; (4) stress cost-effectiveness and net-benefit maximisation of environmental mitigation and repair; and (5) encourage the participation of the local host population, experts, and also refugees. Table 4.1 summarises the 'environmental measures' that the guidelines recommend as options.

Table 4.1: Environmental measures in refugee responses (UNHCR)[30]

Institutional measures (UNHCR)	Emergency phase	Care and maintenance phase	Durable-solutions phase
• Include environmental concerns in other (sectoral) guidelines. • Promote environment-friendly procurement of goods and services. • Co-ordinate environmental policy with other UN agencies, governments, and donors. • Promote environment-friendly technologies. • Upgrade the environmental database (a kind of GIS). • Train staff in environmental issues.	• Consider environmental aspects in contingency planning. • Include an environmental specialist or 'focal point' in the emergency team. • Establish a working relationship with environmental authorities and other actors. • Conduct a post-emergency assessment.	• Assign an environmental co-ordinator or 'focal point'. • Prepare an Environmental Action Plan and in some cases an Environmental Master Plan. • Establish a local Environmental Task Force with representatives of local authorities, other agencies, the host population, and refugees. • Include environment in budget planning.	• After refugees have left, undertake environmental rehabilitation (with others). • Follow 'development' guidelines of other agencies regarding environmental considerations in local settlement and in repatriation of former refugees.

The guidelines stress that mitigating what is usually negative environmental impact should not happen in isolation; it should rather be integrated with other sectors' concerns and activities. The guidelines present a range of activities that can be tried in these sectors to reduce environmental impact and in most cases actually improve the sector's efficiency and reduce short-term and longer-term cost, as summarised in the next table. For livestock, forestry, and energy there are now also separate guidelines, which are more detailed and prescriptive.

Table 4.2: Sectoral activities to reduce the negative environmental impact of refugees[31]

Sector	Measures to reduce negative environmental impacts
Supplies and logistics	• Adequate supplies to avoid burden on local environment. • Avoidance of excessive transportation. • Environment-friendly procurement policy.
Physical planning of refugee settlement	• Respect the 'carrying capacity' of site and surroundings, e.g. in terms of wood and fodder supply and waste-sites absorption capacity. • Avoid environmentally sensitive areas, such as wildlife reserves. • Take special measures, including the supply of environment-friendly or sustainably gathered building materials and construction of drainage channels. • Avoid radical clearing; protect existing vegetation.
Water supply	• Carry out adequate assessment of quantity and quality of water resources. • Protect water sources against pollution. • Control chemicals, including chlorine.
Sanitation	• Establish a system for the disposal of human excreta. • Ensure proper management of waste water. • Set up a waste-management system, with special precautions for medical and toxic waste. • Take dust-control measures (e.g. provide ground-cover). • Take measures to control insects and rodents; include non-chemical methods.
Health	• Identify potential impacts on health, including vectors, climate, local disease patterns, water supply, and sanitation. • Train staff and the refugee community.
Food	• Provide food that requires less or no fuel to prepare (emergency phase). • Promote energy-efficient and low-smoke stoves and utensils. • Promote energy-efficient cooking methods, including pre-soaking of beans and whole-grain maize, also (community-based) grinding of grains. • Select foods with low transport, handling, and packaging needs.

Table 4.2: Sectoral activities to reduce the negative environmental impact of refugees (continued)

Sector	Measures to reduce negative environmental impacts
Domestic energy	• Promote energy efficiency, in particular through fuel-efficient stoves (first choice). • Supply alternative fuels (second choice). • Provide fuelwood in a sustainable manner (third choice).
Forestry	• Assess forest resources and draw up forest-management plan; monitor. • Prevent deforestation with site selection and during site planning. • Mitigate forest degradation through controlled wood extraction, establishing fuelwood plantations, and regulation of charcoal making, wood trading, and hunting. • Rehabilitate forest through tree planting and protection for natural re-growth.
Agriculture	• Do soil and land surveys. • Ensure secure access to agricultural land. • Support sustainable ('low-input') farming methods, supply appropriate farming inputs and extension services.
Livestock	• Determine carrying capacity of camps and immediate surroundings. • Restrict livestock in refugee settlements, in order to avoid animal-borne human diseases (e.g. tuberculosis). • Reduce livestock pressure on the environment by negotiating or supporting the sale of livestock, slaughtering, alternative grazing land, pasture improvement. • Promote health care for animals.
Community services	• Identify locals and refugees with skills and experience in environmental activities. • Encourage the establishment of a local environmental task force, representing the full range of refugee and local community interests; encourage refugees to take part in cleaning and resource protection'. • Facilitate interaction and conflict resolution on environmental issues between the local population and refugees. • Assist in the mobilisation of refugee labour for environmental projects.

Table 4.2: Sectoral activities to reduce the negative environmental impact of refugees (continued)

Sector	Measures to reduce negative environmental impacts
Education	• Develop environmental teaching materials and environmental education programme. • Train teachers to deal with environment-related subjects.
Income generation	• Promote income-generating activities that contribute to sound environmental management. • Identify and discourage environment-hostile income-generation activities. • Design and implement environmentally sound vocational training.

UNHCR has now developed a training module for increasing the environmental awareness of its own staff (UNHCR, 1998d). It complements an important effort to improve the plight of refugees, host populations, and 'the environment'. Nevertheless, there is only scant evidence available that all this is actually implemented *and* achieving reduced long-term environmental degradation. There is no doubt that occupational environmental aspects and (short-term) health concerns are of key importance, and it is thus a reasonable assumption that implementing the above suggestions will help refugees and local hosts immediately. Also, *irreversible* and *long-term* environmental impacts of refugee settlements tend to be limited, whereas the conversion or substitution of natural capital to infrastructure (i.e. *physical capital*; see section 3.2.4) can by no means be called environmentally negative in every case and every sense. In fact, a large influx of refugees in an area with poor infrastructure, inadequate markets, and limited livelihood opportunities may in some ways be a boost for local economic development, although the poorest of the host population tend to suffer from increased commodity prices and reduced quality and availability of environmental resources. Furthermore, guidelines in general, and environ-mental guidelines in particular, are not used often: the impact of notional policies and good intentions is limited, and real change comes from good management and such measures as encouraging a 'learning culture', even in situations where there is great pressure to deliver practical results.

Participation in humanitarian responses
Perhaps the most challenging issue, one that is not fully explored in the UNHCR guidelines, is not specifically related to the environment: it is the matter of involving the important stakeholders in genuine participation, and not mere consultation. Limited experience of introducing negotiation and

mediation processes into work with refugees, host populations, and a range of national and international actors suggests that this is a difficult matter indeed. Initial lessons from such experience do not appear to be fundamentally different from what is being learned in 'development' contexts, but they manifest themselves more sharply in highly pressured situations. The lessons include the following:[32]

* High expectations are often generated among people who are invited to take part – expectations that cannot be met by the emergency-response projects.

* Project managers need to be flexible in response to the stakeholders' analysis, especially where participating host populations want support that is seen as 'non-emergency' and outside the mandate of (for example) the UNHCR.

* It is important to cross-check data from multiple meetings, methodologies, and sources, which is a challenge for any good analysis.

* Participatory processes must be managed to ensure the involvement of women, and in general a 'positive bias' towards the weaker stakeholders. Participation costs time.

These are important lessons, but expectations of genuine participation in emergency responses must be kept low, for example because the staff of disaster-response agencies usually have limited experience of using participatory approaches, and because they are always acting under pressure, working against the clock in difficult circumstances.

Minimum standards in humanitarian relief

The UNHCR guidelines and the idea of improving stakeholders' participation are about improving practice – doing things better. Important benefits can also come from simply adhering to the recently developed minimum standards for work with displaced people by the so-called Sphere Project, which is a collaborative effort by several relief and development agencies. Table 4.3 shows some examples of key indicators that express *minimum* standards (as distinct from *best* practice).

4.3 Projects, participation, and the sustainability of livelihoods

Following the explanations of EIA-for-community-development projects in section 4.2, it can be said that there still is a strong need for an approach that combines the strengths of EIA with those of participatory approaches, and tools to improve understanding of social relations and interactions between people and their physical environment. A hybrid form of existing approaches and tools is thus required, and some of the literature has attempted to develop that.[33]

Table 4.3: Sphere Project: examples of agreed minimum standards for emergency relief[34]

Sector/activity	Examples of indicators/standards with environmental relevance
Water supply	• At least 15 litres of water per person per day is collected. • There is at least one water point per 250 people. • The maximum distance from any shelter to the nearest water point is 500m.
Excreta disposal	• Maximum 20 people per toilet. • Toilets no more than 50m from dwellings. • Toilets available in public places such as markets.
Vector control	• Vulnerable populations are settled outside the malarial zone. • Vector breeding and resting sites are modified where necessary and practicable. • Intensive fly-control is carried out in high-density settlements when there is risk or presence of diarrhoea epidemic.
Solid-waste disposal	• Domestic refuse is removed or buried. • No contaminated or dangerous medical waste left at any time in the living area or public spaces. • There is an incinerator within the boundaries of each health facility.
Drainage	• No standing waste water around water points. • Storm-water flows away.
Family shelter	• If demand for construction materials is expected to cause deforestation, some or all basic materials are supplied to families within two days of their arrival. • There is immediate protection of vegetation that is important for erosion control, wind breaks, or shade.
Household items	• People have access to and make use of fuel-economic, low-smoke stoves, and cooking pots with lids.

Table 4.3: Sphere Project: examples of agreed minimum standards for emergency relief (continued)

Sector/activity	Examples of indicators/standards with environmental relevance
Site planning	• It is not less than 3 metres above the anticipated ground-water table in the rainy season.
	• Land rights and permitted use are firmly established.
	• The site is at least 10km from protected or fragile areas.
	• The site is not prone to tidal waves or flooding, is not situated on land at risk from landslides, and is not close to an active volcano.
	• The site provides 45m² space for each person, including infrastructure, shelter, markets, etc., but excluding agricultural land.
	• There are 50m-wide firebreaks at least every 300m.
	• During site planning, trees are spared as far as possible, and measures are taken to protect or conserve forests.
	• Agreed levels of animal husbandry and agricultural activity by the displaced population are environmentally sustainable.

NGOs have made their own attempts since 1992, and this section builds in particular on that experience.[35] The hybrid takes the sustainable livelihoods framework as its main analytical tool, and Participatory Learning and Action (PLA) as its main approach to ensuring that excluded and deprived people take part in decision making; and it uses aspects of EIA to ensure that environmental sustainability remains a core element of change processes. The final sub-section addresses situations of recovery and rehabilitation of livelihoods, where reduced vulnerability, rather than sustainability, is the main goal.

4.3.1 A generic approach: participatory environmental assessment

The hybrid approach presented here combines especially the framework of sustainable livelihoods, participatory tools, and environmental checklists. The latter are strong aids for understanding potential and actual, negative and positive environmental impacts. The sustainable livelihoods framework helps one to ask questions about *what* changed or is expected to change, and *why* those changes (might) happen. It also shows relations between people and various resources (or capitals). The vast literature and body of experience on involving various social actors in projects helps to ensure that change can be pursued in the interests of the most vulnerable and poor people.

Outline of the assessment process

NGOs have undertaken a number of exercises in which these tools were combined in learning processes with staff, counterpart staff, and also citizens' groups and officials. These exercises were training workshops, project identifications or needs assessments, project reviews or sometimes project-impact assessments, i.e. they happened in several of the stages of the project cycle. They took (and take) broadly speaking the steps depicted in Figure 4.4.

Figure 4.4: Participatory Environmental Assessment

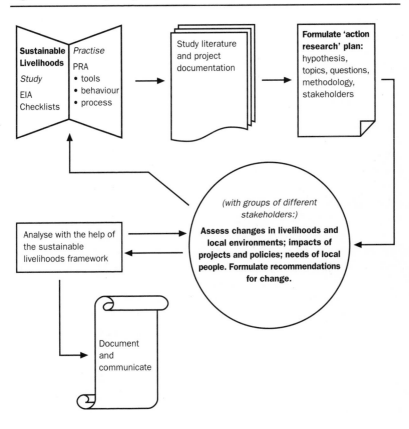

In most cases a group of workshop participants consists of NGO staff, and often also some representatives of beneficiary-communities and local officialdom. These participants are generally of mixed background and skills and are composed of roughly equal numbers of women and men. The workshop participants are in fact the 'outsiders' or facilitators (see also section 3.3.2, where a generalised participatory process of analysis is outlined).

The first steps are to acquire a basic understanding of sustainable livelihoods and EIA processes, in particular checklists, which enable the reading of secondary documentation and the formulation of research questions. Some 'dry-run' practice in the use of the tools and behaviour of Participatory Learning and Action (PLA, also known as PRA) is generally necessary.

This group of people then become facilitators of meetings, dialogues, and interviews with various social *groups*, for example women and men from various neighbourhoods or ethnic groups, and particular social *actors*, including local leaders, citizens' associations, and officials at various levels. Sometimes stakeholders are brought together at a later stage to exchange ideas and experiences, which aims to reach a good level of shared analysis of impacts, needs, and/or recommendations for future action. The facilitators use their PRA skills, knowledge of secondary information, and analysis aided by (for example) the sustainable livelihoods framework in order to prompt questions, structure proceedings, and mediate between the stakeholders. Some of them document the findings.[36]

Participation of stakeholders

Participatory Learning and Action (PLA), also known as Participatory Rural Appraisal (PRA) or (incorrectly) as Rapid Rural Appraisal (RRA), is by now widely known as a methodology or approach used at project level. It has been variously described as a methodology for learning, communication, and research, and it is probably a bit of all of them. There are now vast amounts of literature on PLA, and its strengths and weaknesses are often hotly debated.[37]

Genuine participation of (local) people can be achieved with the use of PLA tools and learning processes through the facilitation of dialogues (also known as 'semi-structured interviews') in which much attention is paid to outsiders' behaviour, good questions, and simple analytical tools (diagrams) that enable the dialogue to focus on a particular subject. PLA tools include mental maps, time-lines that depict historical events, 'Venn' diagrams that depict the relations and power structures of organisations, and various matrices and other aids that enable the comparison of options and the articulation of preferences. The tools are the 'tricks' that can be learned, adapted, and interpreted quickly and easily (see also section 3.3.2 for more on PLA). The best ways to appreciate their finer points are probably to learn by doing and also to observe other people using the tools.

'Behaviour' needs to be understood in two distinct ways. The behaviour of persons who initiate dialogues with stakeholder groups in which tools may be used is of central importance in achieving constructive dialogue, real learning by all involved, and 'trustworthy' data. The behaviour of these often self-appointed facilitators should be to listen to and enable others, prompting them with open and intelligent questions. Of equal importance is the facilitators' awareness of other people's body language: the non-verbal communication of all those present. Sensitive and facilitative behaviour is not easy for all to learn, and it appears to be independent of educational level, social class, or gender: good and bad communicators can be found everywhere.

Facilitating or guiding groups of stakeholders through a process of progressive analysis and learning may, however, be the most difficult of the three aspects of PLA. It requires a good use of authority and understanding of relationships to be able to separate and (later) bring together social actors and disaggregated social groups. Succinct reporting on dialogues is difficult, and bringing several reports together even more so. Triangulating information and opinions from various sources and arriving at trustworthy conclusions that are acceptable to all is arduous, even in the most stress-free and harmonious of cases.

The tools, behaviour, and analytical process that make up PLA have been usefully applied in a very wide range of situations, from organisational analysis and project analysis to needs assessment; they have been used with non-literate people, intellectuals, and bureaucrats; in early stages of projects and in later stages; in the industrialised North and the developing South. The PLA approach can also help to produce large amounts of relevant and valuable information and insights on environmental and socio-political matters, past and present.

However, several aspects of PLA are contested (see also section 3.3.2). It is not always well integrated with existing project cycles, for example, although recently applications of the approach in Participatory Monitoring and Evaluation (PM&E) are being explored with renewed enthusiasm.[38] Experience suggests that enabling the participation of the most deprived and excluded becomes a bigger challenge after the early needs-assessment and needs-identification stages.[39]

PLA is often perceived as limiting participation exclusively to villagers or local people. Also, it may not manage to identify and work with the most important social *actors* and may merely work with social categories such as 'poor women' or 'young men' that are not necessarily socially cohesive and active groups of actors. Although this criticism is not always justified, in practice a broader outlook on key actors and stakeholder participation must be ensured, for which theoretical frameworks exist (see section 3.3.1) and practical training tools have been developed.[40]

PLA does not offer clear guidance on how to ensure high-quality data and trustworthy conclusions. What happens depends very much on the lead facilitators, although possibilities for various forms of cross-checking information ('triangulation') have been explored.[41] PLA became only recently more explicit on the analysis of social differences.[42] Furthermore, it is usually not supported by an explicit analytical framework and, for example, does not address questions about the meaning of (environmental) sustainability, or the relevance of environmental degradation in poverty alleviation. However, interesting work on participatory monitoring and evaluation of environmental change is now being documented, and looks very promising.[43]

4.3.2 Livelihood outcomes and environmental impacts

Concerns that conventional monitoring and evaluation do not always provide good insights into the actual differences made by development activities have prompted development agencies to focus more on project *impact*. An increasing number of development programmes around the world are yielding lessons on how to assess impacts, and recording lasting and fundamental changes as a result of some development activity. Impacts can be changes of any kind, and include changes in livelihoods, in people's institutions, and in policies.

Indicators of change
In much current practice of impact assessment, the importance of participatory approaches is stressed, with an increasing recognition that this implies something more sophisticated than merely the participation of a homogeneous group of beneficiaries. It is important to develop (and negotiate) impact indicators and ways to measure or assess those indicators. Impact assessment is concerned with changes both planned and unplanned. It has a strong analytical focus: one critical aspect of impact assessment is to find ways of actually attributing changes to development interventions. Much of this work takes a 'process' approach, conceiving longer-term processes in which multiple stakeholders operate in some kind of facilitated negotiation about changes, attribution of those changes to certain activities or policies, and modifications of development practice. The variables or indicators of change are negotiated in such a process, which means that indicators cannot be fully predetermined, or that agreed indicators may at a later stage be disregarded.[44]

The sustainable livelihoods framework that is discussed in section 3.2 presents a number of desired outcomes of people's livelihood strategies. These are generalised and 'ultimate' changes or improvements, which may be seen as areas or dimensions in which specific indicators are likely to be developed.[45] They include the following.

- more income
- increased well-being
- improved food security
- improved social equity
- reduced vulnerability
- improved sustainability of environmental resources
- secured 'non-use' values of nature.

Related to those livelihood outcomes may be changes such as 'greater livelihood diversity' as a proxy for *sustainability* of livelihoods, which is directly related to the *livelihood strategies* in the framework. In addition, projects may aim at impacts or changes that are intermediate to livelihood outcomes and that relate more to the *capitals* or to the *policies, processes, and structures* in the sustainable livelihoods framework. These desired changes may include strengthened capacities of project staff and beneficiaries to manage environmental resources, improved capacities to enable learning processes such as those associated with PLA, and greater capacities to run people's organisations and stimulate effective networking. Changes in public policies, such as those related to land reform and its implementation, can also be seen as fundamental or structural changes, and therefore as impacts if they are provoked (in part) by a project or campaign.

Important project achievements might be 'better communication between project staff and other stakeholders', 'better data quality', and 'more synergy from project activities' (that is, one project objective helps to achieve another). These are all removed from real impacts on livelihoods, however: they are *achievements* and possibly intermediary impacts, but not necessarily lasting or significant changes as far as poor and vulnerable people are concerned. They thus demonstrate the nature of projects: they are tools for achieving a greater goal.

Desired impacts or livelihood outcomes need to be articulated in detail and in very practical terms in any particular situation, such as a village, a community of minority people, a group of urban poor women, or a geographical part of a country. Indicators that say something intelligent and substantial about whether or not the desired impact of a project is being achieved need to be acceptable for all stakeholders. Roche (1999) writes that useful indicators that tell us something about impact should be both 'SMART' and 'SPICED':

SMART indicators: **s**pecific; **m**easurable and unambiguous; **a**ttainable and sensitive; **r**elevant and easy to collect; and **t**imebound.

SPICED properties of indicator development: **s**ubjective (stressing the particular position of an informant); **p**articipatory (those who formulate the indicators assess them); **i**nterpreted and communicable; **c**ross-checked and compared; **e**mpowering; **d**iverse and disaggregated (by gender, ethnicity, etc.).

Developing indicators of change

Impact indicators must be negotiated between different stakeholders, and must be flexible in the sense that in the course of projects they may have to change in the eyes of some or all stakeholders as a result of changing circumstances. Developing indicators of general change and impact can be done with certain practical tools from PLA, in particular through well-being ranking of households within a community or the ranking of communities within a district or province, following the same principle. The 'logical framework', a project-planning tool that is used by donor organisations and increasingly by national government departments and also by NGOs and grassroots organisations, expresses impact or general change-indicators at the highest levels of its hierarchy of objectives; it also makes explicit how intermediary achievements are expected to contribute to the greater goals. Consider the following example.

Developing impact indicators with NGOs in Honduras

OCDIH, an NGO from Copan in Honduras, developed a log-frame (logical framework) for its activities. It aims to strengthen organisations in 12 communities, to improve citizen participation and self-management for development and local government, to strengthen a new culture of participation, and to improve soil conservation and sustainable production through farmer-to-farmer exchanges.

Its overall goal is to establish favourable conditions for sustainable human development. This goal and the more specific aims are what would have to be considered in an impact assessment; for that purpose, impact indicators are needed. They articulate indicators of the extent to which women and young people participate in leadership, the dynamism of enterprises, and the existence and functioning of local organisations. Indicators that relate to food security include 'numbers of farmers practising sustainable agriculture and also traditional farming techniques', and 'percentage of families with access to staple food'.

Some of their indicators relate to what the sustainable livelihood framework models under *capitals*, including capacities of farmers' groups and individual farmers in terms of agricultural techniques. The assumption that improved capacity leads to higher levels of food security and sustainability would of course have to be tested, but the link is not unlikely. Impacts on environments *per se* are not made explicit, but environmental sustainability is implied in the use of productive and environment-benign agricultural technologies.[46]

Project managers were asked to rank communities where OCDIH works in terms of their 'relative civil participation'. Occasional questions in the course of ranking (*why is* this or that community ranked higher or lower?) resulted in indicators that included *'OCDIH is comparatively well known in the community'; 'people participate more'; 'they forward more proposals'; 'more productive structures'; 'better (strong) leadership'; 'people are more aware of their civil rights'.*

Answers to the *why?* question obviously result in subjective opinion, but the same exercise can be done with other stakeholders and at other moments, and thus cross-checking can increase trust in the resulting indicators. The actual question that initiates the comparing and ranking of communities determines the type of indicators, too. If the communities were ranked in terms of household food security, agricultural production, or environmental security, different answers would suggest different indicators; indeed, such comparing was also done.

In the example above, indicators emerged from a process of interaction between NGO leaders and representatives of a donor organisation. More negotiation has happened and should happen in similar situations between those and other stakeholders, in particular strong social actors within the communities concerned (representatives of a women's union or a church group, municipal councillors or officials, or a rich landowner). Reconciling and prioritising indicators for practical monitoring and evaluation is then the critical task, which will require negotiation, mediation, and generally speaking a lot of facilitated (and structured) interaction between stakeholders. In such a process, 'positive biases' are likely to be necessary, if intra-household changes are to be valued, if the needs of the least influential groups are to be addressed, and if the most deprived are to benefit from changes in livelihoods and environments.

Attribution of change: impacts

Assessing changes in a society and in livelihoods and environments of poor people is one thing, but attributing changes to a policy, project intervention, or campaign is more complex. Studies of impact, whether participatory or not, tend to start with an assessment of change, intended or unintended, by valuing the trend in one or another indicator of 'impact' (or better: of change). After this the reasons for that change emerge from combining various data and doing analysis of causal links, possibly structured by the sustainable livelihoods framework. In section 3.1, three comparatively elaborate case histories are presented, which all show some changes and actual impacts.

The study of improved democratic space in Recife showed that, despite the improvements in popular participation in public life and government, the poor in the *favelas* have as yet seen very few material and environmental improvements. NGOs can be credited with enabling people to take part in forums set up by municipal authorities, and some played a role in the national democratisation process. Nevertheless, they need to collaborate more and help citizens to generate the power that is needed to make sure that budget allocations for improvements increase, and that they are actually spent.

The Niassa Food Security Programme (in Mozambique) had an important impact in recovering crop production and thus livelihoods following the civil war, but the impacts on environment, livelihoods, social relations, or policies of the agricultural extension programme are so far limited. Agricultural technology has not changed much (yet) in the direction of developing more sustainable technologies; nor has women's position in the communities and in households improved much as a result of the programme. This is despite enormous changes in the lives and livelihoods of people, which are largely attributed to the possibilities that were opened up for people's own initiatives following the peace accords. Nevertheless, the need for food is still huge, markets are only just emerging, and social and environmental dangers as well as opportunities exist: there is an important role for this participatory programme in helping deprived people to articulate their needs and to find appropriate paths to better livelihoods, environmental management, technology development, and improved food security.

The various development programmes in Lung Vai commune (Vietnam) have had some important impacts, in particular with regard to land-tenure policy. Changes in livelihoods over five years are very significant, and the programmes have played their part. Wives' names are now included in land-use certificates, and improved land distribution as a result of project support has stimulated farmers to invest in land. Nevertheless, government policies are most important in these changes, apart from people's own initiatives. Subsidising agricultural inputs has been decisive in changes to almost all livelihoods, although the gains of the poorest families in increased food production and income have been very small. The marked reduction in shifting-cultivation practices is a very positive development, since the risks of soil erosion have been reduced significantly, which is mainly due to government policy. The programmes have also helped by setting up tree nurseries, stimulating tree planting, and promoting wider agro-forestry activities; but the effects are not unambiguously positive, because unequal distibution of tree saplings suggests that future livelihood inequality may be expected.

Below are two more examples of livelihood outcomes of people's own efforts and the support of development programmes.

Examples of rural livelihood and environmental outcomes

Short-term review processes that are unlike conventional external evaluations are illustrated by assessment of the impact of conservation farming in Kenya, and also by the review process in a large refugee-settlement project in Uganda.[47]

In what is known as **the organic farming programme in Kenya**, Oxfam supports nine local NGOs and collaborates with larger, national NGOs in efforts to develop local capacities. Agricultural technologies were introduced in a context of community organising, health, and women-centred work initiated by local NGOs. A review in 1997 and a sequel in 1999 revealed a range of positive impacts, including better diets, more (independent) income for women especially, fewer risks to health arising from the reduced use of agrochemical inputs, and less dependency on financial capital and suppliers of inputs. The projects are mainly targeted at an 'average' group of women and men: full-time farmers in the (generally poor) communities, including some of the more vulnerable.

The various stakeholder-participants in the review were challenged in many encounters by differences of opinion and conflicting information regarding the effectiveness of conservation-farming techniques and the potential of the conservation-farming approach for achieving fully closed nutrient cycles and 'going organic'. There were some (limited) positive impacts on the sustainability of soil fertility and on productivity of staple foods. The local NGOs and grassroots organisations had little, if any, impact on national research and extension policies, which would be important for the millions of farmers who are not reached by NGO projects, especially given the relatively large resources for agricultural research and extension in Kenya. As a result of the impact review, NGOs began engaging more closely with national and international research organisations.

In **the Ikafe refugee settlement in Uganda**, conflict between local leaders, international agencies, national authorities, and several rebel forces caught many Sudanese refugees, project staff, and also members of the host community in cross-fire (literally). The review process concerning the international and Ugandan efforts to help the refugees was one of negotiation between conflicting interests, supported by various pieces of research and consultation.

Refugees were supplied with small plots of bush land for agricultural production and also the necessary inputs for farming, in an attempt to make them less dependent on handouts. Forest and wildlife were affected by the influx of people, but only to a limited degree, because of comparatively low population densities. Land was made productive without any apparent risks of soil erosion. Even here, some positive environmental action took place: deforestation and other environmental impacts of the arrival of refugees were mitigated through an afforestation component that was mainly directed towards the local 'host' population.

Nevertheless, here – as in other situations of conflict and breakdown of societies – 'participation' and formal rights to resources were no solution to the problems. Environmental resources (especially land) had become central to a violent power struggle, and poor people who were directly dependent on these resources became more vulnerable; few had a direct interest in considering long-term environmental sustainability.

Critical outcomes: participation and sustainability

The sustainable livelihoods framework describes environmental sustainability as one key livelihood outcome, which acquires particular meaning when we consider future generations, i.e. the children of deprived people, whom most development activity aims to support. In fact, in the schematic framework presented in section 3.2, this means that people who earn a decent living can invest some of their surplus in maintaining and building up the various capitals.

Equally, participation – in the sense of strengthened democracy and the active involvement of deprived and poor people in decisions that affect their lives – may be seen as a goal in itself, or, in other words, as a livelihood outcome.[48] With it, livelihood strategies tend to strengthen and diversify, and material outcomes become more easily attainable. The framework models this interpretation of participation in the civil-society part of *policies, processes, and structures*, because the strength of local people's voice is dependent on national policies and laws. Furthermore, the strength of social networks and the ability of individuals to organise or actually speak out are aspects of social capital and human capital respectively.

Participation and the goal of environmental sustainability both form part of the 'hybrid' described in this section, which suggests that they can and often do mutually support each other.

A process in which decisions are made collectively, or indeed through comparatively harmonious negotiation and compromise between many different stakeholders, must find ways of involving social actors in different ways. In such a participatory process, problems are gradually analysed, in separate groups and together, and solutions arise from research, discussion, and various interactions. These processes are not strictly defined and structured, and decisions emerge gradually from them, instead of being taken at fixed and predetermined moments by particular people. It is no longer obvious that technocrats prepare a set of scenarios for development, with different impacts in terms of the environment and in other respects, from which decision-makers would choose – as is the case in formalised EIA processes (see sections 4.1 and 4.2). Indicators (and environmental standards) of what constitutes good development practice and desired impact are no longer 'objectively verifiable', but they are mostly qualitative and often subjective.

The implications of this for policies under headings such as 'sustainable development' can be huge. Participatory methodologies need their own ways of increasing the trustworthiness of data and conclusions, especially through cross-checking information from multiple sources (which is often called 'triangulation'). When many stakeholders are involved, the aims of just one of them may well be modified, and that can be the strong poverty focus of one actor, or the environmental care of another. This means that some environmental resources may be used unsustainably, or the very poorest in a community may not always benefit from the project, in particular at the earlier stages.

A participatory process in which local (and poor, vulnerable) women and men are central, and in which local NGOs and authorities and possibly national and international organisations have a say, will concentrate on the use and management of *local* natural resources and possibly on national environmental health and well-being. The participatory approach makes it unlikely that international environmental concerns are considered, unless that perspective is somehow added by project management or, for example, national government. Poorer countries, let alone poorer local people, cannot be expected to be very concerned about their contribution to problems such as global warming. In any case, the dominant cause of that phenomenon is high consumption in industrialised countries, where political will is generally not strong enough to curb energy consumption in any radical way.[49] Thus using a participatory methodology has implications for what is called environmental sustainability and for what can be achieved in terms of environmental management at a non-local level. Synergy between environmental care and participation of the poorest and most deprived (or more diverse social groups and actors) is not automatic. Nevertheless, development practice does suggest that, where local women and men do get better access and more control over environmental resources, they start investing in them, and environmental quality and the livelihoods of their children are an important driving force for that.

4.3.3 Recovery and rehabilitation of livelihoods

Both popular participation and environmental care are extremely difficult to ensure and are accorded a comparatively low priority in the extreme situations of conflict-related and environmental disasters (see also sections

2.3 and 4.2.3). However, following the end of war, the return of refugees, the immediate aftermath of an earthquake, or the subsidence of flood-waters, livelihoods are regenerated, and assets and livelihoods are rebuilt. In those situations, popular participation is both important and desired. A path from survival through reduced vulnerability to improved sustainability of environmental resources and livelihood activities is the almost too obvious goal of everyone who is affected by hazards.

Displacement of people, which often occurs as a result of war, is one type of human disaster. People, environments, and livelihoods are also devastated by floods, drought, cyclones, earthquakes, volcanic eruptions, or industrial disasters, which do not necessarily result in large-scale displacement. Common responses in rebuilding rural livelihoods include livestock-restocking programmes, and seeds and tools distribution programmes; in urban areas, rebuilding houses and public infrastructure tends to take precedence. These responses are briefly discussed in this section, through several practical examples.

Recovery of urban infrastructure

The examples of repairing urban infrastructure given below are responses to 'disasters' ranging from war to flood hazards that are exacerbated by human influence and river pollution. The region of the Rimac river in Peru is also prone to earthquakes. It is suggested by these examples that crucial to the successful reconstruction of infrastructure, the prevention of further disaster, and indirectly the rebuilding of livelihoods is some form of partnership between local authorities, NGOs, and community-based organisations. Good, appropriate technical advice, skill development, and (public) education are also central, as is some kind of 'trigger'. A trigger that sets off a human disaster, like a flood, outbreak of cholera, or earthquake can equally be an opportunity for rebuilding, better prevention, and, in a word, environmental improvement.

Examples of the rehabilitation of urban infrastructure

Oxfam's support for the rehabilitation of **the Phnom Penh water-supply systems** in the 1980s and early 1990s was an ambitious and unusual programme for an NGO. It was unusual in particular because of the scale (a total of £1.2 million was spent on the project), because it had such a strong civil-engineering focus, and also because it was about collaboration with a government ministry, in which there was very little community involvement. The main aim was to improve health, but the project did not concern itself with the general health situation and the health needs of individual groups. There were differences between

Oxfam's objectives and operational priorities and the Water Works Department's objectives, and the latter had very few skilled people available. In 1990, training became a focus of the project, but the project was phased out a few years later.

A workshop in 1995 which reviewed this experience maintained that there had been a real imperative for Oxfam to do something, since no other donors were committed at that time to supporting Cambodia, where the infrastructure of the capital city had been completely devastated during the Khmer Rouge regime. There was a felt need for a public campaign in the UK to draw attention to the continued suffering of the Cambodian people, who remained caught in the middle of Cold War politics. However, this campaign began to drive the flagship water project: money that was collected had to be spent, and success had to be televised in the UK. A reasonable degree of technical expertise was available in the Oxfam-Cambodia team, but the weight of the expectations created by the campaign in the UK, combined with difficulties in collaboration with the Cambodian government department, resulted in an assessment of mixed success some years after the closure of the project.[50]

The Rimac river and valley in coastal Peru, near the capital, Lima, is extremely vulnerable to violent floods, locally called *huaicos*. These are floods containing mud, stones, and sometimes rocks that devastate the population and infrastructure of the 'new towns' (*pueblos jovenos*), which are settlements of recent and often poor migrants, in particular in the outskirts of Lima. The floods are exacerbated by changes in land use in the upper reaches of the river. Deforestation for fuel-wood and timber consumption, and human settlements with their houses and streets, reduce the region's water-infiltration capacity, thus contributing to rapid water run-off.

Since the *huaicos* of 1983, PREDES, CIED, and other Peruvian NGOs have been working with local residents' groups, government agencies, and universities in an attempt to reduce people's vulnerability and mitigate the flood hazard. The NGOs have architects, engineers, and social scientists on their staff, and they advise community-based organisations (CBOs). PREDES in particular advised on how to construct flood-mitigation structures and riverbank reinforcements with local materials, on choosing safer sites for homes, and also on lobbying the local and national government.

Community organisation has been singled out as the most important factor for success in all this. PREDES indeed evolved from an organisation focused on disaster relief to one that addresses broader social and economic needs of residents.

The year 1991 saw an outbreak of cholera in Peru that developed into an epidemic in 1992; it was associated with severe pollution of this same Rimac river. OACA, a Peruvian environmental NGO established in 1992, also played an advisory role, supporting communities and municipalities along the whole of the Rimac river. The river is the main water-source for one quarter of Peru's 23.5 million inhabitants; it was also their main sewer and an outlet for pollution generated by various industries and agriculture.

Collaboration between mayors of municipalities and OACA led to the first water-treatment plant in the whole of the river basin, located in a small town in the upper reaches in 1995. The approach is holistic, in the sense that technical advice is combined with training and local skill development; the first treatment plant produces water for tree nurseries which are used to help reforestation of the highlands; and recycled sludge is used as fertiliser in agriculture. Solid waste is traditionally dumped in the river, a problem that is now addressed through a combination of collection, recycling, and responsible disposal.[51]

Recovering agricultural production

In rural areas, humanitarian agencies often distribute crop seeds and agricultural tools in an attempt to regenerate agriculture-based livelihoods. Good practical guidelines are available for such undertakings.[52] One of the first strategic questions (if not the main one) that needs to be answered in rural livelihoods-rehabilitation work is whether seeds and tools distributions are appropriate at all. This depends on whether food security is a problem; what people's productive means and livelihoods were and are; whether soils and climate are favourable to agriculture at all (land may be mined!); *whose* livelihoods need to be revived; and, above all, on what local women and men themselves think about their needs and opportunities.

Once distributions of seeds and tools are seen as a strategic way of supporting livelihoods, issues such as control of land and access to it need to be clarified and possibly addressed; gender roles and relations with respect to food and agriculture must be understood; and a range of baseline data needs to be collected to enable decision making – as in 'ordinary' project cycles. Baseline data should include substantial information on current food sources and types and cover the breadth of the 'food economy' of communities, households, and women and men inside households. Assessment should involve all important social actors and classes. The decision *not* to proceed with the distributions should remain an option throughout this stage, and the assessment should identify the appropriate main beneficiary group of the project.

Section 3.1 refers to a study of the impact of activities related to food security in Niassa, Mozambique.[53] Oxfam began to work there in the late 1980s, with distributions of clothes and food to people who were displaced during the war. The support included fairly large-scale distributions of crop seeds and agricultural tools in 1993 and 1994, when a peace accord was signed and national elections were organised, when people had started returning to their areas of origin, and when relatively severe climatic drought problems persisted. These distributions of seeds and tools were problematic in terms of logistics but were reasonably successful in operational terms. Some of the distributions were part of goods-for-work schemes, which aimed to repair rural roads and bridges, thus rehabilitating transport systems and marketing routes as well. In 1994 a modest scheme to restock small livestock (goats and pigs) also took place. A review of this four years later confirmed that the survival rate of the offspring of the small animals was reasonable, and a livestock-rotation scheme was set up on a larger scale in 1998/9. The distributions of seed and tools have had a significant impact on the recovery of crop production.

Such distributions do not have to be free of charge, as the example from Mozambique illustrates: rehabilitation after disasters, war, and displacement needs much more than the re-commencement of food production, and some of that may be achieved in goods-for-work programmes. Common problems in these projects are several:

- Often assessment and planning are done in haste, and little participation or even consultation takes place, leading to blueprint 'solutions' and inappropriate projects in which (for example) low-priority crop species are distributed.
- A shortage of food or a lack of trust in the quality of seeds may prompt people to consume them.
- Late deliveries of seeds and low germination rates occur in many projects, the latter often due to a lack of technical expertise and extension.
- Projects do not always achieve differentiated responses to the needs of women and men, so, for example, tools that are culturally inappropriate may be offered.
- Tools of inferior quality have been distributed.

'Seeds and tools' projects aim primarily to restore local food self-sufficiency and rural people's livelihoods based on crop production or livestock rearing. The environmental implications of these projects are not usually strongly negative, but they may be – and they can be positive too. Heavy reliance on conventional agricultural technology with fertilisers and pesticides may be undesirable from the perspectives of production, environment, and health.

These 'external inputs' tend to be unavailable under normal conditions, or inaccessible to the most deprived rural dwellers; they do not support the environmental sustainability of production for anyone. Conversely, recovery of agricultural production may also be seen as an *opportunity* to promote the maintenance of the organic contents of soils, inter-cropping, and other methods of intensification with locally available resources. Genetically inappropriate seeds may be distributed, in particular if the seeds are hybrids that need annual replacement (hybrid seeds are usually highly productive, yet almost sterile as a result of in-breeding). Or seeds originate in different agro-ecological zones, they have low resistance to local climatic, hydrological, and pest conditions, and their widespread distribution can erode local 'gene pools'.

Restocking the animal herds of pastoralists and other rural people with cattle, goats, or pigs is an almost equally common rehabilitation effort, in particular in dry-land Africa. Restocking usually follows a drought in which many animals died or were slaughtered, and in environmental terms it is possibly more controversial than distributions of seeds and tools. Restocking programmes are often very costly, and must respond to challenges that they stimulate herders to acquire more cattle than is permitted by the 'carrying capacity' of the agro-ecological zone, i.e. that they stimulate 'over-grazing'. Some critics also hold that restocking is in fact no more than a short-term solution to an endemic problem of recurring drought, population growth, and cattle increase, and limited natural resources.

However, these programmes do not usually increase livestock numbers in the short term; rather they are a mechanism for redistribution. They are often implemented as rotating schemes, where limited numbers of animals are supplied to some families, who are then responsible for giving the first off-spring to others. Most importantly, recent research and changes in theoretical approaches, in ecological science in general and pasture management in particular, suggest that the idea of carrying capacity as a fixed potential is limiting, if not wrong (see also sub-sections 2.2.1 and 2.4.4). Herders generally follow the logic that high numbers of animals and low density of vegetation, combined with dynamic movement of cattle, provide them with maximum security in times of relative drought, and maximum assets and income at other times. This is increasingly thought to be sound practice from the perspective of environmental and economic sustainability, partly because vegetation cover in dry-land zones is extremely responsive to rain (i.e. vegetation recovers quickly), even where all vegetation appears to have disappeared (as a result of herding and drought). Herders are no longer seen as culprits who cause the expansion of deserts. Nevertheless, over-grazing can be a problem, in particular near settlements and water-points: strategies for spreading people and cattle are then important. In more general terms, for the intensification of agricultural systems, increased numbers of livestock can be a beneficial trend, in particular when integrated with crop cultivation, because cattle can be fed crop residues and deliver dung for soil fertilisation. However, in this case patterns of livestock keeping need to change: fodder is to be brought to the animal, at least some of the time, instead of the animal being taken to the pasture. Of major strategic importance in livestock programmes, and indeed restocking programmes, is the provision of veterinary care, possibly through village-based animal-health assistants and with local people's participation.[54]

In situations of disaster and recovery, the livelihoods framework is not the most obvious tool that development organisations look for, and full participation of local people and other stakeholders in project formulation and management may not be achieved, because of pressures of time and a focus on immediate needs. Nevertheless, good analysis of livelihood needs and strategies is essential, including new livelihood strategies such as agricultural intensification and livestock restocking. As a first priority, people's vulnerability to natural disasters such as drought must be reduced, and the sustainability of their livelihoods can grow from there.

5

Policies and strategies for sustainable development

The sustainable livelihoods framework expresses the fact that *policies, processes, and structures* are of key importance if people are to be able to generate various forms of capital, and also that they are central in creating opportunities for alternative *livelihood strategies* (see chapter 3). Policy processes can be seen as mediating between various capitals, including human capacities and environmental resources, and what poor and vulnerable people can actually do and achieve. This mediation happens through governments, private enterprises, and civil society, which (for example) together determine how markets operate. They all develop policies and strategies of various kinds in order to enable their programmes to become more effective, more efficient, and more closely aligned to stated objectives and policies, for example in terms of environmental care. Of course, the three realms of government, the private sector, and civil society overlap and interact. Governments may run or own companies; various interest groups are represented in government and may take part in State administration and policy making; and companies may supply services that are usually expected of government, or they fund political parties and charities. Furthermore, the way in which they interact depends strongly on the political system and on relationships within any particular country.

The distinction between policies and strategies for development is not clear-cut. Usually policies articulate both aims (what to achieve) and means (how the aims are expected to be achieved), but the latter only in the most general terms. Governments at various levels make public policy, which includes plans for legislation and all kinds of actions and services. Strategies (of government, businesses, or charities) are more practical than policies; they consider the capacities and comparative weaknesses and strengths of the various parties involved (the stakeholders). Nevertheless, strategies still do not provide the detail of *what to do* and *how to* achieve goals: they provide the general outline for a certain course of action.

There is a plethora of management tools for the formulation and implementation of policies that are geared towards sustainable development. Section 5.1 presents some general policy aims and strategic tools and approaches that help governments, NGOs, and others to determine their own direction. Some examples of indicators for monitoring sustainable development are also given.

Section 5.2 discusses some important national but still 'macro-level' environmental issues, and the policy-processes that limit or enhance environmental and livelihood changes. There is a clear trend among national and international development NGOs and their local partners, i.e. citizens' groups, towards strengthening campaigns and doing more lobbying of governments and international agencies for policy changes, and towards challenging the activities of transnational companies (TNCs). Section 5.3 discusses international campaigns and lobbying, including those with implications for global trade and food security. Sections 5.2 and 5.3 present examples of actual policies and policy-making processes at national and international levels.

5.1 Planning for sustainable development

This section highlights some general policy aims and strategic tools and approaches that enable governments, NGOs, and others to draw up their strategies for the medium to long term. It is impossible to consider the detail of the environmental policies of the governments of individual countries – how policies are agreed and implemented – but some general strategy-making processes are explained. This section also discusses some indicators that show progress towards policy goals in the realms of sustainable development.

5.1.1 Environmental policies and strategies of governments

Policy instruments
The policy instruments that governments have at their disposal to achieve some degree of sustainable development include the following (see also section 2.2.4).

1. *Regulation*, for example through laws and bylaws that forbid certain chemicals to be used, and set environmental standards and maximum limits for pollution. Laws can also demand certain procedures to be applied, such as Environmental Impact Assessment (EIA – see chapter 4) in the case of large and potentially harmful developments.

2. *Market-based instruments*, in particular taxation and subsidisation. These can include subsidies for the development of environment-benign technologies such as sustainable agriculture, tariffs to limit the importation and use of particular chemicals, and taxes on pollution, deforestation, mining, and other environmental externalities. Tariffs and resource-taxes thus act as disincentives: they discourage what is unwanted, and they provide a signal to markets to develop alternatives, in particular when they become the main source of revenue for government. They are in fact an alternative to income-tax or taxes on trade in locally grown food products, which discourage the development of livelihoods and employment opportunities, and give local people no incentive to maintain environmental resources.

3. *Public campaigns* that help to create awareness among citizens and enterprises of the environmental impacts of their behaviour.

4. Governments can also *invest* themselves, for example in the regeneration of mangrove forests, the clean-up of polluted waters and land, infrastructure to protect human settlements from landslides, or the protection of steep mountain slopes.

5. Many governments consider making claims through invoking the principle that *the polluter pays* in cases of industrial contamination, even when the pollution took place at a time when no anti-pollution laws existed, or when standards were different. This is obviously rather less attractive to governments if they were the historical owner of the industries, as is the case in many developing countries.

National environmental policy documents
Most developing countries and all industrialised ones have produced documents with National Environmental Management Action Plans (NEAPs or NEMAPs), National Conservation Strategies (NCSs), and/or National Strategies for Sustainable Development (NSSDs). This is often done with the financial and technical support of bilateral and multilateral agencies such as the World Bank and the regional Development Banks, UNEP, UNDP, bilateral donors, and also the IUCN and WWF.[1] The NCSs are promoted particularly by the IUCN; they aim to analyse the possibilities for integrating pro-conservation conditions into the economic development process. The World Bank promotes NEMAPs and has supported many low-income countries in developing them; many examples are available through the Bank's publications department and website. In NEMAPs, environmental problems and mitigating policies are formulated with the aim of mainstreaming environmental management in national decision making.

NSSDs relate to the implementation of Agenda 21, the main document agreed at UNCED in 1992 (see also section 2.1.2 and Appendix 1). They integrate environmental, economic, and social objectives into national policy making. There is now international agreement that by 2005 all countries will have begun implementing their own NSSDs. The UN Commission on Sustainable Development (CSD) sees them as particularly important for national capacity building, and a key step towards meeting the international development target of reversing the degradation of environmental resources at national and international levels by the year 2015. NSSDs should be regarded as complementary to other national strategy and planning documents, and they should ensure that ideas about environmental sustainability are fully integrated into mainstream policy. It is felt that NSSDs should be developed in wide consultation with officials, experts, and ordinary citizens, that implementation should happen at all levels (from the national to the local), and that local capacity building is essential.

Government strategies are informed by national statistics, with data coming from a range of departments, research institutes, and universities, and often also from research and documentation carried out by international agencies (see Appendix 2 for sources of data, including websites). Much of the data and documents that support policy development are descriptive and inform NSSDs and the like; they are not necessarily a reflection of political compromise and agreed policy, since they are generally compiled by experts who are somewhat removed from policy making. Nevertheless, they are often extremely informative – and the information can prove very powerful, if interpreted correctly and used at the right time. Environmental Profiles, for example, available for many countries, are generally descriptive, and indeed informative, since they tend to give a brief but complete overview of important environmental issues, policies, and organisations, as suggested in Table 5.1. The integration of environmental considerations into national strategies, as outlined in the table, is important, because it provides a framework for development in a range of areas. In fact, the national strategies as such can also be seen as national policy, depending on the political status that they are given.

Strategic Environmental Assessment

Strategic Environmental Assessment (SEA) has been described as a process to aid the integration of environmental considerations into specific (sector) policies, laws, plans, and programmes, 'on par with economic and social considerations'.[2] This tool should lead to more concrete results than the various national strategies or general policies can provide, yet SEA does not operate at project level. It nevertheless seems to have grown out of decades of experience with Environmental Impact Assessment, which is a project-management tool (EIA; see chapter 4). SEA is a fairly recent development and

Table 5.1: Environmental Profile: sample outline[3]

Introduction	Objectives of the Profile, which may include (a) to identify recently developed environmental management processes and management knowledge; (b) to identify resource use and resource management; (c) to assist planning to reverse environmental degradation and work towards sustainable development; (d) to develop and strengthen monitoring and evaluating environmental impacts; (e) to inform debates on the relationship between poverty and environment. This section should also include the status of the document in the department or organisation and decision-making processes.
Description of environmental issues	Environmental changes and their impact on social changes, for example changes in agro-ecosystems, habitats, demography and urbanisation, health, water quality and quantity, land and soil degradation, deforestation, fisheries, marine resources, water for agriculture, agro-chemicals, wildlife, energy, mining, and urban and industrial pollution.
Environmental policies	Past, present, and future policies of the government, political parties, NGOs, and donor agencies, including legislation, regulation, and responsibilities.
Institutions and organisations	Capacities of groups (in the particular region or country and internationally) which deal with environmental issues: environmental action groups, information centres, research and training institutes; and the actual and potential co-operation between them.
Recommendations	Concrete suggestions for planning, monitoring, and evaluation of environmental impacts, setting up or strengthening of relevant institutional structures and future policies.
References	Sources of information used for the profile, and bibliography for further consultation.

is so far not being applied by many developing-country governments. However, SEA does appear to be useful, and a number of industrialised countries have developed legislation and institutional arrangements for it, while development agencies such as the World Bank have initiated sectoral and regional (strategic) environmental assessment. Some guidelines now exist, and the literature is developing.

The steps to be taken in the SEA process are very similar to those of EIA, yet characteristics differ, as outlined below.

Steps in Strategic Environmental Assessment[4]

Screening

Assess which strategic decisions may have significant environmental consequences.

Scoping

Research and provide information in order to judge (a) whether an initiative (policy, plan, or programme) should proceed, and (b) whether alternative approaches may be better for the environment. Sufficient environmental and socio-economic information must be generated; the assessment must be timely; it must involve consultation of stakeholders; and it must set out mechanisms of accountability. Analysis of the wider social-environmental context and environmental problems and opportunities must include current trends, environmental norms and standards, and the capacities of various social actors.

Decision-taking

Actual decisions are taken following analysis of the implications for environmental sustainability of policies, laws, programmes, and their alternatives.

Action plan for enhancing sustainable development

This must include details of proposals for the programme, policy, or law and must show how these are expected to support environmentally sustainable development.

Post-decision

Information on the actual impact of the decisions, policies, laws, or programmes is collected for further learning and possible changes.

Table 5.2: A comparison of Strategic Environmental Assessment (SEA) and Environmental Impact Assessment (EIA)[5]

SEA	EIA
Is proactive and informs development proposals	Usually reacts to a development proposal
Assesses the effect of a policy, plan, or programme on the environment, or the effect of the environment on development needs and opportunities	Assesses the effect of a proposed development on the environment
Addresses areas, regions, or sectors of development	Addresses a specific project
Is a continuing process aimed at providing information at the right time	Has a well-defined beginning and end
Assesses cumulative impacts and identifies implications and issues for sustainable development	Assesses direct impacts and benefits
Focuses on maintaining a chosen level of environmental quality	Focuses on the mitigation of (negative) impacts
Has a wide perspective and a low level of detail, to provide a vision and overall framework	Has a narrow perspective and a high level of detail
Creates a framework against which (negative) impacts and benefits can be measured	Focuses on project specific impacts

In both SEA and EIA, national regulations and practice determine the rights of citizens to participate in the actual process of assessment and decision making, or to be informed about the outputs of these processes, i.e. the detailed information that is produced. Civil-society organisations vary in terms of their ability to exercise those rights effectively.

Specific laws and programmes that thus fill in the details of national strategies for conservation or sustainable development and that are developed with the aid of SEA may still not stipulate environmental standards. Standards of maximum permitted pollution or otherwise can be enshrined in law, but they are generally at a further level of detail, and they may have to change from time to time on the basis of new scientific findings. It is generally within the powers of, for example, the national Ministry of Environment to set standards, but it does not necessarily have the capacity to enforce them.

5.1.2 Environmental policies and strategic plans of development organisations

Few development NGOs have detailed policies on environmental sustainability, although most subscribe to some interpretation of sustainable (human) development, be they local or international NGOs.[6] Reasons for this include a limited internal capacity for addressing what is not always seen as central to the organisational mandate, which may be 'to eliminate poverty', or 'to reduce human suffering'. There is often limited understanding of the interaction between social change and environmental change. Development NGOs have fewer links to the world of environmental campaigners than some might have expected, following the positive dialogues at the UN Conference on Environment and Development (UNCED) in 1992 (where a Global Forum was organised, dominated by NGOs – see section 2.1.2). UNCED was about environment *and* development. Even so, it is acknowledged by many in development circles that such links are valuable, if only for the 'opportunities' that cases of extreme environmental degradation 'offer' for addressing poverty issues.

The main policies and medium-term strategic plans of development organisations usually include some reference to sustainable development and environment. Oxfam's overall strategic aims include 'achieving sustainable livelihoods'.[7] Under this broad 'umbrella', several strategic aims are formulated, most notably to improve income, employment opportunities, and food security, while improving or maintaining social equity and environmental sustainability. These aims then translate into strategies and a practical approach to development that makes use of various analytical and participatory tools, as it does in several programmes of the international NGO CARE, and also UNDP and DFID.[8]

The strategies of NGOs consist of projects and campaigning efforts to promote or challenge policies that affect livelihoods and environments. For example, many development NGOs promote forms of sustainable, low-external-input agriculture in support of poor subsistence farmers and commercial smallholders.[9] Another example is Oxfam's analysis of the causes of global poverty and links between (mostly Northern) consumption and (mostly Southern) poverty, in preparation for a large-scale international campaign. The key document for that campaign, *The Oxfam Poverty Report*, contains a chapter on ecological footprints.[10] The idea here is that global environmental change such as climate change or the use of rainforests by international logging companies is largely driven by the consumption demands of affluent peoples. Thus sea-level rises, increased river flooding, and the depletion of fish stocks can be seen as primarily caused by the 'ecological footprint' of high-consumers. These consumption patterns are maintained and stimulated by international economic policies, including trade regulations. Since poor nations and vulnerable groups of people are the first to suffer from these environmental changes, a programme to alleviate poverty must logically include a campaign against unsustainable resource consumption by the better-off.[11]

International aid agencies require strategy documents in their country programmes, and these strategies need to comply with the laws and policies of the governments with which they work. NGOs may work primarily with certain elements of civil society, but they too are generally expected to work within the government's policy and legal frameworks. UNDP's multi-year planning instrument for technical co-operation with a country is called 'Country Programme': a document that spans five years and supports a portfolio of projects. The UK's Department for International Development (DFID) produces Country Strategy Papers over three-year cycles, defining a medium-term development strategy in and with the country concerned. In Oxfam GB, Strategic (Business) Plans exist for country programmes, regional programmes (i.e. several country programmes combined), and the entire international programme.[12] Most international NGOs have similar planning systems, and many of their national counterpart organisations have adopted medium- to long-term planning procedures too.

These plans help individual organisations to take decisions about (for example) allocating grants, recruiting and training staff, and various development activities. 'Activities' can be in geographical areas or in particular sectors of the economy; they may be projects involving particular groups of people, or they may be campaigns for changes in public policy. The plans usually set out a contextual analysis and formulate medium- to long-term aims and activities; they may cover a period of three–five years. The process of medium-term strategic planning is expressed in Figure 5.1.

In **Step 1** of this process, an analysis is made of what the organisation or country programme is expected to do, or not, in accordance with internal policies and regulations, legislation, and the requirements of the main stakeholders (including donors, beneficiaries, citizens' groups, and possibly trustees of the charity concerned). An NGO's country or regional programme is bound by what directors and trustees have agreed as the organisation's mission statement, and bilateral aid programmes are expected to take heed of the general policies of both the host and the donor government. The mandate of the organisation or programme and the scope of strategic planning are thus bound by what is 'given' and is not negotiable.

Figure 5.1: Developing strategic, medium-term plans

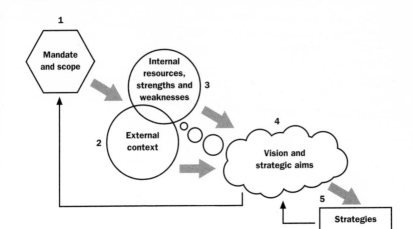

Step 2 concerns analysis of what is called *vulnerability context* in the sustainable livelihoods framework: possibly trends in the wider organisation and also in other organisations, plus analysis of what poor people and governments are doing to address poverty and manage environments. In this step, national policies must be analysed, and the capacities and limitations of (potential) counterpart organisations. The needs of poor and excluded women and men to which the organisation could possibly respond will relate to the various 'capitals' in the sustainable livelihoods framework and to (national) policies and structures of governance: these together enable people to pursue their livelihood strategies.

Step 3 focuses on what is possible, depending on internal financial and human resources, strengths and weaknesses. It involves a review of the existing programme or portfolio of projects. The second and third steps interact strongly.

In **Step 4** a distinction is made between a vision (what the organisation or country programme wants to contribute towards, together with many others), leading to a so-called mission statement, and the programme's strategic aims. The latter highlight what is really fundamental to change in a given society, and what can be changed – although not usually in the short term. They express what is *possible* to change and what is prioritised, given the organisation's capacities, experience, and resource limitations. Strategic aims are likely to identify a focus on geographical areas, particular social groups, types of livelihoods, and environmental issues.

Strategies are the way to achieve the aims; they are formulated in some detail in **Step 5.** They are normally accompanied by a budget outline. Strategies must also include an indication of partnerships that are important, plus information on institutional learning, the strengthening of internal capacities, and the capacities of counterparts.

It needs to be stressed that these steps are not entirely chronological, and indeed the diagram indicates that certain iterations are expected to take place during this planning. It could even be argued that, as with analysis following the sustainable livelihoods framework, an analysis and planning exercise needs to start with desired outcomes, i.e. changes in livelihoods and environments, and then work 'backwards', in order to identify the obstacles that are strategically the most important and the most amenable to change.

The strategic planning guidelines of Oxfam GB contain guidance on the meaning of sustainable livelihoods and the relevance of this framework for some of the steps of the strategic planning process.

Oxfam GB: strategic plans and sustainable livelihoods[13]

For Step 1: Mandate and scope

Country and regional programmes should follow the organisation's mandate, general policies, and strategic choices, which have included working towards sustainable livelihoods for several years now, as one key interpretation of 'working towards overcoming poverty and suffering'. One of Oxfam's core aims is to support people in asserting 'the right to a sustainable livelihood', with two key outcomes: (1) 'increased food and income security for primary producers, landless and urban dwellers, who live in poverty', and (2) strengthened 'access of poor people to secure paid employment, labour rights, and improved working conditions'.[14] Also articulated is the need for social equity and environmental sustainability (with the rights of future generations particularly in mind).

For Step 2: External context

Analysis of the causes of poverty, environmental change, and livelihood needs should include an assessment of the overall trends in environmental and market-related factors (*vulnerability context*). For particular social groups, analysis should determine their capacities (for example health, knowledge, and strengths of social networks) and identify the trends in their claims and relative control over assets (that is, *social* and *human capital*), and the quality of environmental resources (that is, *physical* and *natural capital*). It is important to understand which livelihoods prevail in the region or social group concerned, and people's ability to offset risks and cope with shocks in climates, markets, and so on. Furthermore, the main 'macro' *policies and processes* that affect them need to be understood. The capacities of partner organisations with regard to supporting livelihoods and environmental sustainability need to be assessed.

For Step 3: Internal resources, strengths, and weaknesses

Determine which internal resources, strengths, and weaknesses exist in terms of understanding and supporting livelihood strategies of particular groups of people, and influencing *policies, processes, and structures* that affect the environmental sustainability of livelihoods.

For Step 4: Strategic aims

Strategic aims can be formulated in basic terms, such as 'improve food security' or 'support the livelihood of …', and they can also be formulated as 'alternatives'. For example, 'support the development of livelihoods of smallholder farmers who produce organic coffee and who market this through fair-trade channels'. Strategic aims may focus on a particular type of livelihood or commodity, and will also express a focus on *capitals*, on *policies*, or a mix of the two. Strategic aims, alternatives, and indicators for success in improving livelihood sustainability must follow from close consultation with the people concerned.

For Step 5: Strategies

Strategies are normally composed of a range of approaches that operate at various levels, and they articulate intermediate objectives, i.e. changes in particular policies of governments, improvements in the practice of counterpart organisations, or immediate improvements in the survival chances of victims of disasters. The approaches include practical emergency-relief responses, rehabilitation efforts after a crisis, capacity building of partner organisations or grassroots groups, networking with other organisations, and also campaigning at national and international levels – all of which are expected to work towards a common, strategic aim. Alternative livelihood strategies are based on changes in policies, markets, technologies, and other social and human capacities.

Thus a range of strategies is formulated that all work towards the same aim, for example the aim of supporting the sustainability of livelihoods of the poorer women-headed households in a particular region. In this example, strategies could include local campaigning to strengthen women's legal rights and improve their actual control of land; development of the technological and managerial capacities of women members of farmers' groups; and international lobbying to limit the control of international companies over (local) genetic resources. Campaigns should aim to prevent smallholder farmers becoming dependent on companies for acquiring seeds, which is particularly risky for women-headed households with very low cash incomes. Successful implementation of such strategies depends on good partnerships with developmental and environmental organisations and activists.

Strategic planning is essentially an internal process for organisations, but various stakeholders are consulted at several stages of the process described above. The strategies expressed in these plans involve a number of stakeholders or social actors, and should in principle be agreed with them. Of central importance in formulating strategies is identifying the relative strengths and weaknesses and the comparative advantages of organisations, in terms of particular livelihood and environmental problems and opportunities. A good strategy thus articulates collaboration, partnerships, and networking. About many development NGOs it is fair to say that until now they have rarely had strong links with environmental activists and movements in the developing world, and that these links need to be strengthened.

Strategic plans need to include a clear articulation of rights to environmental resources, which are a key necessity for livelihood security, in particular land in rural areas and housing in urban areas. Rights to those resources are usually different for women and men, both their respective legal rights and their actual access to the resources. These rights are essential for livelihood security, especially for the most deprived, which tend to include women-headed households, and they are also key to achieving better environmental management.

Strategic plans are also expected to conceptualise the links between national policy and local environmental management. In Oxfam's programme in the Philippines, for example, strategic plans of the last decade or so have expressed a combination of practical regeneration of fishing grounds by grassroots groups, support from intermediary NGOs for fisherpeople's organisations, and national networking and campaigns on fishing rights. These various actors and activities were partly funded, and also supported in other ways, by international organisations. All share the goal of supporting poor fisherfolks' livelihoods and the natural resources on which they depend – with some success: synergy has been achieved between a range of activities in working towards those twin goals.[15] However, despite attempts to work towards improvements in livelihoods as well as in the status of both women and men, fishing is primarily a male domain, and women have benefited mainly indirectly through improved household income security.

In Oxfam's Vietnam programme, support in the northern province of Lao Cai and specifically in the commune Lung Vai for the implementation of land-reform legislation has stimulated farmers to plant trees and helped to reduce a local form of 'slash and burn' cultivation (this case history is discussed in detail in section 3.1). Oxfam's experience of supporting land-tenure claims at the local level led to engagement with provincial and national authorities and contributed to a country-wide shift in the implementation of land-tenure policy. This is expected to be a gain for women in particular, because their names are now included in Land Use Certificates. In Kenya, following a review of support for nine grassroots NGOs working in conservation farming, Oxfam and partners planned to strengthen their policy analysis and national influencing capacity, which indeed began happening with a particular focus on international trade and also land-tenure policies.[16] However, national and regional development programmes still make few links between national policies, global (international) environmental change, local poverty, and local environmental change, even though the importance of national policies is generally acknowledged.

To influence policy, good knowledge of the environmental specifics is needed. The UNDP develops five-year country programmes through a similar internal planning process. In Step 2 of the strategic planning process (see above), they propose the drafting of an 'Environmental Overview of the Country Programme (EOC)' (which is in fact an example of Strategic Environmental Assessment and shows strong similarities to Environmental Profiles – see section 5.1.1.) In outline, EOCs are expected to cover the following factors.[17]

UNDP – Environmental Overview for Country Programme

a. Brief description of the natural environment of the country

This section provides basic physical characteristics with a focus on the most important environmental resources (including mineral resources that can be mined) and phenomena (for example, regular drought and flooding). It should present environmental baseline data and some detailed information on land, water, non-renewable resources, and biodiversity issues.

b. Main environmental issues

Here the five most important environmental issues of the country are described in more detail, for example air pollution, potential for recycling of waste, water-treatment infrastructure, and so on.

c. Economic development and the environment

In this section the environmental implications of national planning, economic policies, and regulations are discussed.

d. Ability of the country to achieve environmentally sustainable development

In this section are discussed the existing environmental policies, laws, and regulations, the main environmental actors (including international agencies), environmental education and awareness, and institutional issues pertaining to environmental management.

e. Identification of environmental impacts associated with the programme

The potential impacts should take into consideration alternatives proposed by the programme.

(Total length should not exceed 10 pages)

5.1.3 Indicators of sustainable development

As in logical frameworks (a project-management tool; see chapter 4), central features of strategic plans are indicators of success in achieving aims – indeed, a reason for developing medium-term plans in the first place is to enable organisations and regional or country programmes to monitor change and assess their impacts.

The sustainable livelihoods framework suggests some general livelihood outcomes that would indicate people's success in pursuing their livelihood strategies (see section 3.2, and also section 4.3.2 on livelihood outcomes and impact indicators). Impacts of national or regional development programmes on successful improvements are difficult to determine, because they are just one 'actor' among many, and indeed development organisations pay due attention to partnerships in their strategy formulation. Nevertheless, strategic plans need to suggest indicators that show general and lasting change and that at the same time make some causal link to the activities of one or more social actors. Indicators of change or impact of strategic programmes are thus very similar to 'livelihood outcome', but must be formulated in more detail for a particular situation than is possible with the framework.

Nevertheless, categories of change or outcome indicators can be useful. Desired changes in environmental resources can include (for example) 'more access to safe drinking water'; 'more renewable environmental resources available'; and 'reduced resource degradation'. Other indicators express the notion of access and control to resources and the outcomes that are more directly related to livelihoods, including 'stronger women's rights and control over land' and 'less malnutrition'. Literature provides very large numbers of indicators of sustainability or of sustainable development (see also section 3.1), most of which are very similar to livelihood outcomes. Furthermore, some desired changes relate to *policies, processes, and structures*, and the various capitals in the sustainable livelihoods framework.[18] The synopsis in Table 5.3 categorises indicators of sustainable development per main group of the framework. (No indicators are listed for *vulnerability context*. Some of the trends and hazards under *vulnerability context* are caused by human action and can be improved with certain policies; but it is generally very difficult in the short to medium term to make any confident claim for improvements following policy change, even if the improvement itself can be asserted.)

Table 5.3: The sustainable livelihoods framework and categories of indicators of sustainable development

The sustainable livelihoods framework	Examples of indicators of (national or regional) sustainable development:[19] change, and possibly impact
Livelihood outcomes • More income • Increased well-being • Reduced vulnerability • Improved food security • Improved social equity • Improved sustainability of environmental resources • Non-use values of nature secured	• Improved human-development index, which is made up of factors expressing income, life expectancy, and access to education, etc. (UNDP, 1998, 1999). • Increased per capita income (GNP per capita) or per capita purchasing power; reduced income poverty. • Improved employment opportunities and reduced unemployment rates; creation of new jobs. • Diversifying national economies. • More equitable distribution among social groups of costs and benefits of nature conservation. • Reduced incidence of disease and death from environmental vectors and pollution. • Improved industrial-safety measures and reduced industrial accidents. • Genetic diversity of crop varieties and plant species maintained. • Negative effects of mining (including oil exploration) on local livelihoods are reduced or mitigated. • Improved conservation of areas with irreplaceable environmental phenomena.

Table 5.3: The sustainable livelihoods framework and categories of indicators of sustainable development (continued)

The sustainable livelihoods framework	Examples of indicators of (national or regional) sustainable development:[19] change, and possibly impact
Livelihood capitals • Natural • Physical • Social • Human • Financial	• Improved human-development index, which is made up of factors expressing income, life expectancy, and access to education, etc. (UNDP, 1998, 1999). • Per capita natural-resource consumption, for a given standard of living, is dropping. • Natural resources like fish and forest are 'harvested' at or below the rate of their renewal. • Soil fertility maintained from using more local biomass, successful use of practices such as nitrogen fixation and intercropping, or improved nutrient recycling. • Increased proportion of the population has access to clean drinking water and adequate sanitation facilities. • Increased and freer flow of 'clean' technology to developing countries. • Improved national and human capacities regarding 'clean' and 'sustainable' production technologies. • Improved national capacities for environmental monitoring and auditing. • Diversification in livelihood skills and enterprises in communities.
Policies, processes, and structures (rules and regulations that make up social institutions) • Government: laws, regulations, and policies • Private sector: behaviour and markets • Civic and political institutions	• Improved laws and procedures to integrate environmental values in policy, planning, and national accounting. • National economic indicators express environmental values and stocks better. • Taxation and tariff systems provide more incentives for 'cleaner' technology and reduced use and degradation of environmental resources. • Subsidisation encourages transfer and development of 'clean' technology. • More effective environmental monitoring and auditing systems. • Improved compliance with internationally agreed environmental practices and standards. • Increased voluntary agreement in sector-associations of business to improve environmental behaviour. • More equal rights of access for women, ethnic groups/castes to resources (land, water, fishing grounds, public infrastructure). • Intensified civic participation of vulnerable people in resource management and allocation. • Increased access to regulated financial services of the poorest 20 per cent of the population. • Fewer conflicts over resource claims.

5.2 National policies and campaigns for sustainable development

Many national policies and structures contain some environmental element. Conversely, campaigns by civil-society groups for more or better environmental care are rarely purely environmental. They are more likely to be campaigns for access to economic development processes, but on the terms and in the interest of local, excluded people. Environmental degradation is usually one among several reasons for protest, and proposals for alternative paths of (local) development. 'The environment' can thus be seen as one 'entry point' to poverty-related campaigning, which calls for strong links between development NGOs and the local environmental activists and NGOs,[20] and also sector ministries and government services with a stake in improving environmental conditions.

This section presents some thematically grouped examples of national environmental policies and local campaigns, which in some cases have international dimensions and links to international actors. Several of those themes and examples concern local people's control over land, and issues of compensation for the loss of it. Campaigns are often informed by EIAs (environmental impact assessments), which are now legally required elements of planning processes in most nations of the world (see also chapter 4).

5.2.1 Land and livelihoods

Campaigns for securing access to agricultural land, 'ancestral domain', forests, and pastures are widespread and are among the most important ways to secure the livelihoods of poor and vulnerable women and men. National governments are the main target of campaigners, as they make and implement laws on land ownership, tenure, and use rights, although that often happens in some (informal) arrangement with traditional leaders. The World Bank, bilateral donors, and other international development agencies often play an important role too, as they support research and the development of new legislation.

Land provides for livelihoods, and indeed for cultures, in ways that are as many as there are peoples in the world. Nevertheless there are parallels and lessons to be learned from others. One lesson from Vietnam (see section 3.1) is that help with implementation of land-reform legislation at a very local level, combined with dialogue at national level, can result in altered and indeed improved implementation strategies. However, in many other cases land is contested strongly, ownership patterns cause extreme poverty and deprivation, and the struggle for land can lead to civil war.

Mining and traditional land rights

In **Zambia**, the national copper-mining company ZCCM is the largest landowner apart from the State. People, including retired miners, have lived and earned part of their livelihoods from some of that land for years, often without full awareness of its legal status. The Copperbelt is a comparatively urbanised part of Zambia, where farming and local trade and services usually make up the mix of livelihood strategies for families of miners and ex-miners, in particular with the decline of mining profitability and employment opportunities. Research shows that these people for various reasons do not wish to go back to the remote rural areas from where they migrated decades or so ago. The new Land Act now makes the sale of this land possible, and many people are threatened with eviction from their small plots and homesteads. Many have entered designated forest areas to engage in charcoal burning, and stayed put as farmers after the forests were cleared. They are thus illegal squatters on 'gazetted' land controlled by the Forestry Department. The situation is made more complex because of promises made by politicians that people can stay where they are, or be resettled, and that certain forestlands will be 'de-gazetted' (brought back legally into the private domain, so that they can be controlled and used by individual households or small communities). Legal procedures for acquiring title deeds to what is designated agricultural land (including de-gazetted forest) are complex, expensive, and confused. For example, few officials seem to know that women can have legal title at all, even though under customary law they are not entitled to own property. Local authorities are currently discussing resettlement of people living on ZCCM land, and World Bank money will be forthcoming for 'emergency support' of victims of eviction and also for the increasing numbers of unemployed miners. Much of the forest reserve in this area is now depleted of forest, under threat, or designated for de-gazetting; policing of tree stands has proved not to work. New initiatives are being taken regarding community forestry management on the basis of a new Forestry Act. Oxfam[21] has initiated a 'livelihoods improvement programme' that attempts to aid thousands of poor farmers to get title to their land, for example through legal support. It engages in national awareness and advocacy programmes in order to address the effects of land privatisation, and also to encourage the implementation of the national gender policy, which states that 60 per cent of women who apply should receive land title.[22]

There are copper-mines in other parts of the world too, with different problems. Bougainville is a little-known island that forms part of **Papua New Guinea** (PNG). Conzinc Riotinto of Australia (CRA) began mining there in 1964 as the majority shareholder of Bougainville Copper Limited (BCL), with the national government as a minor partner. BCL was granted the licences that it needed, miners from other parts of the country were attracted, and one of the biggest copper-mines in the world was established by the 1970s. The open-cast mining created a hole with a surface area of 7km^2, 500m deep (i.e. about 2.5 square miles in extent and 1500ft deep). The disposal of 150,000 tons of rock-waste per day caused a massive environmental disaster, with losses of land, drinking water, and forest. Tributaries to local rivers were blocked, erosion and waste caused very high sediment levels, water and sediment were contaminated with heavy metals, and fish stocks were depleted. CRA/BCL became hugely profitable, and profits from licences and direct earnings for the national government amounted to almost half of PNG's national export earnings. However, the local (provincial) government was receiving only a fraction of the earnings, and local landowners even less. The traditional way of life of the indigenous population was severely threatened. Land was lost for agriculture, people were alienated from their land, land was polluted, and yields declined. The locals remained a minority among the mines' employees, while management remained entirely in the hands of expatriates. Roads were built, health and education services for the local population were established, access to markets and communication improved, and these changes were appreciated: 'Bougainvilleans are unlikely to seek to withdraw towards self-sufficiency and subsistence economy' (Böge 1999). It is, however, not surprising that the local population felt neglected and exploited, and that a nationalist independence movement emerged. The reasons for this are of course far more complex than simply 'environmental degradation': they include issues of identity and ethnicity. The traditional land-control patterns are highly complex, and payment of (limited) compensation caused tensions among the locals too. A young generation formed a 'new' association of landholders, which developed into an armed independence movement. Talks could not prevent civil war from the late 1980s onwards, fought by the PNG forces with help from Australia. Later negotiations resulted in a failed attempt to establish a regional peace-keeping force, and a further escalation of hostilities. Gross violations of human rights by the PNG forces and attempts to use foreign mercenaries were reported around 1996 (for example by Amnesty International), but the political scene in PNG changed with the elections of 1997. Hostilities have still not been resolved, and the State and the independence forces each control a part of the island; but several initiatives to find a solution are being taken by churches, women's organisations, and village leaders. Nobody is earning much from mining these days, the environmental problems have not been resolved, and war has devastated social services and livelihood opportunities.[23] Negotiations, a peace settlement, and an inclusive development strategy are the only way out.

In the **Philippines**, where large national and international companies are expanding their mining activities, concerted efforts by local, national, and international NGOs and local leaders of ethnic minorities have achieved important legislative changes regarding the recognition of rights over 'ancestral domains'. In this success there was and is an important role for artists and participatory theatre companies to express cultural values, to raise public awareness, and to mobilise support. Nestor Horfilla, an activist, actor, and theatre director in Mindanao, commented that 'the primary reason why ancestral domain is a major cause of contention is because ancestral territories are considered public domain. It is from this generalisation in law that concern has arisen over the indigenous people's rights and their pursuit of self-determination.' Theatre, music, and storytelling are used to reassert and rediscover identity, and also to communicate to the wider public the spiritual and practical values of land for indigenous people and the conflicts that arise from the entry of mining companies (whose 'rights' are granted by central government). Practical improvements in livelihoods are sought through forms of sustainable agriculture, and national lobbying for changes in land legislation has begun to result in recognition of the rights and needs of indigenous minority people. Crucial to these successes are the enthusiasm, professionalism, and dedication of NGO staff (activist-actors, or ATORs), the strong links between local leaders and NGOs, and national networking.[24]

Rainforests in Brazil

Rainforests are regularly in the news. Their destruction intensifies the global 'greenhouse gas' problem and accelerates global climate change, because they act as an important 'carbon sink'. They are depleted by tree loggers, or destroyed and converted into tree plantations, as in Indonesia, where the forest fires of the late 1990s were associated with such conversion. Rainforests contain a large proportion of the world's total wildlife and biodiversity, with implication for pharmaceuticals and tourism. Above all, rainforests are the homes and livelihood sources of indigenous people, who have lived in and with them for thousands of years and who are powerless against the economic and political interests of so-called developers. Feeney (1998) shows that the World Bank, the European Union, and bilateral donors, in collaboration with national governments, often fail to involve affected people in development projects, in particular in the earlier stages, when important decisions are made. Participation, intervention, and lobbying by local, national, and international development NGOs has influenced legislation and project-management procedures, and has attracted and sparked off people's movements, for example in Rondônia State in the Amazonian region of Brazil. A regional development project funded by the World Bank began in 1980 with an initial budget of more than 1.5 billion US dollars, in response to the impact of colonisers and in particular the expansion of ranching at the expense of rainforests and the indigenous population. In the 1980s, migration into the area intensified, deforestation continued apace, and landlessness and inequality became a big problem; but the project's funds were used to further the political aims of the elite. NGOs challenged the World Bank on its project design and behaviour, and also called the local authorities to account. Since the mid-1980s the MST (Movimento Sem Terra), a national movement of landless people, has been working in Rondônia. Its methods include direct acts of resistance, such as occupations of land,[25] which have been violently opposed and have led to the deaths of squatters. In 1992 the World Bank and Rondônia State authorities conceived a new approach to the project, renaming it as PLANAFLORO, with pro-poor and environment-friendly aims, and with participation of rural poor people as a declared objective. NGOs achieved the right to participate in the project and continued to lobby the World Bank. International NGOs, including Oxfam, funded meetings and training of local stakeholders, and initiated a study of civil-society participation in the project. The latter revealed 'great dissatisfaction with the project's failure to incorporate grassroots proposals into the planning process'.[26] (Grassroots groups are rural workers, including women and men, indigenous people, and rubber-tappers.) Feeney (1998) concludes that there remained an excessively top-down and technocratic project-based approach, even though high-level World Bank officials were concerned and concessions were made, and the project 'was fashionably restyled as a participatory project'.[27] It is obviously difficult to turn around such a large project towards real and effective empowerment of local people, even though poor and marginalised Rondônians themselves have taken initiatives, and local, national, and international NGOs supported them.

Pastoralism and wildlife in Tanzania

The interest groups who argue for nature conservation and the tourist industry are mostly based in the industrialised West, but they have particularly strong influence in Africa, where several of the most renowned wildlife parks can be found. There is a growing level of recognition that local farmers, hunters and gatherers, and pastoralists can no longer be simply excluded from the land that once was their main source of livelihood, and that they can and should play a crucial role in the actual conservation of lands, forests, and wildlife. Large international organisations such as IUCN and WWF now promote 'community-based conservation'.[28] The Campfire programme in **Zimbabwe** is probably the most frequently cited example: local associations of rural people manage resources, get benefits in terms of jobs and finance for social services, and indeed maintain good stocks of wildlife for tourists to admire. There is criticism of the programme: some hold that the actual success of Campfire in benefiting local livelihoods *and* wildlife is overstated. Elsewhere there are still many examples where local people are marginalised by the entry of external investment in nature-tourism and by corruption of officials.

In **Tanzania**, Oxfam is supporting lobbying and court cases brought by community groups and national NGOs regarding the appropriation of grazing land by commercial companies. The land is in the so-called buffer zones, just outside the Serengeti National Park. It was legally allocated to Maasai communities (i.e. land is held collectively). The Maasai had already been deprived of their traditional pastures when in 1959 the colonial administration banned them and their cattle from what became this world-famous wildlife park. Through persuasion and fraud, commercial companies acquired documents in support of their land claims; for them, access to administrative and legal structures is much easier than it is for the largely illiterate, traditional, and remote Maasai communities. The legal support for the communities has paid off, and at least one of the court cases filed by the people of Ololosokwan village against a wealthy land investor has been won. Nevertheless, the land remains insufficient for re-establishing the pre-1959 livelihoods, when moving cattle over very large distances was part of a strategy of maintaining large herds even in times of drought. Drinking-water for people and cattle is still insufficient in the buffer zones of the Park and in the nearby Ngorongoro Conservation Area, where herding is still possible, but agriculture is not. Women usually stay near homes in the buffer zones and have taken up agricultural crop cultivation, which plays now an essential part in survival. Their burden increased, but their rights and social status did not improve, for example in terms of decision making over household money or community affairs. National and international political and economic interests are such that it is very unlikely that the Maasai can ever return to their traditional livelihoods, and social changes among their communities will prevent that too. Livelihood alternatives are sought, in particular in tourism and so-called community conservation projects. If local people are to benefit from those initiatives, and indeed get new livelihood opportunities and the opportunity to change their lifestyles at a reasonable pace, then secure rights to land and to wildlife are required. The Maasai themselves generally do not hunt (and therefore do not directly harm wildlife), but if existing hunting rights were to be transferred to them, then they could earn income from tourist hunters, develop this form of tourism on their own terms, and ensure that hunting was limited to a sustainable level. Strong support for local education, skill development, and participation in structures of governance is also essential if change is to take place on the terms of the Maasai women and men themselves.[29]

Also in Tanzania, in the Singida region, land of the Barbaig people has been turned into large-scale wheat farms, run by the government with foreign support. The Barbaig are pastoralists, as are the Maasai, but they keep far fewer cattle now than they did in earlier days. Pastures, forests, and the habitat of large wildlife have all suffered as a result of the wheat farming; men have become dependent on alcohol; women's burden has increased; and conflicts with other ethnic groups have arisen. However, the Barbaig have started a litigation process in order to get compensation for the land; there is now a community development programme that seeks to support alternative livelihood strategies; and the Barbaig case is supported by the lobbying efforts of national NGOs.[30] During the 1990s, controversy arose over the radical recommendations of the 1991/92 Presidential Land Commission of Tanzania. These proposals were greatly weakened through the intervention of international experts who promoted strong privatisation of land, and through secretive dealings in the Ministry of Lands. Actual government policy and new legislation continue to promote the centralisation of land control and 'modernisation', by giving extensive rights to (foreign) private companies. However, the fight of NGOs for legislation that serves land users rather than bureaucrats continues, in part through the work of the National Land Forum (NALAF) and also the Land Rights Research and Resources Institute (LARRI) in Dar-es-Salaam. Recently a new version of the Land Act has been passed through parliament, incorporating many of the proposals of NALAF and LARRI. This Act regulates the rights of land users and the various conditions under which land may be alienated (i.e. claimed by or transferred to – for example – private or State enterprises) for three categories of land: 'village land', 'reserve land', and 'general land'. Some international development agencies have long supported their research and proposals for legislative change, in the interests of decentralising and democratising access to and control over land, with specific attention to the land rights of women.

5.2.2 Biodiversity and agriculture

The Green Revolution
The so-called Green Revolution of the 1960s and 1970s is widely seen as having made a major contribution to increased food production, for example in India and Indonesia. It promoted hybrid seed varieties (High Yielding Varieties – HYVs – which are normally grown from in-bred seeds with very weak reproductive capacities), widespread use of fertilisers and chemical pesticides, increased irrigation, and a basic level of mechanisation. It has contributed significantly to national food security in several countries. The Green Revolution has, however, not managed to eliminate rural poverty and rural food insecurity. It promoted agricultural practices that were based on external inputs (i.e.

external to local agro-ecological systems) of agro-chemicals; natural soil fertility and organic-matter content has been depleted; soil erosion is enhanced; and health risks (indeed, incidence of death from poisoning) have increased with the use of pesticides. The technological package that was promoted was relevant mainly to land of higher potential, which led to geographical and social inequality, because such land tends to be in the hands of the better-off farmers. Farmers' dependency on external inputs (provided by the State or private enterprises) sharply increased. The medium-sized to large farms benefited, while smallholders and subsistence farmers did not gain any advantage at all, and some actually became worse off. Total, national production increased in several Asian countries, but that effect was not substantial in much of Africa; even where it happened, inequality sharply increased. Landlessness increased in the wake of inequality, in part attributed to the Green Revolution, especially because mechanisation increased productivity per worker, so that the share of income from agriculture that went to (wage) labour declined.[31]

'Green Revolution' ideas and technologies are still dominant in the research and extension services of many developing countries, and also in donor organisations. However, increased inequality and environmental degradation pose questions about the appropriateness of the approach and technologies, and in particular about the level of consultation or participation of women and men farmers in research and extension. The degradation of soil fertility and increased pest resistance have provoked more dependency on fertilisers and pesticides, and are jeopardising further increases of area-productivity. The production increases that followed the introduction of newly bred strains of rice and other food crops are no longer as dramatic as they were when the HYVs first appeared. Furthermore, productivity increase per labour input is stalling or slowing down now, partly as a result of reduced expansion (potential) of irrigation systems, while a lack of alternative employment opportunities forces agriculture in many countries to absorb labour surplus (and this keeps wages of agricultural labourers very low).

Food security and sustainable agriculture

Famine is rarely a question of overall supply or food availability, because food security depends on people's 'exchange entitlements', i.e. whether they can actually claim the available food or not.[32] The rural poor are often strongly dependent on home production for their food security, which in turn depends on their exchange entitlements to three particular assets (i.e. *capitals*): (a) **land for cultivation** (and therefore the quality of land and land-tenure relationships), (b) **capital for investment** in inputs and infrastructure, and (c) **human capital** (i.e. the potential to work, the knowledge of farming techniques, etc.). In many developing countries, NGOs and grassroots groups play a significant role in the development of 'low-external-input sustainable agriculture' (LEISA) (or organic farming, conservation farming, permaculture, or some other label for this alternative form of production, technology development, and social organisation). These forms of sustainable agriculture depend particularly on a fourth asset, a form of natural capital, which is (d) **biodiversity**. The productivity and resilience of conservation farming depend on the diversity and the particular qualities of crop varieties that have been selected and bred over thousands of years, and on the diverse organisms in local ecosystems, which include predators and repellents of crop pests. Biodiversity plays a central role in livelihoods of fisherfolk and forest dwellers too, where food-gathering activity, combined with a certain management or harvesting strategy, is the main form of human interference. In agriculture, however, human interference with ecosystems goes much further.

'Sustainable agriculture' comprises a range of techniques and approaches that have been promoted by the FAO, UNDP, and Agenda 21 (at UNCED), and particularly by the more progressive non-government development organisations. Interpretations of sustainable agriculture differ, but most agree on the following aspects:[33]

1. Research and development of technologies that maximise *local* resources (inputs), improve soils, reduce pollution and health risks, etc. (Examples of such techniques are crop rotation, integrated pest management, green manuring, agro-forestry, alley cropping and intercropping, diversification of crops, and locally improved varieties.)

2. Participation of women and men farmers in technology development and technology adaptation, leading to technologies that are particularly relevant to poorer farmers (who usually have comparatively little labour available in their families).

3. A gender-sensitive approach to technology development and extension (responding for example to the need of women farmers to combine food production with daily reproductive tasks).

4. Improved land-tenure security, for women and men, particular minority ethnic groups and marginalised castes.

5. Decentralisation, of research and extension services in particular.

6. Improved infrastructure related to financial services, processing, and marketing.

7. Promotion of agro-ecological systems that combine livestock, crops, and sometimes forestry and fish farming.

8. National and international pricing and market policies that stimulate local production and product diversification.

A biotechnological revolution

Biotechnological developments are regarded by some as the source of the next technological revolution, comparable with the electronic, computer, and information revolution in the twentieth century. Others describe the health and environmental risks of 'genetic modification' as 'paralleled historically only by the splitting of the atom' – according to one genetic scientist, who goes on to comment: 'It will be a high price to pay for the arrogance of a species which meddles with the blueprint of nature disregarding the responsibilities that come with such power'.[34] There are obvious risks from these technological developments, and potential benefits too. FAO data for 1999 show that 790 million people worldwide are suffering from food insecurity. Staple-food production is globally sufficient and continues to increase, but at a slower rate than in the 1970s, and global food stocks are relatively low. On the other hand, global cereal prices at the end of the 1990s were below where they were at the beginning of the decade, and the trend is further downwards.[35] Proponents argue that we need rapid technological innovation to feed growing populations; opponents argue that there are severe environmental, health, and socio-economic risks attached and that the apocalypse is not close at all, while alternative routes to increasing production exist. Table 5.4 summarises the arguments in favour and against relatively unregulated genetic modification of crops.

Table 5.4: Food security and the genetic modification of crops[36]

Opportunities and gains	Risks and losses
• Higher yields and labour productivity, e.g. from GM crops that are salt-tolerant, resistant to pests and drought, or nitrogen-fixing. • Investment, research, and rapid technology development fuelled by profits accruing to holders of patents for genetic materials and production processes.	• Many unpredictable effects, including unexpected side-effects (since nobody knows in advance exactly on which chromosome, and where, to put the exotic gene); genetic instability (after some generations, the crop has fewer or more copies of the inserted gene); a weakening of other plant traits as a result of 'overwork' (as in the case of permanent production of a pesticide by the plant itself); and, in particular, the risk of genes being transferred to other plants, with unknown consequences (which happens in nature in various ways). These unknowns imply threats to human and animal health, to wild plants, crops, and agro-ecosystems, even though probabilities of severe problems are small.

Table 5.4: Food security and the genetic modification of crops (continued)[36]

Opportunities and gains	Risks and losses
• Reduced costs for producers e.g. from reduced dependency on external inputs such as fertilisers and pesticides, and increased effectiveness of herbicides; possible benefits from reduced pollution with agro-chemicals. • Cheaper products, including staple foods, for consumers in developing countries that are net importers of food, because of higher productivity in industrialised countries. • Improved quality of fruit and vegetables on supermarket shelves from suppression of ethylene-producing genes. • Improved flavour, texture, and nutritional content; elimination of allergens and toxic substances; etc. • Production of vaccines, biodegradable plastics, etc., from GM plants and crops.	• Large-scale GM-crop farming makes GM-free and organic farming *de facto* impossible. • Natural soil fertility declines through the reduction of the activity of nitrogen-fixing bacteria. • Monocultures and contracts with large companies lead to further losses of agricultural biodiversity. • GM crops that are resistant to herbicides and pesticides will stimulate their use, causing increased natural resistance of weeds and pests to these same agro-chemicals, which in turn stimulates their use, and can lead to 'super-weeds', such as rye grass in Australia. • GM technology and its products are monopolised through patenting by transnational companies, whereas *public* research and publicly available knowledge was the main driving force behind the (qualified) success of the Green Revolution. • Financial benefits are denied to developing countries and the generations of farmers who have domesticated crops and improved genetic traits through selection. Patenting systems and current breeders' rights systems allow pirating by companies that transfer or delete a few genes among thousands. • Increased liberalisation of food markets and greater corporate control of the production process leads to more cash-crop production and fewer food crops grown on farms, which increases smallholders' vulnerability to crop failure and sudden food price rises. • Corporate control over production inputs, markets, and products increases, at the expense of smallholder producers, through input-packages (certain seeds respond positively to branded agro-chemicals).

Table 5.4: Food security and the genetic modification of crops (continued)[36]

Opportunities and gains	Risks and losses
• Development of GM plants for removing toxic chemicals from soils.	• GM varieties extend the range of crops and crop products that can be produced in Northern temperate zones, and these compete with or substitute for developing-country export products (e.g. rape-seed engineered to produce lauric acid, which is traditionally derived from coconut oil from the Philippines and other tropical countries). • GM crops are introduced faster than the development of the regulatory capacity in poor countries and also in many rich countries. • Biotech companies bear little or no liability for any damage to the environment or public health resulting from use of the GM technology or crops. They deny liability even though they argue that there are no risks.

The alternatives to patented crops controlled by a handful of international companies are in the realms of sustainable agriculture. International companies who modify and patent the genetic materials spend much of their energy on developing herbicide-resistant or pesticide-producing varieties. These applications risk damaging ecological diversity and resilience, and they are at best irrelevant for the smallholder farmers who cannot afford the input packages and whose families make up the majority of the almost 800 million undernourished people of the world.

The advantages and disadvantages listed above suggest that the advance of genetically modified crops and plants is neatly intertwined with the development of international economic policy, in particular trade-related policy that is now regulated under the World Trade Organisation (WTO). In India and Brazil, for instance, farmers are protesting against the prospect of genetically engineered varieties by burning experimental fields, and governments in Europe and elsewhere are trying to accommodate public anxiety about international trade agreements and the Convention on Biodiversity (CBD). This international dimension is discussed further in section 5.3.

Examples of sustainable agriculture

Alternative agricultural technologies are available and are developing rapidly, and some believe that their spread through formal extension services, international organisations, and particularly through NGO networks is already so substantial that the 'high tech' of genetic engineering will not be as dominant as the Green Revolution technology was, despite the efforts of 'big business'. Documentation is being produced to show that hundreds of thousands of farmers all over the developing world are adopting technologies that all in one way or the other minimise the use of pesticides, increase the effectiveness of local resources to maintain soil fertility, or improve the water-holding capacity of soils. The increases in yield achieved by alternative technologies are very substantial,[37] and that simple fact is likely to be the single most important reason for their spread.

The idea of sustainable agriculture and that of partnerships between researchers and farmers has found support in many national and international NGOs and coalitions. Lobbyists have also called for arrangements that will enable developing countries to export to rich countries, and for comparatively long (transitional) periods of import protection in order to develop alternative crop-production systems, for example in the case of the banana trade to Europe from small island states in the Caribbean. NGOs and activists in India and Brazil run campaigns against the excesses of biotechnology and its corporate proponents, and in favour of alternative systems. Many of those, including MST in Brazil (a movement of landless people), have campaigned for years for improved access to land, as the key productive resource for poor rural people; they also have taken a public position in opposition to genetically modified crops and in favour of sustainable agriculture. MST trains thousands of women and men farmers in appropriate technologies, and its success seems to derive from the combination of that very practical work with land-occupations and campaigning.

The *campesino a campesino* (farmer to farmer) movement in **Central America and Mexico** has assumed the role of an alternative to government extension and technology development, and has influenced research and extension policies of governments across the region.[38] In farmer-to-farmer extension, volunteer farmers who are trained and who have increased productivity on their own farms promote changes in technology and management with neighbours; this happens largely without remuneration, on the principle that success should sell itself. In Cuba, alternative low-external-input agriculture has developed in a very short period of time, owing to the intensive efforts of government research institutes, forced by the collapse of the Soviet Union, the drying up of cheap oil imports, and the continued trade blockade of Cuba by the USA.[39] In a project in a mountainous and densely populated part of **Albania**, permaculture design principles and sustainable agricultural techniques are being developed for application on local farms. This project stimulates local horticultural production and also that of staple foods under difficult agro-ecological and economic conditions, and with success.[40] Its achievements are partly due to the fact that there is a good market for the produce in this area, which has a substantial population and difficult transport connections.

In **Kenya**, many local and national NGOs work on conservation farming, with considerable success in improved vegetable production, increased household incomes and women's incomes, and improved environmental health. They are part of a reasonably well-functioning network in which some national organisations with international contacts have key roles. In Zimbabwe, national NGOs and alternative networks have promoted organic farming for years, helped by international contacts. In all these cases, some form of beneficiary participation in technology development is seen as an essential and integral part of projects. The Kenyan NGOs (and also NGOs in other countries) are attempting to increase the staple yields of thousands of farming families, and have initiated close collaboration with researchers from government and international research organisations and also from the alternative NGO circuit (which focuses on organic farming). However, national and international movements for alternative forms of agriculture do not always amount to campaigns that aim to change the behaviour of government extension services and their research policy. In the Kenya case there is still a lot of unexplored potential in this sense. Furthermore, the Kenyan NGOs, like their counterparts in India and Brazil, have started to work on the policy context of trade regimes and farm-gate prices, advocating more research in support of environmentally sustainable agriculture.[41]

In **Brazil** the so-called Hunger Campaign reached a peak in terms of media attention, private donations, and grassroots activity around 1993-94. After the election of President Cardoso in 1995 and the death of the movement's leader, the human-rights activist Betinho, in 1997, the campaign lost its momentum. That is of course in the nature of campaigns: a period of growth and success, followed by one of decline and then transformation. The campaign developed out of a movement called Citizens' Action, in 1989, and became known for its highly creative and diverse initiatives, different in every State, yet spanning virtually the whole country. The Hunger Campaign set up a plethora of local, diverse initiatives aiming at achieving food security. This included the stimulation of rice cultivation by Kaiapo indians in Goiânia.[42] In Bahia State, a Carnival Without Hunger campaign was launched, and food distributions were organised in communities living around refuse tips in Mato Grosso State. In Alagoas a project called 'The Community Sings' was allocated land to establish an agricultural co-operative. The national campaign lost momentum, but several local initiatives continue, with funds raised from local business and councils, and through mergers with other groups. They have raised national awareness of poverty and destitution and its causes, and helped many poor and vulnerable people, rural and urban dwellers alike.

In most countries, the focus of the alternative agriculture movement is on the poorest farmers, or at least smallholders, prompting a debate about whether it is exclusively concerned with technology for the poor, or whether it should be seen as an (environmental) alternative for all scales of agricultural production. It is true that technologies for the rich and for the poor are and should be different, because these groups do not share equal access to labour, capital, land, and other resources. However, there are benefits for all from various alternatives. Government resources are usually directed at technologies that are accessible for better-off farmers only, failing to support alternatives that are primarily of interest to the agriculture-based livelihoods of large numbers of people, if not the majority in the country (in Africa, and also much of Asia and Central America).

Wealthy and poor farmers have different investment abilities, aims (sustaining production or maximising profit?), consumption needs, abilities to operate in markets, and labour availability. Many of the principles and techniques of sustainable agriculture are, however, interesting in terms of cost and productivity, apart from environmental and health benefits, which should make them useful to all farmers, even though they need to be slightly altered, depending on the farmer's capabilities and resources. For example, nitrogen-fixating 'green manure' (such as a bean crop that is ploughed into the soil before maturing) aids productivity and improves environmental sustainability, and can compete with the use of chemical fertilisers (depending on transport, subsidy, and tax arrangements). Nevertheless, ploughing the green manure into the soil at the appropriate moment requires equipment, time, and/or investment, which poor farmers may not have. The very poorest are often left out in high-input farming, because they lack financial capital to invest, and may also be excluded from the benefits of low-external-input alternatives because of the high demands made on learning time and ability, and also on labour, which is not available in families of elderly widows, single mothers with very young children, the sick, or more generally the most destitute rural population.[43] Support for agricultural production can help to alleviate their poverty and improve their food security only indirectly. Economic growth is particularly associated with a shift away from an agriculture-based economy to an urban economy, with manufacturing and services that require energy and cheap foods. This so-called modernisation process comes with many problems for poor people and negative impacts on environmental quality, as the following themes and examples illustrate.

5.2.3 Industrialisation and urbanisation

Dams and electricity

The term 'river development' covers a wide range of environmental interventions: the canalisation of rivers; reduction of natural floodplains; construction of dams and reservoirs for electricity generation, irrigation, and possibly the provision of safe drinking water; the use of river water for industrial processes; and also the river's use as a conduit for sewage. Huge dam projects have not been relegated to history yet, despite many well-known problems such as people displacement, reservoir siltation, and other externalities (i.e. real costs which are generally not incorporated in financial calculations – see also section 2.2.4). National governments continue to conceive large dam-building projects, and often get financial backing from multilateral development banks and bilateral development agencies. At the heart of the arguments for proceeding with them (indeed for being enthusiastic about them) is the need for cheap and reliable electricity and water for urbanising populations and for industrialisation. This collaboration between national governments and international development agencies makes all the more obvious the need for a coalition of national and international activists who challenge the negative impacts on people, livelihoods, and environments.

Near a dam in the **São Francisco River in Brazil**, people are still fighting for compensation for the loss of land and livelihood, although the dam was completed in 1986 (this example is also referred to in section 4.1). The biggest ever such scheme is being implemented in **China: the Three Gorges dam project**. The dam in the Yangtze River will create a reservoir whose area will exceed 650km^2 (more than 250 square miles) and is expected to displace one million people by the year 2010, mostly from Sichuan province. The project is fraught with problems, not least because of corruption and the related compromising of technical standards by contractors and officials. Ecological systems will be upset, and – because people are expected to be moved higher up the hill and mountain slopes – soil erosion is predicted to increase substantially. Homes, factories, roads, and other infrastructure will all be submerged. River navigation is expected to improve, and vast quantities of electricity will be generated. However, as with other dam projects, critics point out that the same hydro-electricity can be generated by several smaller dams in the river's tributaries, which would reduce the risk of collapse and disaster for millions of people downstream, and limit disturbance to local residents and eco-systems. If earlier experience in other countries is anything to go by, and the criticism of activists and even of the Chinese Prime Minister Zhu Rongji[44] is only partly vindicated, the displaced will not be fully compensated for the loss of land and livelihood, and many will live in communities where they are unwelcome, or on lands where reconstructing a livelihood will prove to be very difficult.

Equally controversial and on a similar scale is the series of dams in the **Narmada River and its tributaries, in India**. The scheme consists of more than one hundred dams, some huge, and thousands of minor structures. It is designed to produce hydro-electricity and provide irrigation and also drinking water to a very large area. Here, too, poor people are suffering from ecological degradation, siltation, and disruption of local livelihoods. The total number of people who will be displaced by the dams, including the Sardar Sarovar dam, is now estimated to be 200,000, according to the authorities – but many more, according to others. The scheme was initially supported by the World Bank, but pressure of grassroots groups, national NGOs, and also international NGOs and changes in the Bank itself led to its withdrawal from the project. Protests and court cases have interrupted the construction of the Sardar Sarovar dam, and local NGOs have worked with affected people to get some compensation at least. The large majority of the people affected by this dam and the thousands of others that were built in India (especially since Independence) are 'tribal' minorities and Dalits (untouchables). In other words, the social under-classes of India are bearing the brunt: 'India's poorest people's are subsidising the lifestyles of her richest'.[45] Their lands, culture, and lifestyles are being disrupted severely, no matter what compensation is offered. Nevertheless, the Indian government is persisting in its determination to produce electricity for urban populations and to 'modernise' agriculture with large irrigation systems.

National activists in China with strong concerns about the Three Gorges project have great difficulty operating in a country that tolerates only very limited opposition against government decisions and projects. In India, coalitions of activists have proved to be difficult to maintain, which means that there is not always a single opposition front. Despite a large political space for NGOs, activists, and ordinary people and a greater degree of political openness than in China, the Indian establishment manages to force its case through political decisions, bureaucratic support, and court cases: construction is continuing, despite some delays.

Industrial pollution

Industrialisation often leads to increased competition over natural resources such as water and (agricultural) land between (formerly) rural people and industries, and it also causes environmental pollution. It thus affects negatively the livelihoods and environments of poor and vulnerable women and men on the fringes of cities. This happened and is happening in Java, **Indonesia**, for example, where households replace fuelwood with kerosene, have to accept lower quality of domestic water, reduce the numbers of their domestic animals, and change the management arrangements for common resources. However, not all change is bad. One conclusion is that women cannot simply be assumed to be the victims of changes in the availability and quality of natural resources; in the process of industrialisation, gender roles change, (employment) opportunities appear, and both women and men adapt to the changing circumstances.[46]

Once established, industries tend to be surrounded by residential areas of poorer people who are interested in working in them, but who also suffer the often unseen effects of pollution. The occupational environment of workers is of central importance in large-scale industries, but also in small-scale and 'informal' workshops, as is argued in section 3.1.1 with the example of engineering workshops in Bangladesh. There is increasing evidence that exposure to toxic substances in and around industrial areas affects brains and intelligence (especially of children), and that male fertility is affected by the presence of agro-chemicals, female hormones, and other pollutants in drinking water in urban areas. There are in particular reports of effects on children, with asthma, lead poisoning, and a range of other health problems. Children, women, and more generally the poorest and most vulnerable often find employment in the harshest of circumstances, with severe impacts on their health.[47]

Industrial disasters have, of course, the biggest impact, as in **Bhopal, India**, where toxic gases escaped from a pesticide plant owned by the US company Union Carbide on 2 December 1984. Thousands of people were killed and many more suffered respiratory and eye ailments. In the aftermath there were also reports of miscarriages and female infertility; true or not, young women's marriage prospects were affected. Compensation fell well short of what was expected, and was in fact jeopardised by Indian legislation adopted *after* the disaster: 'special legislation *diminished* the rights of victims through giving the state absolute control over claims and denying liability for future generations'.[48] This terrible disaster sparked various spontaneous protests immediately following the gas leak. Several activists got involved, but they were by no means all local, and they had different and conflicting opinions and priorities. In fact, the initial public action was centralised and dominated by middle-class groups, and consequently it missed opportunities for building local and international solidarity links. Later the survivors began to organise themselves, but again conflicts between different organisations and leaders hampered the success of their demands for recognition, compensation, and jobs. They did not manage to forge a strong international and national solidarity movement, which would be an obvious goal, given the scale of the disaster and the fact that Union Carbide is a company with activities in more than 100 countries. A further lesson to be learned from this disaster is the need for the generation and dissemination of information, in order to create links with other groups and especially to establish liability. Both the company and the Indian authorities continued to suppress the publication of crucial facts.[49]

Homes, services, and infrastructure

In broad terms, there are three ways to reduce (urban) poverty: (a) increasing income and/or assets; (b) upholding human rights, particularly civil and political rights; and (c) improving housing and basic social services.[50] Prominent in the latter category is the *securing* of housing *tenure* as a basis for progress in so many of the other areas, because security of tenure means that financing for housing improvements can really take off: for many people, secure housing provides a basis for income generation, and neighbourhoods can develop strong action to claim improved infrastructure and services. Only with secure housing (tenure rights) can urban infrastructure in poor settlements be expected to improve, and as a consequence environmental risks will generally be reduced.

Increasingly important in struggles for secure tenure are local campaigners who organise citizens and demand (legal) recognition from municipal authorities, and NGOs who train and advise the grassroots groups, often with support from international organisations. NGOs also support a plethora of groups and neighbourhoods to improve water supply and sanitation systems in their settlements.[51] There are obvious reasons for this: the main health risks in poor neighbourhoods relate to hygiene, i.e. vector-transmitted and water-borne diseases such as malaria and diarrhoea.

In Recife, in **Brazil**, SCJP (*Serviço Comunitário de Justiça e Paz –* Community Service for Justice and Peace) is one of several NGOs that give legal and practical support to citizens' groups struggling for the improvement of their *favelas* (slums). New legislation from 1987 onwards defined the terms for citizens' participation in municipal policy making. It is seen as a very significant achievement that *favelas* have been made legal, that citizens' participation has been institutionalised, that plans are being made for improvements to infrastructure, that some investments have been made, and that the authorities are now really listening to the views of local people. Nevertheless, despite more then ten years of hard work and lots of talking in all kinds of forums, drinking water, sewerage systems, and electricity supply remain very basic. More and better co-operation between NGOs is needed, together with a stronger focus on practical achievements, according to a recent evaluation.[52]

In Cairo, **Egypt**, a community of garbage collectors has suffered from environmental health risks ever since it emerged in the 1940s. The settlement of the Zabbaleen was not officially recognised, and the service that the people supplied to the city (collecting, sorting, and recycling garbage) is still not generally appreciated. Hardly any government support is supplied to this community. In response to public campaigning, supported by NGOs and the Coptic Church, the electricity network reached the neighbourhood in the 1980s, settlement rights were given, and people started improving their houses and developing some businesses. By 1996 much had improved, but only some minor sewerage work had been done and drinking-water supply was insufficient, falling short of promises and plans that had been made, and harassment by certain authorities continued. There were also contradictions and tensions between different groups seeking influence in the community, including NGOs. However, residents have made enormous progress in terms of developing the ability and confidence to articulate their needs and challenge the negative portrayal of their community in the local press and on national television. However, this has not been appreciated by all supporting NGOs, most of whom are interested less in campaigning and more in 'doing' development projects. The local residents' struggle to get recognition of their role and support from government services in health care, sewerage systems, and better water supply continues.[53]

5.3 Global environmental policy and campaigning

This section discusses international policies that affect environments and livelihoods, and campaigns and lobbying for change. The main international issues relate to climate change, biodiversity, and macro-economic policies.

5.3.1 Managing the global environment

The Earth Summit, held in Rio de Janeiro in 1992 under the official title of the United Nations Conference on Environment and Development (UNCED),[54] followed a similar conference 20 years earlier in Stockholm, and preparatory work by the Brundtland Commission, which produced the report *Our Common Future* in 1987.

At UNCED the Rio Declaration was agreed; it states 27 principles for sustainable development, but is not legally binding. Possibly the most significant output was Agenda 21, which is a programme for promoting sustainable development from 1992 through the twenty-first century. It contains chapters on almost all environmental topics, from seas, atmosphere, human settlements, and land to desertification, mountain development, sustainable agriculture, biotechnology, and hazardous wastes. There are also special sections on combating poverty, meeting the needs and rights of women and children and those of indigenous people, international relations, and partnerships with NGOs.

It is important to stress that implementation of Agenda 21 is to a great extent a local matter. Local authorities and citizens' groups are encouraged to address issues that range from pollution and transport to improvement of human settlements and waste collection and recycling. Unsurprisingly, this is happening in particular in the industrialised world and middle-income countries, where more resources are available.[55] With support from the World Bank and bilateral development agencies, many countries have produced or are producing national sustainability strategies (see also section 5.1.1), and developing national structures and skills with the support of the Capacity 21 programme, an initiative of UNDP.

Much environmental management in developing nations relates to reducing vulnerabilities and hazards, which often play a role in conflict generation, extreme suffering, and environmental destruction, as is discussed in sections 2.3 and 4.2.3. Environmental causes of disasters include climatic drought, volcanic eruptions, earthquakes, and cyclones. Human causes include mismanagement, over-consumption, and deforestation (leading to climate change, death from toxic spills, and river floods). Disasters are another source of environmental impacts, including the consequences of human displacement such as deforestation and soil erosion, and impacts from floods and oil spills on biological diversity and soil quality. The causes of disaster and extreme suffering are thus a mix of factors, local and global, human and natural. Some of them can be addressed by policy-influencing activities. Important lobby targets and international response agencies in this field are the UNHCR, World Food Programme (WFP), UNEP/OCHRA, the European Union (EU), and also national governments.

Many Third World countries remain marginal to most international discussions and negotiations, except for nations such as China, India, and Brazil that are significant in terms of population, economic power, and military strength. Furthermore, many Southern leaders seem to believe that 'the environment' is the problem of rich nations in the North, and if there are global environmental problems *for* the South, it is still the North that causes them. That sort of reasoning enables the governments of developing countries to deny their responsibilities and the need to act, yet it does not necessarily put them in a position to influence global problems. Moreover, some are rapidly catching up with the industrialised world in creating and enhancing global (and local) environmental problems.

Some of the main global environmental threats are related to climate (as is shown in section 5.3.2), and they are not alleviated by human activity. They include cyclones, droughts, and floods. River management, river floods, and dam failure can have international consequences for obvious reasons, as can industrial pollution of water and air, all of them affected by human interference, or even caused by people. For example, toxic effluents can kill fish in rivers and coastal waters and destroy the livelihoods of fishing communities. The nuclear disaster in Chernobyl affected natural resources, animals, and crops, locally and across northern Europe. Volcanic eruptions and earthquakes are not caused in any significant way by people, and their effects are usually local only. Nevertheless, large volcanic eruptions can have a global impact because of the gases and ash that enter into the atmosphere, and which lead to global climatic changes for periods of possibly several years.

Very important policy developments that affect the global environment and local resources are taking place in the realms of international trade, with the WTO at the centre, and also in the regulation of financial flows and investments and 'structural adjustment', with the IMF and World Bank in the limelight. Global trade regulation under the WTO at best ignores environmental change where it is stimulated by trade regulation; in several cases the WTO has ruled that trade restrictions on environmental grounds are not allowed, which appears to contradict international treaties on environmental protection and sustainable development. The impact on environmental sustainability of the various policies that are included in 'structural adjustment' appear to be mixed, but far too little is known for the real effects to be asserted with confidence (see also section 5.3.2). Environmental change remains marginal to many of those policy developments, even though there are enormous implications for 'global commons' and poor people's environments.

5.3.2 Global climate change

Among the key trends and shocks that are outside the sphere of influence of poor people and citizens' groups and also that of most developing-country governments are changes in climates and their effects on people and their environments. These changes are to some extent the result of human behaviour, however. There is widespread agreement that the so-called 'greenhouse effect' *is* real and *is* leading to a rise in the average Earth temperature, and this appears to be associated with increasingly erratic climatic behaviour. Exactly how much change is taking place is not agreed, and the actual consequences for particular countries and regions are both uncertain and in some cases controversial. The facts add up to an alarming picture. This section discusses global climate change, global warming, the greenhouse effect, sea-level rise, the *El Niño* phenomenon, and some of the ways in which the impact of these changes might be mitigated.[56]

1998, a year of climate change

In 1998 there were several 'natural' disasters, which – according to Munich Re, a German insurance company – caused economic damage costing almost $US 100 billion. However, insurance cover was less than $15 billion, and related mostly to disasters in the USA. The company claims that three times as many natural disasters occurred annually in the 1990s as in the 1960s, and that annual economic damages (adjusted for inflation) are now nine times what they were 30 years ago. Insurance cover is lowest in developing countries, where the greatest damage is done and most lives are lost. In 1998, Hurricane

Mitch hit Central America and George hit the USA and Caribbean; a cyclone hit Gujarat, India, and there was bad flooding in Bangladesh. Russia, Indonesia, and the Amazon region suffered drought-induced forest fires, and in some Latin American countries crop harvests were reduced by droughts. Scientists warn that warming of surface water in the oceans affects coral reefs, which are important breeding grounds for fish.[57]

According to the World Meteorological Organisation (WMO), 1998 was by far the warmest year on record (systematic measurements began about 160 years ago), and the ten warmest years have all occurred since 1983. Temperature increases happen unevenly: that is, some areas will become significantly warmer, while others may not notice much change. The temperature changes are associated with relatively rapid shifts of agro-ecological zones and shifts in the potential for food production: some areas may be able to produce better as a result of longer summer periods, while others may be less fortunate. There are also risks that disease vectors are enhanced, in particular that tropical diseases such as malaria will spread to temperate climatic zones. However, far greater risks are posed by the increasingly erratic behaviour of climates as a result of the greenhouse effect and average global warming.

The greenhouse effect

Water vapour and certain gases in the air 'trap' the long-wave radiation from the earth's surface into space. (The radiation came from the sun in the first place: sunlight bounces back from the earth's surface, but in the process the wavelength becomes shorter, making it eligible for 'trapping'.) This happens in the same way that the glass walls of a greenhouse 'trap' radiation that bounces back from the ground surface. As a result, the earth and air get warmer. Water vapour is naturally in the air, as are small amounts of the so-called greenhouse gases, but this effect is enhanced by the (extra) gases that human beings have contributed to the atmosphere since the Industrial Revolution of the eighteenth and nineteenth centuries. The main greenhouse gas is carbon dioxide (CO_2), which is produced by burning fossil fuels. Also important are chloro-fluorocarbons (CFCs, from industrial processes, fridges, air-conditioners, and sprays) and methane (CH_4), which is produced in rice paddy fields and by ruminating animals (of which cattle and goats are the best-known examples).

Global warming

A rise in the average temperature of the Earth is the result of the global greenhouse effect. The rise since the 1880s is generally agreed to be about 0.5 degrees Celsius, and a further rise of 0.5–2.0 degrees is expected by 2050. It is hard to predict the exact rise of the average temperature, because of the many uncertainties that are associated with various 'feedback mechanisms'. For example, cloud cover will be affected by temperature rise and changes in regional weather patterns. If the total global cloud cover increases as a result of warming, it means that less radiation can come in from the sun, and the warming effect is thus reduced.

Temporarily lower average Earth temperatures can be caused by several phenomena, including volcanic eruptions that bring very large amounts of gases and ash into the atmosphere which screen off radiation from the sun (and potentially cause a 'volcanic winter'). This happened following the eruptions of the Pinatubo volcano in the Philippines in 1991 and 1992. Nevertheless, volcanic eruptions also bring large amounts of greenhouse gases into the atmosphere, which have a warming effect.

A far more alarming possibility (although of low probability) is suggested by analysis of historical global temperatures. They have been comparatively very stable over the past 10,000 years, but immediately before that they fluctuated heavily by up to 8 degrees Celsius over periods of mere decades. The last 10,000 years is roughly the period since the start of agriculture, and this period is extremely short when put in the perspective of the age of the Earth and its atmosphere – about 4.5 billion years, during which climatic stability must have been rare. Some scientists believe that human influence on global climates will not just cause a gradual warming but could trigger some kind of collapse or sudden change in the Earth's weather systems and ocean currents, and the heat exchange between the two. This kind of 'collapse' is most likely to result in rapid cooling of the Earth.[58] (The 'collapse' possibility fits in with the Gaia hypothesis of Lovelock, which is briefly discussed in section 2.2.1.) The mere possibility of this happening should obviously be enough reason to take radical measures to reduce the impact of the greenhouse effect of traffic, manufacturing industry, electricity generation, and other consumption.

Climate-pattern changes
The temperature of the Earth will obviously not change everywhere by the average amount, and indeed the expected temperature changes are larger in the cold parts and less so in the tropics. However, temperature is just one factor in Earth's infinitely complex weather systems. It is almost certain that changes in climates will happen, but there is much uncertainty about *how* weather patterns will change. There is a strong probability that average rainfall (on a global scale) will increase, but that big increases are likely at high latitudes (i.e. in the far North and far South of the planet) and in what are now the humid tropics (that is, areas where rainfall is plentiful already). In the mid latitudes (between 30 and 60 degrees) and the interiors of Northern continents, rainfall is likely to decrease, causing drought. It is also possible, though not certain, that the frequency of extreme events such as droughts, floods, and cyclones will increase.

El Niño

The so-called El Niño Southern Oscillation effect (ENSO) is an as yet unexplained rise in surface-water temperatures in the Southern (equatorial) Pacific Ocean, off the coast of Peru. These higher water temperatures change weather patterns, and, in particular, they block the so-called South-East Trade Winds: that is, they block wet rains that originate from the south-eastern Pacific and prevent them reaching Indonesia and neighbouring countries. Furthermore, the El Niño phenomenon is increasingly seen to correlate with extreme weather conditions in all parts of the world, in particular with droughts and floods. For example, there was drought during the 1982–83 'El Niño year' in Central America and East Africa. Flooding in Bolivia and Peru would have been caused by increased heat flow from the surface water in the Pacific Ocean into the atmosphere, resulting in all kinds of knock-on changes in weather patterns. Later El Niño years were 1987–88 (which lasted into 1989), 1991–92, and (less strongly) 1993 and 1994. 1997–98 is seen as an unusually strong El Niño year; and El Niño reigned again in 1998. Following the latter, forest fires raged through parts of Indonesia and Amazonia, unimpeded by the expected rains, which did not arrive. Scientists have suggested that it is possible that the El Niño phenomenon is increasing in frequency from an historical 20-year cycle to maybe even one in every two years in future: the sequence of El Niño years in 1991–92 and 1993–94 is very unusual. Indeed, the frequency of El Niño has increased strongly since the 1970s. This increased frequency of occurrence is now being associated with global warming and the greenhouse effect. However, predicting the effects of El Niño events is still difficult: a drought and famine were expected in Southern Africa following the 1997–98 El Niño, but they failed to materialise.

Whether the reduced 'upwelling' of cold and nutrient-rich bottom waters has positive or negative effects on the ocean's capacity to be a vital 'carbon sink' is unclear as yet. It is possible that less carbon dioxide (the main greenhouse gas) is released from the South Pacific ocean than in normal years, while it absorbs carbon dioxide at other times in the Northern regions. Thus El Niño may constitute a blessing in disguise, even though it is a temporary effect. However, the droughts in 1997/98 in Brazil and Indonesia that are also associated with El Niño strongly exacerbated fires in (rain)forests that led to an enormous release of carbon dioxide – and the rainforests are supposed to be important global carbon sinks and oxygen producers, the 'lungs of the Earth', instead of the 'chokers' of the Earth.

El Niño was identified by fishermen who noticed unusually warm water off the South American coast, and correlated this fact with their markedly reduced fish catch. Because this was occurring around Christmas time (once in so many years), they gave the phenomenon its name: El Niño, 'the boy child', which is a reference to Jesus Christ. More recently scientists have also identified another phenomenon, La Niña, the 'little girl', which is more or less the opposite of El Niño, i.e. unusually cold surface-water temperatures in the (equatorial) Pacific Ocean. La Niña would have some correlation with the increased frequency of tornadoes in the particular regions of the Americas, and is associated with less-than-normal moisture in the air over the South Pacific Ocean, resulting in less rain along the coasts of North and South America. 'La Niña events' occurred in 1985, 1988–89, 1995, and late 1998.

Sea-level rise

The current estimates of the future rise in sea-levels as a result of global warming range from 5 to 40 cm (2 to 16 inches) by 2050, but it is agreed that the increase might be much more than this, depending on various uncertainties. Global warming is causing thermal expansion of the sea water, and ice from mountain glaciers is melting; both effects can be estimated fairly well. More uncertainty exists over the rate at which the ice caps of the landmasses of Greenland and Antarctica are melting, while increased precipitation (snow and hail) in the areas near the North Pole and the South Pole can rebuild ice caps to some extent. Analysis of historical changes in global temperatures suggests that the possibility of the collapse of the so-called West Antarctic Ice Sheet is a real threat, although of unknown probability. It could lead to a sudden rise in sea levels of 6–7 metres (18–21 feet),[59] which would flood many countries.

The effects of sea-level rises can be devastating, especially if a somewhat high estimate of the rise – say one metre – over the next century turns out to be the case. Enormous costs will be incurred by several small island States, which will struggle for survival, and a large area of deltas such as those in Bangladesh and Egypt will be inundated, or at least threatened, if no measures are taken.

Global climate negotiations

All the above changes are associated with greenhouse gases and global warming, which in turn are in large part influenced by the release of carbon dioxide (CO_2) from burning fossil fuels. It is thus crucial for the world community to negotiate reductions of CO_2 production. The Climate Change Convention was adopted in 1992 in response to growing concerns over emissions of carbon dioxide, methane, and other greenhouse gases. So far, 175 countries have signed and virtually all have ratified the Convention: it took official effect from 21 March 1994. Its implementation is being taken forward by a series of special conferences. The so-called Parties of the Climate Change Convention met for the first official conference in Berlin in 1995, then in Geneva in 1997, in Kyoto in 1997 for the third conference, in 1998 for the fourth in Buenos Aires, and in late 1999 for the fifth official conference in Bonn, Germany.

It was agreed by the 159 countries represented at the Kyoto conference to reduce their collective emissions of greenhouse gases by 5.2 per cent of the 1990 level by the period 2008–2012. For 38 rich countries this reduction is compulsory; for developing countries it is voluntary. However, each country has a target, and in some cases an increase in emissions was permitted. Also established were the Kyoto Mechanisms, in order to reach emissions-reduction targets: the Clean Development Mechanism (CDM) aims to contribute to reducing emissions of greenhouse gases and promote sustainable development in the South. It will grant better-off countries credits, which will finance developing-country projects that avoid emissions and promote sustainable development. The principle of Joint Implementation and Emissions Trading offers credits for reduction in emission levels through projects in industrialised countries – credits which they can trade with other industrialised countries (including the countries of Central/Eastern Europe and the former Soviet Union). Thirdly, an international emissions-trading regime will allow developed countries to buy and sell emissions 'credits' among themselves. The Parties to the Convention are now elaborating the nature and scope of these 'flexibility mechanisms', the criteria for project eligibility, the roles of various institutions, and an accounting system for allocating credits. This negotiation is taking place mainly in technical committees.

The Kyoto Protocol was signed by 83 countries, plus the European Commission, and more governments are expected to sign up, which is necessary for the Protocol to become legally binding. Unsurprisingly, the strongest opposition to real reduction in emissions and progress in the negotiations comes from the biggest fossil-fuel consumer (in total and per capita), the USA, and from several oil-producing countries, all strongly influenced by the powerful lobby of large oil companies. The Buenos Aires Plan of Action, adopted in November 1998, set a deadline of late 2000, at the sixth official conference, for finalising agreement on all these issues, so that the mechanisms can be fully functional when the Kyoto Protocol enters into force.

Consumption, climate change, and campaigning
The consumption of fossil fuel is the main cause of the greenhouse effect, and of the increase of the average global temperature, more erratic climate patterns, possibly enhanced 'El Niño events', sea-level rises, and more. The implications of all this are very significant for the most vulnerable people living in the deltas of poor countries, in areas prone to drought and flood; but most fossil fuels are consumed by other nations. Furthermore, the high-consumers of the world must also take responsibility for the destruction of forests, the expulsion of original land-users and owners from wildlife parks, the deprivation that follows the construction of dams and reservoirs for electricity generation, and the devastating impacts of mining. The fact that high consumption is also

responsible for those local environmental changes is not obvious to all, and it is less dramatic if viewed from a global perspective, but the changes are no less significant for developing countries and poor people. High-consumers are implicated in deforestation and the destructive effects of mining, dam building, and wildlife parks through their engagement in markets, the operation of their transport systems, their financial investments, and – above all – by virtue of their strong influence over policies that govern the mechanisms that drive environmental degradation. Their 'ecological footprint' is enormous.[60] High-consumers can be found primarily in industrialised nations, but the middle classes in developing countries have similar consumption patterns, and their numbers are rising, especially in cities.

Campaigns to reduce environmental degradation include the initiatives in developing countries mentioned in the previous section (concerning dams, extractive industries, nature parks, etc.) and also campaigns to reduce (fuel) consumption and protests against the expansion of road networks in highly industrialised countries. In all those campaigns, local concerns are central, and the international dimensions and global implications of consumption are not the only grounds for social action. This is understandable; indeed, whatever vice is addressed, over-consumption is often responsible for a combination of local and global environmental impacts. Deforestation enhances the greenhouse effect, because it removes a carbon sink, increases the risk of soil erosion and river flooding, and destroys traditional forest-based livelihoods. New motorways may be planned to go through 'sites of special scientific interest' or residential areas, in particular in poorer neighbourhoods. Local concerns about the health risks created by traffic and industrial air pollution are likely to cause more civic action in Southern and Northern cities than does the 'hole' in the atmospheric ozone layer over the South Pole (which allows harmful radiation to reach the surface of the Earth). Furthermore, some causes of global climate change (with its local effects) are very unlikely to be taken up by local campaigns at all. The greenhouse effect is enhanced by methane gases in the atmosphere, emitted from ruminants and issuing from paddy cultivation, which are both increasing as people in poorer countries 'move up the consumption ladder' (i.e. eat more meat and replace grains and roots such as cassava with rice). There are no reports of demonstrations against increasing cattle herds and paddy fields by campaigners concerned about global climate change!

A recent research project has produced 'ten suggestions for policy makers' addressing climate change, some of which reflect also the importance of local issues and the importance of changes in other 'capitals' (see chapter 3), as summarised below. This still means that the problem of climate change and the mechanisms that cause it should be addressed by lobbyists intent on influencing global policies that affect climate change; in fact, they might use the suggestions below in their engagements with influential people and organisations. Central to negotiations about climate are of course the governments of the high consumers – the G8 (i.e. the G7 plus Russia), and also China, India, Brazil and other large, industrialising, and middle-income countries. Furthermore, the World Bank, which manages the Global Environmental Facility (GEF), UNEP, and the Intergovernmental Panel on Climatic Change (IPCC, set up by the World Meteorological Organisation and UNEP) are important actors too. The strongest opposition to reductions comes from the obvious sources: oil-producing countries and companies.

Ten suggestions for policy makers concerned about climate change[61]

1. View the issue of climate change holistically, not just as a matter of reducing harmful emissions.
2. Recognise that, for policy making on climatic issues, institutional limits to global sustainability are at least as important as environmental limits.
3. Prepare for the likelihood that social, economic, and technological change will be more rapid and have greater direct impacts on human populations than climate change.
4. Recognise the limits of rational planning.
5. Employ the full range of analytic perspectives and aids to decision-making from the natural and social sciences and humanities.
6. Design policy instruments for real-world conditions, rather than trying to make the world conform to a particular policy model.
7. Incorporate concerns about climate change into other more immediate issues, such as employment, defence, economic development, and public health.
8. Take a regional and local approach to climate-policy making and implementation.
9. Invest resources in identifying vulnerability and promoting resilience, especially where the impacts will be largest.
10. Use a pluralistic approach to decision-making.

5.3.3 Macro-economic policies

Economic liberalisation, mounting national debts, and economic structural adjustment programmes (SAPs) are all part of a wider process of so-called modernisation and globalisation, and are possibly most notable for the gradual loss of national sovereignty in economic and political affairs. Large and rich countries are dominant, of course, in bilateral relations and also in multinational structures and development banks; nevertheless, they are also part of these unstoppable trends. The main structures that have been created for the regulation of and co-operation in the globalising economy (i.e. the IMF, World Bank, and WTO) were set up when some of the driving forces of globalisation were not yet known about, such as present-day information technology.

This book does not set itself the task of unravelling all the strands of the economic change-processes, and in fact there are so many links between them that it is extremely difficult to assess their environmental effects. It is, for example, a very complex task to assess the environmental impacts of economic adjustment programmes and separate those from the impacts of the 'Uruguay Round' of world trade negotiations.[62] However, we do need to consider what effects are possible and have been observed in poor people's livelihoods and environments.

Impacts of Structural Adjustment

Stabilisation and Structural Adjustment Programmes (SAPs) are probably the most wide-ranging expressions of economic liberalisation and modernisation: they promote the principle of 'balancing the books', but also advocate liberalising trade, stimulating exports, and prioritising debt repayment and reduction. More generally they stimulate countries to sign up to mainstream global treaties and conventions. Impacts on livelihoods and environments are clearly not simple or straightforwardly good or bad; they differ from case to case and are highly context-specific. Possible (observed) impacts may be summarised as follows.[63]

- The impact of devaluation may be higher producer prices, increased costs of imported production inputs (such as fertiliser), expansion or reduction of cultivation in ecologically fragile areas, increased use of local resources for soil fertility, or increased soil-nutrient mining. Higher farm returns (from higher producer-prices and increased exports) may result in farmers' investments in land, such as soil and water conservation measures.

- Impacts of price and trade liberalisation may include higher product-prices, in particular for cash (export) crops, but may also include (initial) failure in marketing, increased costs of imported inputs, and an increase in livestock keeping.

- Cuts in public expenditure can lead to a reduced ability to manage forests, reduced research in (sustainable) agriculture, reduced agricultural extension, and less investment in (urban) flood control and (rural) soil and water conservation.

- Impacts on employment can be positive, in particular if land-tenure relations allow urban to rural migration, following higher producer-prices; however, inequality may also increase in response to cuts in expenditure and privatisation, because only the large (rural) producers can maintain the import of production inputs, and because social services (which are particularly important for the most vulnerable people) will inevitably deteriorate.

- Intensification of agriculture can mean more cash-crop cultivation (displacing food crops), and – despite increasingly expensive imported inputs – it can lead to greater use of agro-chemicals. However, increased use of local organic materials is also a possible effect. Farmers may diversify, but adjustment policies usually encourage a focus on a narrow range of cash-crops. Because of improved agricultural terms of trade, migration from towns to rural areas may occur.

- Debt can be an incentive for unconsidered, exploitative mining, deforestation and fishing, strong support for uncontrolled (and polluting) industrial development, and for export-oriented 'high-chemical-input' agriculture in order to earn foreign exchange at the lowest possible expense. Debt reduction or rescheduling may therefore reduce these pressures.

- Aid money is just a very small fraction of international financial transfers. Finance and trade are dominated by banks and transnational corporations (TNCs) from OECD countries which own patents on technologies and on genetic materials. The products of these technologies (such as genetically modified crops) and the technologies themselves are difficult for the South to acquire, but may be essential for countries that are trying to pursue more sustainable development paths, if they are applied in ways that support livelihoods and environmental quality, instead of merely boosting the profits of TNCs.

Obviously macro-economic policies can have significant impacts, either positive or negative, on environmental quality and local livelihoods, depending on the situation. A group of NGOs assessed the impacts of adjustment and stabilisation policies on Nicaragua, in particular on the viability of peasant agriculture and basic-grain production.[64] It was concluded that the combined impacts of price and tariff policies affected agricultural goods strongly, putting producers in a highly unfavourable position with respect to international markets. Peasant labour was exploited as a result of credit restrictions, and weak marketing systems were seen as limiting the livelihood development of rural women especially. The report calls for price controls, especially with regards to basic grains; better rural infrastructure (storage, transport) in order to access local, regional, and international markets; and an improved credit-delivery system.

Conditionality, SAPs, and trade

An important issue in all international relations and negotiations, and certainly where structural adjustment programmes are concerned, is 'conditionality'. Richer, larger, and more powerful nations can demand that certain conditions are met before other countries are granted a place at the table, let alone before they can benefit from preferential trade agreements, aid, or debt-relief and restructuring packages. 'Green conditionality' has appeared too and in some cases has been likened to 'green imperialism', in particular in the context of North–South relations. Most environmental regulations are stronger in the richer countries; this has been construed as an argument for saying that environmentalism is a rich-country luxury and a new way of keeping developing countries poor and backward. Of course the main reason for comparatively strong regulation in the North is that environmental risks are so much higher, with high degrees of industrialisation and resource consumption, and extensive transport systems based on fossil fuels.

The differences over environmental regulation between North and South lead to controversy in trade negotiations, in which there is a risk for developing countries that the markets of rich nations will be closed to them if they do not follow the environmental (and social) standards of the rich nations. Why would Malaysia (for example) refrain from using or selling all the trees from its natural forests, when Great Britain did the same thing a two–three hundred years ago? Why would any newly industrialising country adhere to the current pollution standards of the USA, a nation that was polluting its own soils and waters most harmfully just a few decades ago? For answers to such questions, one needs to look first at the needs, environments, and livelihoods of the populations of Malaysia and other developing countries, and the interests of their children. It is obvious that pollution and large-scale deforestation are not usually in their interests, nor in the interest of the national economy. (This becomes visible if environmental externalities are properly accounted for.) However, financial resources to invest in the latest and 'cleanest' technology are also limited, and some sort of compromise between short-term production gains and longer-term economic and environmental sustainability will need to be found. The international community can help, for example by finding ways to make the latest technology available to developing countries.

Northern environmental standards were not set objectively: they are the outcome of political choices made by the people and governments concerned, even though discussion and decision will always be based on some scientific evidence. Standards for acceptable pollution of surface water, for example, change continuously in response to new scientific evidence of the effects on health, the election of new governments, and changed economic conditions. Also, the standards need enforcing, and this can happen only with local political support. Where ethical, environmental, and health issues are of concern to consumers, it is reasonable to expect that their voice is heard and that production conditions are explained on mandatory labels (as in 'fair' or 'ethical' trade). However, labelling can be seen as one of many restrictions on import, and exporting countries do not want importers to dictate how they should produce their goods. A famous case where import restrictions were not allowed on environmental and ethical grounds under GATT rules is the US ban on imports of tuna from Mexico, where tuna fishing was harmful to dolphins. The US ban implied an extension of the jurisdiction of a country beyond its borders, and it was not allowed by the global trade regulators.[65] The same type of dilemma dominated the 'shrimp-turtle case', where the WTO ruled that the USA cannot ban imports of shrimps caught with techniques that harm migratory sea turtles, following a challenge from exporting countries, including India, Malaysia, and Thailand. This case also showed several flaws in the legal capacity of the WTO to rule on environmental matters.[66]

Trade policies, biotechnology, and biodiversity

Trade-related international policies and policy-making processes have very strong implications for food security and biodiversity, as the following shows.[67]

The USA and the EU now have policies in place that make both plants and plant-breeding processes patentable, although the EU directive still meets opposition in some of the member countries, who are all expected to incorporate it in their national legislation. Biotechnological processes (i.e. technologies) and their products (i.e. genetically modified, or GM, crops) must be novel, inventive (not a discovery), and capable of industrial application in order to be eligible for patenting. An example from the USA is the grant to W.G. Grace & Co. and Monsanto of a patent on *neem* products, with applications for use as pesticides and also in human health – despite the fact that the *neem* tree and its many products and applications have been publicly known for centuries in India. The standard criteria for patenting (especially those of novelty and invention) were obviously not applied.

Not all countries have well-developed patenting systems, and few have included life-forms as patentable (notably the USA, Japan, and European countries). The existence of a patent in a country has implications for trade with others, even though the patent applies only to that country. For example, when the harvest of a particular crop (variety) is traded with a country that recognises a patent (i.e. private rights) on its genetic make-up, the patent holder can claim royalties or import restrictions, even though the patent is not legally reinforceable in the country where the crop was grown. This became a real threat in the case of the export of harvests of the staple food quinoa in Bolivia, when US researchers effectively patented (in the USA) the Apalawa variety and indirectly other traditional varieties.

The agreement on Trade Related Intellectual Property Rights (TRIPS) is incorporated in the WTO regulations: its article 27.3b requires all countries to 'provide for the protection of plant varieties either by patents or by an effective *sui generis* system'. *Sui generis* refers to a system that at least regulates intellectual property rights in some way. There are opportunities for developing effective systems that do not demand full patenting, but they are complex and costly, and will effectively have to be endorsed by the international community. The text is thus very ambiguous and will be renegotiated (which may result in more flexibility for developing countries, or force them to edge closer to including life-forms in national patent systems). With most industrialised countries now in agreement over the patenting of life forms, the opposition from the rest of the world will have to be very strong indeed to protect local biodiversity, farmers' rights to save and re-use seeds, and traditional processes to extract plant properties. The Indian government and particularly Indian activists are in the forefront of the opposition to protect the livelihoods of small farmers, together with farmers themselves. The existing TRIPS agreement must be implemented in developing countries by 2000, or 2006 for the least-developed countries.

The UPOV Convention on Plant Breeders' Rights was agreed in 1991 and many countries had signed up for it by 1999. UPOV is a system that could be the '*sui generis*' system that is required under the TRIPS agreement of the WTO. It allows individual entities (which means in practice large farms and seed companies) to claim rights over the crop varieties that they breed from older varieties. Unlike patenting systems, UPOV does not allow claims of intellectual rights over the processes or techniques to create new varieties, i.e. traditional breeding or modern biotechnological processes. However, this is not a mechanism that can protect farmers' seed-saving rights; nor does it recognise the efforts of generations of farmers in selecting and breeding crop varieties, because registration requires crop varieties to be distinct, uniform, and stable, which traditional varieties generally are not. This system of regulating breeders' rights (and patenting even more so) effectively enables those who manage to alter two or three genes out of the thousands of genes of a particular crop species to claim rights over that variety's seeds and the off-spring of the seeds.

The WTO–TRIPS agreement and the Convention on Biodiversity (CBD) are both signed by most countries of the world and are both legally binding, but they conflict with each other, and neither is very clear. The CBD, finalised in December 1993, is a legally binding treaty to stop the destruction of biological diversity and to protect species; it established guidelines for the sharing of research, information, profits, and technology in genetic research. However, it has not been signed by all interested governments, and most notably the US (Senate) has so far opposed it. The CBD promotes the sharing of benefits of genetic resources, but TRIPS promotes their commercialisation and privatisation. Calls to strengthen the CBD cite various cases of 'bio-piracy'. Bio-prospecting is mostly carried out for the pharmaceutical industry, but it is expected to play an important role in the research and development of genetically modified (GM) crops and plants.

The International Undertaking on Plant Genetic Resources (IU) stresses national sovereignty over the 'common heritage' of seeds and plants, in line with the CBD, and aims to preserve, collect, and make plant species widely available for breeding and other purposes. Current negotiations are seen as a key opportunity to gain sufficient guarantees for farmers' rights, in particular if the EU supports African nations and many other developing countries in accepting the IU as a legally binding protocol under the CBD. By late 1999 the IU was still a non-binding agreement, and some important countries had not signed it, including the USA, Japan, Brazil, China, and Malaysia.[68]

The parties to the CBD are negotiating a so-called Bio-safety Protocol, aiming at the safe transfer, handling, and use of living modified organisms, and focusing on trans-boundary movement. Many NGOs argue that a global moratorium on commercial releases of GM crops and trade in their products is needed until the risks are properly known, and issues of liability and also intellectual property rights have been agreed. They would welcome a Bio-safety Protocol that covered issues of liability and compensation for the calamities that can result from the transport and release of GM crops. Negotiations stalled in 1999, but appeared to reach a reasonable compromise in early 2000.[69] The Food and Agriculture Organisation (FAO) plays an important role as co-ordinator of some of these discussions, partly because of its technical expertise, and also because it controls the so-called gene-banks of the international agricultural research centres of the CGIAR system.[70]

Trade and agriculture

The WTO's Agreement on Agriculture (AoA), signed in 1994 at the Uruguay Round, is currently being reviewed. It commits signatories to a substantial reduction in the protection of domestic agriculture, with some safeguards for developing countries. Industrialised countries are expected to reduce export subsidies, other financial support for agricultural products, and tariffs on imports more rapidly than developing countries, in six instead of ten years from 1995.[71] However, the levels of subsidies and support for agriculture and farmers by the rich countries were and are likely to remain substantially higher than what most other countries are or would be capable of, leaving them with tariffs as the main way to protect their farmers and food markets. But tariffs must be reduced, according to the agreement.[72] High levels of subsidies in the EU and the USA lead to artificially low world-market prices and effectively to dumping of their surplus production. This creates a very 'uneven playing field' for Third World farmers, who already have difficulty in competing, because they produce with lower educational levels, less investment capacity, and less-developed extension services, and they trade through less-developed infrastructure and with fewer services.

The safeguards in the AoA for developing countries include the proviso that reform from 1999 should take into account trade and non-trade concerns, and should consider the initial impacts of the AoA on employment, livelihood opportunities, and the national balance of payment. The impacts on world trade and non-trade concerns are of course very difficult to assess, but calls for in-depth research have so far met with only a limited response by the WTO and the rich nations, even though the new round of negotiations is underway (despite setbacks in starting up the negotiations in Seattle in 1999, which were disrupted by vigorous popular protests, and where developing countries voiced strong criticism of the dominance of the USA and EU).

The AoA is expected to have a particular impact on the prices of certain commodities, on world-market price stability, and on the food-import bills of the Least Developed Countries (LDCs) and Net Food Importing Developing Countries (NFIDCs).[73] Initial analysis suggests the following:

- Prices of commodities such as cereals and meat rose as a result of the AoA, in particular because of a reduction of subsidies in the EU and USA, but a reduction of world-market prices from 1996 till late 1999 (and further downward pressures) suggests that this impact may have been temporary and that other factors may be more important.

- The expectation of greater stability in world-market prices has been questioned, in particular in the short term, for example because of the potentially destabilising effects of reduction of government stocks following liberalisation. The few data from the short period since implementation of the AoA are insufficient to draw any conclusions in this regard.

- The effects on the food-importation bills of developing countries have been negative. Because of their continuing debt burden, these countries are rendered more vulnerable to sudden calamities such as drought that would result in steeply increased food bills. The LDCs and NFIDCs have depended heavily on concessional food sales and food aid; since 1994 they have been paying higher food prices, and their import volumes have risen. The rise in their average food bill is thus largely attributed to a reduction in food aid, which in turn relates to a (gradual) reduction in over-production, following reductions in agricultural subsidies in rich food-exporting countries. A significant problem is the fact that producers in LDCs and most NFIDCs operate under such disadvantaged circumstances that world-market prices do not translate into effective production incentives.

The AoA allows domestic support measures that have no direct impact on production and are not seen as support measures that distort trade, for example government payments for environmental protection, regional assistance, and training and research programmes. Other domestic support measures that are exempted under the AoA include agricultural input subsidies to low-income producers. These exemptions are (almost) all based on government payments, i.e. subsidies to the agriculture-plus sector, and are less achievable for developing countries, because of a lack of financial resources,[74] although in some developing economies they have been shown to be important. For example, analysis of the impacts of agricultural extension activities and government policies on extremely poor farmers in a remote area in Vietnam showed that even some of the very poorest families within those communities managed to increase productivity and income over the period 1994–1998 (but the increases were smaller than the achievements of the better-off farmers). This was attributed to a number of government policies and measures, in particular to modest subsidisation of hybrid seeds, fertilisers, and livestock medicines (see also section 3.1).[75]

Some activists come close to the position of rejecting altogether the trade policies on food and agriculture as promoted by the WTO. They want policies that aim for national food self-sufficiency and exclusively local food production and consumption chains. In order to safeguard the interests of developing countries and poor women and men farmers and consumers, most lobbyists aim more realistically for amendments. They argue for strengthening of the CBD, a greater role for developing countries in international negotiations, and additional international agreements. Amendments and additions to the AoA should concern in particular the conditions under which domestic support for farming can be provided, in order to strengthen local food systems (including production) and environmental quality.

Lobbying of the main players in international negotiations usually takes place on the basis of analysis of global processes, of detailed information collection, and with case studies of developments in particular countries. An example of this concerns the links between farm subsidies in the industrialised world, global trade rules, and the predicament of farmers and consumers in the Philippines and Mexico.[76] It has been concluded that the WTO and regional trade associations should 'allow developing countries to protect their food systems up to the point of food self-sufficiency for social, ecological and economic reasons', and that the USA and EU should end agricultural subsidies and the dumping of surpluses. Some international campaigning efforts are carried in part by grassroots action. In the case of GM crops and patenting of life-forms, farmers in India play a key role, with their vocal leaders. A large part of the people's movement in India has adopted Gandhian tactics of non-violent civil disobedience and campaigns for self-reliance, despite instances of State violence (see also chapter 2). Hundreds of heavily indebted farmers committed suicide after the failure of harvests of hybrid cotton that proved to have little resistance to pests and drought. This tragedy created an important impetus for protests against Monsanto, national patent laws, and WTO policies, and received broad international media coverage.

Sometimes international campaigns focus on just one particular regional case, in order to address an urgent problem. An example of that is the preferential banana trade from Caribbean island States to Europe. These countries and their farmers are extremely dependent on the trade with Europe, but are relatively uncompetitive compared with large US-based corporations with plantations in Central America and elsewhere. The former British and French colonies were allowed quotas for export to Europe for a certain period of time (allowing for gradual diversification and to make investments to improve productivity and competitiveness), and US corporations complained of being excluded from a large market. This preferential treatment of some former colonies developed into a serious dispute between the USA and the EU. The WTO ultimately decided that the USA was justified in imposing retaliatory trade sanctions on exports from the EU of wholly unrelated products, in respect of forgone trade in bananas that are not even grown in the USA.

Oxfam and several other international NGOs have supported Caribbean NGOs and States in their efforts to convince the EU of the validity of their cause, and they made initially good progress. Work to develop alternative trade in coffee from those and similar countries has also been on-going for some years, and channels for fairly traded bananas have been opened up too. This is based on collaboration between national producers' groups and fair-trade organisations in several European countries, including Max Havelaar in the Netherlands and the Oxfam Fair Trade Company in the UK. Fair trade aims to by-pass the 'middlemen' and pay fairer prices directly to producers, and also to ensure decent working conditions and environment-friendly production. Fairly traded coffee has achieved a significant market share in several European countries, and in the case of bananas there is hope that some of the problems of Caribbean farmers caused by the decision of the WTO will be alleviated.[77] Many 'fair traders' have also taken steps to ensure that their food products are GM-free, and in many cases they are organically grown – with benefits for consumers, producers, and environments.

Epilogue

The global environmental changes and macro-economic policies discussed in the last section of this chapter are often beyond the immediate experience of poor and excluded people, and also beyond the interests of development professionals who work to reduce poverty. That does not make the global environmental changes less pertinent, or the macro-policies that influence them less important.

The sustainable livelihoods framework suggests that macro-policies and structures of governance can influence the trends and shocks to which poor people are particularly vulnerable. The less-natural disasters such as droughts and floods appear to increase in unpredictability and severity with climate change, which is at least partly the result of human action. Human action can by definition be influenced by policy. For example, airline fuel could be taxed, which would limit excessive air travel and false competition with other modes of transport, and would help society to take responsibility for economic externalities borne by the environment. There are macro policies that can influence all kinds of global or regional trends and shocks. All of these policies are primarily made by national governments, and sometimes in international forums, such as the World Trade Organisation.

There is ample evidence to show that poor and excluded people can influence policies of their governments and the multilateral agencies created by them. Marginalised people do not generally want to influence policies for the sake of the global environment, but rather because they want to protect and improve their own livelihood opportunities and local environments. However, the power and agency of social classes or 'target groups' is generally limited: they are not usually social actors. Poor and excluded people need representatives and the support of agencies and organisations that have an interest in helping them to improve their situation and that have (or can generate) influence.

The effects of the policies of governments and large enterprises on local environments and livelihoods must be understood, and warnings must be issued as soon as the indications are negative. Public policies can also support livelihood strategies; they can stimulate regeneration of natural capital, or they can for example help to enhance awareness of environmental change (that is, they can help to build up knowledge and human capital). Nevertheless, poor people themselves are the main resource and the main force for improvement of their livelihoods and environments.

People are their own human capital; they decide their own livelihood strategies; they invest their time and their savings in physical, social, and natural capitals. They bring up their children and provide them with education, and thus reproduce life and society. That completely obvious truth is also the main reason why people – and certainly poor and marginalised people – will generally be a force for environmental conservation.

This book has attempted to explain some of the complexity of livelihoods, the relationships between poverty and environmental change, and some of the variety of responses of deprived people to environmental challenges. It set out to explore the reasons why environments are important in poverty alleviation, and also to offer some guidance to development professionals in helping people to improve both their livelihoods and their environments. I hope that its contents will prove to be of value.

Appendix 1:
Selected international agreements on the environment[1]

Early agreements

1911 Convention for the Protection and Preservation of Fur Seals

1923 Convention for the Preservation of the Halibut Fishery of the Northern Pacific Ocean and the Bering Sea

1931 Convention on the Regulation of Whaling

1940 Convention on the Nature Protection and Wildlife Preservation in the Western Hemisphere

1951 International Plant Protection Convention

1954 Convention for the Prevention of Pollution of the Sea by Oil

1958 Convention on Fishing and Conservation of the Living Resources of the High Seas

1959 Antarctic Treaty

1963 Treaty Banning Nuclear Weapons Tests in the Atmosphere, in Outer Space and Under Water

1964 Agreed Measures on the Conservation of Antarctic Fauna and Flora

1967 Treaty on Principles Governing the Activities of States in the Exploration and Use of Outer Space, including the Moon and other Celestial Bodies

Species and habitat

1971 Convention on Wetlands of International Strategic Importance Especially as Waterfowl Habitat (Ramsar Convention) – managed by IUCN/IWRB

1972 Convention Concerning the Protection of the World Cultural and Natural Heritage (World Heritage Convention) – managed by UNESCO

1973 Convention on Endangered Species (formerly known as Convention on International Trade of Endangered Species of Wild Fauna and Flora (CITES))

1979 Convention on the Conservation of Migratory Species of Wild Animals (Bonn Convention) – managed by UNEP

1980 Convention on the Conservation of Antarctic Marine Living Resources (CCAMLR) – managed by CCAMLR secretariat

1991 Protocol to the Antarctic Treaty on Conservation

1993 Convention on Biological Diversity

1996 Convention to Combat Desertification in those Countries Experiencing Drought and/or Desertification Particularly in Africa (opened for signature October 1994 and entered into force December 1996)

Marine pollution and conservation

1972 Convention on the Prevention of Marine Pollution by Dumping Wastes and Other Matter (London Dumping Convention)

1973 International Convention for the Prevention of Pollution from Ships and the Protocol of 1978 Relating Thereto with Annex (MARPOL 73/78) – managed by IMO

1982 Convention on the Law of the Sea (entered into force in 1994) – managed by United Nations Office of Ocean Affairs and Law of the Sea (OALOS)

1991 International Convention on Oil Pollution Preparedness, Response and Co-operation – managed by IMO

1992 Convention on the Protection and Use of Transboundary Watercourses and International Lakes

1994 Buenos Aires Convention on the Protection of Underwater Cultural Heritage

1995 Agreement for the Implementation of the Provisions of the United Nations Convention on the Law of the Sea Relating to the Conservation and Management of Fishing Stocks and High Migratory Fish Stocks

Hazardous substances

1986 Convention on Early Notification of a Nuclear Accident

1986 Convention on Assistance in the Case of a Nuclear Accident or Radiological Emergency

1989 Convention on the Control of Transboundary Movement of Hazardous Wastes (Basel Convention)

1991 Ban on the Import within Africa and the Control of Transboundary Movement and Management of Hazardous Waste within Africa (Bamako Convention)

1996 Convention on Liability and Compensation for Damage in Connection with the Carriage of Hazardous Noxious Substances by Sea

1996 Comprehensive Test Ban Treaty

Pollution of the atmosphere

1979 Convention on Long-Range Transboundary Air Pollution (LRTAP) – managed by UN/ECE

1985 Helsinki Protocol on the Reduction of Sulphur Emissions or Their Transboundary Fluxes by at least 30 Per Cent

1985 Vienna Convention for the Protection of the Ozone Layer

1987 Montreal Protocol on Substances that Deplete the Ozone Layer

1988 Sofia Protocol Concerning the Control of Emissions of Nitrogen Oxides or Their Transboundary Fluxes

1992 Framework Convention on Climate Change

1997 Conference of Parties to the Framework Convention on Climate Change (resulting in the Kyoto Protocol)

1998 Draft Protocol to the Convention of Long-Range Transboundary Air Pollution on Resistant Organic Pollutants

Environment and development: general

1991 Convention on Environmental Impact Assessment in a Transboundary Context

1992 Draft Declaration on the Rights of Indigenous Peoples

1993 Convention on Civil Liberty for Damage Resulting from Activities Dangerous to the Environment

1994 Draft Declaration of Principles on Human Rights and the Environment

Global conferences

1972 United Nations Conference on the Human Environment (UNHCE) (Stockholm)

1976 Human Settlements Conference, Habitat I (Vancouver)

1987 IUCN Ottawa Conference on Conservation and Development

1992 United Nations Conference on Environment and Development (UNCED), the Earth Summit (Rio de Janeiro)

1994 International Conference on Population and Development (Cairo)

1994 International Conference on Chemical Safety (Stockholm)

1995 The World Summit for Social Development (Copenhagen)

1995 Fourth World Conference on Women (Beijing)

1996 Habitat II (Istanbul)

1996 World Food Summit (Rome)

1997 Earth Summit II, United Nations General Assembly Special Session (UNGASS, New York)

1997 Conference of the Parties of the Climate Change Convention (COP 3, Kyoto)

2000 Five Year Review of the 1995 Copenhagen Summit for Social Development

2002 Earth Summit III

Appendix 2:
Sources of information on environment and development

National environmental data and other data are now in part available in a user-friendly way in publications produced by the UNDP, World Bank, UNEP, and other organisations. Specific data that inform (or should inform) national environmental strategies and descriptive documents tend to be bulky, difficult to access, and – if accessible – technical. Less specific data are not always useful, given the fact that national and regional policy by its very nature needs to be based on aggregated data; but they inform policy making.

The internet is an extremely useful source of information. The UN agencies and some of the development banks have set up websites for specific country programmes. Private organisations, including NGOs and networks of municipalities, research organisations, and bilateral development agencies, tend to provide documentation on a range of subjects, apart from an overview of their own programmes and policies. It is possible to give only a small selection of websites here, but most of them provide links to others.

Multilateral organisations

Website	Name	Type of information available
http://www.unep.org http://www.unep.ch	United Nations Environment Programme (Nairobi, with an important sub-office in Geneva)	• Global and regional environmental data, reports, and literature references, including the annual *World Resources* report with comprehensive data. • Information on international environment conventions.

Website	Name	Type of information available
http://www.fao.org	United Nations Food and Agriculture Organisation (Rome)	• Information on food security and agriculture, including national and international food stocks, prices, production, and 'undernourishment'. • Also information on nutrition, fisheries, land tenure, sustainable development, etc. • Text of FAO reports.
http://www.undp.org	United Nations Development Programme (UNDP; New York)	• The UNDP's *Human Development Report* is published annually and is thematic; for example in 1998 it was concerned with consumption, and in 1999 with globalisation. It always contains data that enable conclusions on environmental pressures and changes. • Many other reports can be downloaded too.
http://www3.undp.org/	UNDP	• Information from the UNDP sustainable-development networking programme, which helps to develop electronic networks in many countries.
http://www.undp.org/sl/	UNDP	• Information from the UNDP sustainable-livelihoods programme, as part of the UNDP's poverty-eradication strategy.
http://www.undp.org/popin/	UNDP	• All sorts of population statistics available in graphic form.
http://www.worldbank.org	International Bank for Reconstruction and Development (IBRD; Washington DC)	• The annual *World Development Report* provides global statistics based on national aggregates; the version for 2000/01 focuses on poverty. • Many other reports and publications can be downloaded or ordered.
http://www.worldbank.org/poverty/	World Bank	• A site specifically focused on poverty alleviation, with an increasing amount of information.

Website	Name	Type of information available
http://www.worldbank.org/html/pic/ENVIR.html	World Bank	• Focus on research and policy for environmentally and socially sustainable development; most documents can be downloaded.
http://www.un.org/esa/sustdev/csd.htm	UN Commission for Sustainable Development (CSD, New York)	• The CSD was set up in Rio (UNCED, 1992) at ministerial level. It has annual meetings. The secretariat is central to the implementation of Agenda 21 and helps to organise follow-up meetings to UNCED, such as 'Earth-Summit+10' in 2002. The website provides information about the current topics of concern.
http://www.unchs.org/	United Nations Centre For Human Settlements (Habitat; Nairobi)	• This UN agency leads on urban development, provides access to publications, and runs campaigns, for example on tenure and urban governance. It has many programmes, including its sustainable-cities programme. It has six regional offices.
http://www.unhcr.ch/	United Nations High Commissioner for Refugees (UNHCR), responsible for the protection and welfare of refugees.	• The UNHCR has a policy and operational guidelines to minimise the impact of refugees on the environment; the guidelines can be downloaded.
http://www.cgiar.org/	Consultative Group on International Agricultural Research (CGIAR)	• A collective of publicly funded agricultural research organisations that work on crops, crop bio-diversity conservation, and biotechnology. Through this website and the links to member organisations, many reports and publications are accessible.
http://www.gefweb.org/	Global Environment Facility	• A fund for large projects with (global) environmental benefits, particularly concerned with energy (climate) and biodiversity.

Website	Name	Type of information available
http://www.wmo.ch/	World Meteorological Organisation (Geneva)	• Much information and links available, for example on the El Niño effect.
http://www.ipcc.ch/	Intergovernmental Panel on Climate Change (IPCC, of WMO/UNEO)	• This panel of experts compiles international research on climate change and provides much relevant information.
http://www.unfccc.de/	UN Framework Convention on Climate Change	• Information on progress in the negotiations to reduce greenhouse-gas pollution and climate change.

Research and information on environment and development

Website	Name	Type of information available
http://www.wcmc.org.uk	World Conservation Monitoring Centre (Cambridge, UK)	• Established by UNEP, WWF, and IUCN, with a focus on providing information about bio-diversity information, but also on climate change.
http://www.wri.org	World Resources Institute (Washington DC)	• Many publications and reports accessible, on a range of environmental subjects. • Provides links.
http://iisd1.iisd.ca/	IISD (Canada)	• Publishes on the Web a very large number of documents from inter-national negotiations on environ-mental issues and provides access to academic research and publications. • Provides links.
http://www.iied.org/	International Institute for Environment and Development (IIED, London)	• Many publications and reports may be ordered, on a range of environmental subjects.
http://www.worldwatch.org/	The Worldwatch Institute	• Publishes the annual *State of the World* reports.

Appendix 2: Sources of information on environment and development

Website	Name	Type of information available
http://www.odi.org.uk/	Overseas Development Institute (ODI; London)	• Publishes on many subjects related to natural-resource management, and particularly on sustainable livelihoods.
http://www.ids.ac.uk/ids	Institute of Development Studies at the University of Sussex, UK, including the Rural Sustainable Livelihoods Programme	• Access to the Development Studies library database, IDS publications, and to ELDIS, a gateway to development organisations. • IDS is at the forefront of research, with publications on participatory methodologies and sustainable livelihoods.
http://www.oneworld.org/panos/	Panos Institute (London, with regional centres)	• Information on sustainable development, with a global outlook.
http://sdgateway.net/webring/default.htm	Sustainability web-ring	• Provides access to many websites on sustainable development.

NGOs working on environment and development

Website	Name	Type of information available
http://www.oneworld.org	Oneworld	• An internet community of hundreds of development organisations and also environment NGOs.
http://www.iucn.org	World Conservation Union (Gland, Switzerland)	• Offers on-line publications on a range of environmental subjects. • With regional or national centres.
http://www.panda.org/	World Wide Fund for Nature (WWF-global)	• Network of 27 national organisations. • Research and project information available from around the world, including *The Living Planet Report*, 1999.
http://www.greenpeace.org/	Greenpeace – International	• Campaigns on climate change, genetic engineering, forest conservation, etc. • Many national affiliates.

Website	Name	Type of information available
http://www.foei.org/ http://www.foe.co.uk/	Friends of the Earth (FoE) – International, and FoE-UK	• FOE-International has 61 groups in as many countries. • Campaigns and information on climate change, trade and environment, mining, and sustainable agriculture, etc.
http://www.climatenetwork. org	Climate Action Network	• With 269 members and a focus on lobbying the parties to the Climate Convention.
http://www.twnside.org.sg/	Third World Network (TWN)	• Networks with various organisations, particularly in the South. • Publishes on biotechnology, environment and trade issues, etc.
http://www.rafi.org/	Rural Advancement Foundation International (RAFI; Winnipeg, Canada)	• Campaigns on agricultural biodiversity, and concerned about the impact of intellectual property rules and practices on agriculture and world food security. • Many papers available on-line.
http://www.ukfg.org.uk http://ds.dial.pipex.com/uk fg/ukabc.htm	UK Food Group, with UKabc (agricultural biodiversity, conservation)	• Documents and links on food security, agriculture, and agricultural biodiversity.
http://www.grain.org/	Genetic Resources Action International (GRAIN; based in Spain, the Philippines, and Uruguay)	• Campaigns on the loss of biological diversity. • Many papers available on-line.
http://www.bluekey.co.uk\ gcuk	Green Cross UK aims to prevent and respond to environmental disasters and raise public awareness.	• Information on the Environmental Response Network (ERN), which provides information, responds to queries, and has a database of environmental specialists.
http://www.oneworld.org/ cse/	Centre for Science and Environment (New Delhi)	• Campaigns and provides information on a range of subjects, including biodiversity and climate change.

Website	Name	Type of information available
http://oxfam.org.uk	Oxfam GB (member of Oxfam international)	• Provides policy papers on trade, debt, education, and other campaigning issues, including genetically modified crops.
http://www.oxfam.org.hk	Oxfam Hong Kong (member of Oxfam International)	• Information on campaigns, addressing food security and sustainable agriculture.
http://www.novib.nl/	Novib (Dutch member of Oxfam International)	• Information for partners in several languages.
http://www.actionaid.org	ActionAid (UK-based international development NGO)	• Information on a range of policy issues, including biodiversity and biotechnology.
Http://www.oneworld.org/ itdg/	Intermediate Technology Development Group (ITDG, UK)	• Operates research, project management, and publishing programmes.
and http://www.itdg.org.pe	Specialises in appropriate-technology transfer. The ITDG-Peru website is partly in Spanish	• Runs Intermediate Technology Consultants (ITC), providing technical and business support for small-scale enterprises in Africa, Asia, and Latin America. • Intermediate Technology Publications publishes a wide range of books on environment and other development issues.
http://www.ifrc.org	International Federation of the Red Cross and Red Crescent	• Information on environmental health in emergency situations.
http://www.iclei.org	The International Council for Local Environmental Initiatives (ICLEI)	• Gives information on local initiatives and provides links to various partners.

Website	Name	Type of information available
www.care.org	CARE (a federation of 10 international development NGOs)	• Supplies project examples and brief reports on responses to natural disasters, sustainable livelihoods, etc. CARE's work on sustainable livelihoods is particularly developed in Southern Africa.
www.scfuk.org.uk	Save the Children Fund UK (a member of a network of similar international development organisations)	• Publishes various manuals on project planning and on what is known as 'the household economy approach', which is somewhat similar to the concept of sustainable livelihoods.
http://www.dfid.gov.uk	DFID (UK government's Department for International Development)	• Has a special site on sustainable livelihoods: go to 'Strategies for Achieving International Development Targets' from the home page.

Publishers who specialise in environment and other development issues

Routledge: http://www.routledge.com

Earthscan: http://www.earthscan.co.uk

Oxford University Press: http://www.oup.co.uk

Island Press: http://www.islandpress.com

IT Publications: http://www.oneworld.org/itdg/publications.html

Oxfam Publishing: http://www.oxfam.org.uk/publications.html

Notes

Chapter 1

1   From an exchange meeting under the South-South Environment Linking project of Oxfam (UK & Ireland), Thursday 10.9.92 and Friday, 11.9.92. Translated from the original Spanish text.

2   As far as Oxfam goes, see for example Bull (1982), Jackson with Eade (1982), Davidson and Myers, with Chakraborty (1992). Eade and Williams (1995), *The Oxfam Handbook of Development and Relief,* contains sections on urban and rural environmental change, agriculture, 'ecofeminism', and methodological approaches to finding out about environmental change – all within the conceptual framework of 'sustainable livelihoods'. See also Caroline LeQuesne, 'Ecological footprints', in Watkins (1995a). Oxfam GB (formerly UK & Ireland) has published a range of practical books about agriculture, pastoralism and livestock keeping, seeds and tools distribution for rehabilitation following disasters, and many other topics. Furthermore, a large number of project evaluation reports, commissioned research, and 'unofficial' internal publications form an important body of experience on which this book is based – see bibliography. Also important to mention are four editions of 'Exchanging Livelihoods', collections of case studies written by staff and sometimes partner staff for institutional learning purposes, several of which are referred to in this book. Particularly relevant publications from DFID are ODA (1996), Carney (1998), DFID (1999a, b) and CRDT/DFID (1998). Publications from ITDG and IT Publishing relevant to this book are Hubbard (1995), ITDG-Bangladesh / REMS (1999), Scott (1998), Hall *et al.* (1996), and other books from IT Publishing, mentioned in the bibliography.

3   See e.g. Davidson and Myers (1992) and Borrini-Feyerabend (1997).

4   That there remain important questions concerned with the 'why?' of environment is concluded from, for example, work with national NGOs in Uganda who are partners of Novib (Neefjes and Nakacwa, 1996) and wider assessments internal to Novib; a survey conducted in 1998-99 of Oxfam staff and partners in national

programmes around the world on achievements in learning about sustainable development (Neefjes and Woldegiorgis, 1999); and interviews with higher-level managers in Oxfam in 1999. Learning needs were also exposed in two earlier assessments by student-volunteers of the practice of environmental assessment in ITDG and Oxfam: Pasteur (1994) and Moorehead (1992).

5   In Oxfam GB there is evidence of a marked improvement in attempts to relate poverty to environmental changes as part of this kind of planning during the 1990s.

6   These discussions were with 'Regional Managers' of Oxfam in particular: Neefjes (May 1999), 'On Sustainable Livelihoods, Poverty and Environment, interviews with Regional Managers', unpublished mimeo, Oxfam GB. Gaps were also confirmed in a large number of informal discussions with Oxfam 'Country Representatives' and a number of Novib and ITDG managers over the last few years.

7   The same is true for most other international development NGOs; see Pasteur (1994) about ITDG and also other NGOs; and Moorehead (1992), Neefjes and Woldegiorgis (1999) about Oxfam GB. Training of hundreds of staff and also Oxfam partners in 'sustainable livelihoods', environmental impact, and participatory approaches intensified from 1992 but did not take place in all countries where Oxfam has a programme. A one-page guideline with key questions / issues that need to be addressed during the grant-approval process was forwarded in early 1995 to all staff (David and Neefjes, 1995); and more detailed suggestions are offered in Eade and Williams (1995). See chapter 4 of this book for practical suggestions to improve the appraisal of project grants from the perspective of environmental sustainability.

8   See Oxfam (1996, 1999) 'Exchanging Livelihoods', editions on urban development and natural-resource management; see also Hall *et al.* (1996), which shows examples of urban work of ITDG, Oxfam GB, and other development NGOs based in the UK.

9   Many reports are available in Oxfam, ITDG, and other international NGOs regarding such training workshops, with evidence of positive immediate feedback but no assessment of impacts some time after the training. Neefjes and Woldegiorgis (1999) report a brief impact-study of training in sustainable livelihoods and participatory project approaches, conducted for Oxfam GB. The first Oxfam GB workshop for staff in which the sustainable livelihoods framework was used for analysis of relationships between people and environmental change took place in Cambodia in 1992 for field staff and partners, and for higher-level managers in Thailand, 1993 (Neefjes, 1993a and 1993b). Oxfam adopted sustainable livelihoods as a 'strategic aim' for its international programme in 1993; CARE has also developed similar policies in the early 1990s under the label 'household livelihood security framework', as have UNDP and (later) DFID. Progress with and comparisons between more recent adaptations of the framework are reported by Carney *et al.* (1999) and Ashley and Carney (1999).

10   See for example Chambers and Conway (1992), Scoones (1998), Carney (1998).

11   See Estrella and Gaventa (1997), Abbot and Guijt (1998), and Roche (1999).

Chapter 2

1   P. Lal (1965), p. 54.

2   M.K. Gandhi (1980), p. 181.

3   Guha and Martinez-Alier (1997).

4   Ian Harris, 'Buddhism', in Holm (1994), p.26.

5   *Yang* stands for light, movement, life, masculine, fire, heaven, and 'positive'; and *yin* stands for dark, rest, matter, feminine, water, earth, and 'negative'.

6   See Xinzhong Yao, 'Chinese religions', in Holm (1994).

7   See Martin Forward and Mohamed Alam, 'Islam', in Holm (1994).

8   Quoted in Hayward (1994), p. 30.

9   Ponting (1991), pp. 141-6.

10   Quoted in Davidson and Myers (1992), p.184.

11   Meadows *et al.* (1972).

12   WCED (1987), p. 43; see also sections 2.2 and 2.4.

13   See also A. Gupta and M. Asher (1998) *Environment and the Developing World: Principles, Policy and Management* (Wiley).

14   See Gupta and Asher (1998).

15   For analysis of the Earth Summit II, see D. Osborn and T. Bigg (1998) *Earth Summit II Outcomes and Analysis,* Earthscan, London.

16   Guha and Martinez-Alier (1997), pp. 16-17.

17   Naess (1973).

18   Guha and Martinez-Alier (1997), pp. 92-108.

19   Conservation-based organisations such as the World Wide Fund for Nature and the World Conservation Union (WWF and IUCN) have policies that echo the ideas of John Muir, although they have increasingly become sympathetic to the interests and strengths of local people as wildlife managers. WWF and IUCN have become actual implementers of projects for the conservation of nature, while Greenpeace International is an organisation with national affiliates whose campaigns focus on particular issues of environmental destruction and pollution. Friends of the Earth is a politically more radical international grouping of national organisations, the first of which was a breakaway group from John Muir's Sierra Club, in 1969. Many within this network are concerned about social justice in general, and not exclusively with the preservation of particular environments. Deep ecology and also ideas such as the Gaia hypothesis of Lovelock have found sympathisers among very radical 'eco-warriors' in groups like Earth First in the USA and the UK. Some of those groups have internationalised – they have set up organisations and projects in the East and South, and they have broadened their views and support base. See for example Pepper (1984).

20   Guha and Martinez-Alier (1997), p. 100.

21   Hayward (1994), p. 195.

22 Guha and Martinez-Alier (1997), p.76.

23 Davidson and Myers (1992).

24 Ken Saro-Wiwa, cited in Watts (1998).

25 Watts (1998), p. 257; see also Guha and Martinez-Alier (1997), pp. xviii–xx.

26 Many examples, and lessons on process management of 'alternatives', are articulated by Chambers (1997) and Gibson (1996), Pye-Smith *et al.* (1994), Davidson and Myers (1992), and Guijt and Shah (1998), concerning the South and the North. Schumacher (1973) developed some of the socio-economic rationale for developing 'intermediate technologies'; based on his ideas, the New Economics Foundation (NEF) in the UK is promoting alternative economic models. Schumacher himself set up the Intermediate Technology Development Group (ITDG) in the UK, with branches and sister organisations in several countries.

27 An important development approach that fits this category of 'intermediate alternatives' is PTD, Participatory Technology Development, which aims in particular to develop forms of sustainable agriculture; see for example Reijntjes, Haverkort and Waters-Bayer (1992). See also Neefjes *et al.* (1997); Conway (1997).

28 See also Moore-Lappé *et al.* (1998), who highlight lessons from the Green Revolution and challenge the idea that 'nature' is a main cause of poverty and famine, and that feeding the world's poor would necessarily be environmentally problematic.

29 See Magsanoc Ferrer *et al.* (eds) (1996).

30 Neefjes, Hart, and Dem, in Hall *et al.* (1996); also Davidson and Myers (1992).

31 Davidson and Myers (1992), pp. 115-17.

32 Gibson (1996), pp. 159-65.

33 See Peet and Watts (1996), chapters 1 and 12 in particular; see also Scoones (ed.) (1995).

34 Data are compiled by UNDP and UNEP, FAO, the World Bank, and a number of government or private organisations such as the World Resources Institute (WRI) and the Worldwatch Institute in Washington D.C., USA, and the World Conservation Monitoring Centre, Cambridge, UK.

35 Lovelock in Myers (ed.) (1994) *The Gaia Atlas of Planet Management*, London: Gaia Books, p. 94. This publication also contains a chapter by Oxfam: 'People as planet managers'.

36 Blaikie and Brookfield (1987), p.6.

37 Ibid, p.8.

38 See also chapter 8 and Macrae and Zwi (eds) (1994).

39 Blaikie and Brookfield (1987), p.16.

40 It should be noted that philosophers like Hayward (1994) and political economists gathered by Keil *et al.*, all writing on political ecology, do not even

refer to Blaikie and Brookfield. Keil *et al.* write about global political ecology and are also concerned with including ecological theories as a central feature in neo-Marxist thinking, in particular in response to the failure of neo-classical economics to capture the dependency of the economy on the environment. Their focus is in particular on global issues and political concerns in industrialised, Western nations; the rural Third World land manager of Blaikie and Brookfield does not feature.

41   See Shiva (1988), Agarwal (1998), Rangan (1996).

42   Agarwal (1998), p. 198.

43   Oxfam (1993).

44   Leach, Joekes, and Green (1995), 'editorial', in Joekes *et al.* (1995).

45   Ibid.

46   Schumacher (1973), p.48.

47   WCED (1987), p. 43.

48   Gupta and Asher (1998), p.42.

49   Pearce *et al.* (1989), pp. 29-30.

50   Ibid. p.32.

52   Pearce (1991), p.5.

53   Walker (1989), p.3.

54   See also section 2.4. Also Holt (1999), Maskrey (1989), WFP (1999). Urban vulnerability is particularly enhanced by low income (opportunity), deficiencies in services and infrastructure, bad housing, a lack of provision for earthquake impacts, and a lack of flood protection.

55   McIntosh and Thom (1978) explain as follows. Hurricanes appear in the western Atlantic ocean, and typhoons in the western Pacific, but they are essentially the same, and both are called tropical cyclones – in other words these three words are synonymous. They develop over the western parts of these oceans where the winds of the Northern and Southern hemispheres meet (i.e. in the tropics) and when the surface-water temperatures are at their highest, which is usually in the late summer or autumn (at both sides of the Equator). The air 'inside' the hurricane/typhoon spins extremely fast, inwards, and upwards and causes torrential rains and thunderstorm. At the core of a hurricane is the 'central eye', typically about 40 km in diameter, in which there are just light winds and no rain. They normally move slowly westwards, but when they reach higher latitudes and weaken in force they move eastwards. When they are inland, they rapidly decline in force. Tornadoes are very different, but also involve spinning air and can occasionally be extremely destructive. They develop overland, last rarely more than 15 minutes, and do not usually measure more than 100 metres across. They occur all over the world and particularly in central areas of the USA.

56   Nearly every major flood in Bangladesh has this effect, besides death and destruction.

57 See for example Penning-Rowsell (1998), who also makes the point of slowly emerging impacts on flora and fauna.

58 A highly publicised example of oil spills associated with political violence happened in Ogoni land in Nigeria; several political leaders were killed, including Ken Saro-Wiwa, who was executed by the Nigerian government; see also section 2.3.

59 See for example Dinham (1993).

60 UNEP/OCHA stands for UN Environment Programme, and Office for the Co-ordination of Humanitarian Affairs, accessible through the UNEP website www.unep.ch. The organisation Green Cross UK runs a website with information on disasters, provides access to expertise, and links to other websites: www.bluekey.co.uk/gcuk/ - see also Appendix 2 for websites and data sources.

61 See for example Shestakov (1998), and note also what happened to the Aral Sea to the south of Kazakhstan, where water from rivers was diverted for irrigation, the sea water salinised, and levels reduced to the point that fish died, fishers lost their livelihoods, and transport is now no longer viable; this is a good example of a 'slow-onset' disaster on a large scale.

62 See for example Kennedy (1998).

63 Sen (1981) explains famine as a result of 'entitlement failure', and Leach *et al.* (1997a) build on his theory with application to 'environmental entitlements'.

64 See for example Walker (1989) and especially Hubbard (1995).

65 An excellent and accessible publication on risk management is Periperi (1999).

66 See Baechler (1999), Kennedy (1998), and Neefjes (1999b) for similar character-isations of the diverse linkages between environmental change and conflict.

67 See Brazier (1992).

68 See for example a public statement by M. Gorbachev on 24 April 1999, 'Environmental Implications of the Hostilities in Yugoslavia', Green Cross International, Geneva; and also George Monbiot, 'Consigning their future to death: bombing Belgrade's chemical plants will poison the unborn', *The Guardian*, 22 April 1999.

69 See Macrae, Zwi and Duffield (1994); Neefjes (1999b), also Baechler (1999).

70 This taxonomy and my use of it are taken from Beachler (1999).

71 For a more elaborate version of this case history, see Neefjes (1999b); also Gasana (1995), and André and Platteau (1996).

72 These cases are short versions of what is reported in Neefjes (1999b); see also Richards (1996) on Sierra Leone; Spooner and Walsh (1991), and Neefjes (1998c) on Sudan case history; and Scoones *et al.* (1992) on wild foods.

73 Richards (1996), p.164.

74 From a case history by Douglas Johnson, presented in Oxfam UK&I (1997a): 'Exchanging Livelihoods – food-security edition'.

75 See Spooner and Walsh (1991).

76 Neefjes (1998c).

77   From John Buttery (1995) 'Displacement, relocation and the rights of the urban poor: a Sudan perspective', in Oxfam UK&I (1995a) 'Exchanging Livelihoods – urban edition'.

78   This is taken from Neefjes (1999b) and Neefjes (1997a); see also Black (1998).

79   Hoerz (1995) gives an overview of refugees and environmental change, which corroborates these points and several others.

80   This paragraph is strongly based on Black (1998).

81   See also Neefjes (1999b).

82   WCED (1987), p. 8.

83   Peet and Watts (1996), p. 7 (italics in the original); see also Blaikie and Brookfield (1987).

84   See Wackernagel and Rees (1996); Caroline LeQuesne, 'Ecological footprints', chapter 5 in Watkins (1995).

86   See for example Neefjes, Hart and Dem, in Hall *et al.* (eds.) (1996).

87   Chambers (1997), p. 7.

88   UNDP (1994), pp.23-4.

89   See also UNDP (1998); UNDP (1999).

90   'Environment', W. Sachs, in Sachs (ed.) (1992), p. 29.

91   Pearce *et al.* (1989).

92   'Making development sustainable', Paul Ekins, in Sachs (ed.) (1993).

93   Caroline LeQuesne, 'Ecological footprints', chapter 5 in Watkins (1995); see also sections 2.2.4 and 4.2.

94   Merril, quoted by Sarupria (1994).

95   'Technology', Otto Ullrich (1992), in Sachs (ed.) (1992), p. 280.

96   Wilson (1995), who discusses NGOs in Zimbabwe, including Oxfam GB.

97   See also section 2.1 on alternatives developed by environmentalists and other activists and development agencies; Schumacher (1973), Chambers (1997).

98   Chambers (1997), pp. 24-29, cites many more examples that challenge this neo-Malthusian myth.

99   Reported by Fairhead and Leach (1996).

100   Neefjes (1998b), p. 29.

101   Davidson and Myers (1992), see also Pretty and Guijt (1992).

102   Dobson (1998), p. 15.

103   See for example Worster (1993).

104   Worster (1993).

105   See for example Scoones (ed.) (1995).

106   FAO (1999). There is a vast literature on the Green Revolution and alternatives to it. See Bull (1982) and Conway and Pretty (1991) on pesticides; Shepherd (1998), Moore Lappé *et al.* (1998) and Conway (1997) for general critiques.

107 'Terminator genes' is a reference to a genetic trait bred into some experimental crops that render seeds sterile and thus offer patent holders or breeders the opportunity to force farmers to buy new seeds annually (even if a patent is not awarded!). This genetic trait has not been released for commercial crop-growing yet, and some limited trials in the USA have been discontinued. However in the USA and some other countries, government support for biotechnology is very strong.

108 Also known as conservation farming, low-external-input sustainable agriculture (LEISA), ecological farming, or organic farming.

109 The alternative future scenario for agriculture has been dubbed 'The Doubly Green Revolution' by Gordon Conway, now President of the Rockefeller Foundation.

110 A report that refers to many of the most recent developments and achievements is CIIFAD (1999).

111 Rabinovitch (1998): 90 per cent of the poor of Latin America, 45 per cent of the poor of Asia, and 40 per cent of the poor of Africa, or on average 50 per cent of the poor in developing countries will live in cities around the year 2000.

Chapter 3

1 Tacoli and Satterthwaite (1999).

2 This case history is based on Caccia Bava (1999); Oxfam has been an important donor of SCJP over several years.

3 Nine UK-based international development NGOs brought together some of their (and their national partners') experience in urban poverty alleviation in Hall, Hart, and Mitlin (eds.) (1996).

4 Based on Hall, Hart, and Mitlin (eds.) (1996); also Oxfam (1995): 'Exchanging Livelihoods' – urban edition.

5 See Neefjes and Sabri (1996). Recent publications have also paid considerable attention to 'environmental victimology' with a particular focus on health risks from pollution in urban centres; see C. Williams (1997) and C. Williams (ed.) (1998).

6 ITDG-Bangladesh REMS (1999).

7 See also Scott (1998).

8 This is based on an analysis of key lessons from a range of urban-poverty projects under various conditions, as documented by Hall, Hart, and Mitlin (eds.) (1996).

9 The two case histories presented here are documented in Neefjes (1998a,b).

10 See also section 5.3.2 on climate change. Analysis of rainfall data, combined with some crude assumptions of soil-moisture retention and crop-water needs in different stages of crop development led to the analysis that the worst seasons in Niassa were 1979/80, 1993/94, and 1994/95, and also bad in terms of drought stress were 1980/81, 1981/82, 1987/88, and 1991/92 (Neefjes, 1998a). It seems an extreme coincidence that all but the first two overlap fully with the 'El Niño years' (considered in section 4.3.2): 1982/83, 1987/88, 1991/92, and less strongly 1993 and 1994. Also interesting to note is that, whereas governments and development agencies prepared for drought in Southern Africa during 1997/98 –an 'unusually strong' 'El Niño year' – that drought did not happen.

11 Carney *et al.* (1999).

12 The early forms of the sustainable livelihoods framework were all based on Chambers and Conway (1992).

13 See for example section I.4.3.4 on EIA in Eade and Williams (1995); Maesson (1992); Borrini-Feyerabend (ed.) (1997); IUCN (1997); Donnelly (1998); and Goudie (1997). The latter is an anthology of papers about human impacts on environments, presented in five groups: (1) geomorphological and surface impacts, (2) soil impacts, (3) water impacts, (4) climatic and atmospheric impacts, and (5) biological impacts.

14 See for example Pickering and Owen (1994).

15 This definition is similar to (but not the same as) Carney (1998), which in turn is based on Chambers and Conway (1992). Internal debates in Oxfam in 1993 and 1994 led to the definition of a livelihood as '*a means of living, not just of production*', and sustainability as '*the ability to maintain and improve livelihoods while maintaining or enhancing the global assets and capabilities on which livelihoods depend*'. Oxfam (18.2.1994), 'Discussion Paper on Sustainable Livelihoods', Oxfam, Policy Department. Comparable definitions appear in Scoones (1998) and in Leach, Mearns, and Scoones (1997b).

16 This diagram is based strongly on Carney (1998), but important subtle differences make this version less obviously rural and opens possibilities for urban livelihoods and livelihoods based on non-natural resources to be addressed. The diagram of Carney (1998) is in turn based on Chambers and Conway (1992), Scoones (1998), and the work of a committee on sustainable rural livelihoods set up by DFID in 1998. The rest of section 3.2 is (also) based on Carney (1998); and Scoones (1998), Chambers and Conway (1992), Eade and Williams (1995), DFID (1999).

17 Roche (1999).

18 Scoones (1998) quotes Lipton, who explains that 'capital' is conventionally seen as the stock of productive resources built up by human action by investing current income streams, and so increasing future benefits from a given input of labour or raw material. Such capital may depreciate, be consumed, or be sold off. Under such a definition, it can be argued that natural and social 'capital' are not always appropriately termed 'capital' resources.

19 The definitions are based on Carney (1998) and DFID (1999), but are not the same.

20 Holland (1999) defines it as 'knowledge, skills, virtues and habits needed to realise natural and human made capital'.

21 From Leach *et al.* (1997a,b) and Scoones (1998).

22 'Human-made capital' is however defined by Holland (1999) as 'artefacts and physical infrastructure, and also including human capital'.

23 In fact a pasture thus described is a mixed form of natural and human-made capital, described by Holland (1999) as 'cultivated capital'.

24 The language of endowments and entitlements is borrowed from Sen (1981), who discussed the causation of famines. See in particular Leach, Mearns and Scoones (1997a,b) and Scoones (1998).

25 'Institutions' can be understood as 'the rules of the game' (formal or informal rules) and thus include markets, land tenure, and also for example conjugal arrangements (various types of marriage and relationships in a society). They will normally include organisations (for example central banks or village councils) but are not equated with organisations.

26 See e.g. Eade (1998).

27 This description of trends, seasonality, and shocks draws strongly on DFID (1999).

28 Sen (1981), Hubbard (1995) and Oxfam UK&I (1997a) elaborate on food security and food insecurity; Macrae *et al.* (1994) are excellent on complex emergencies.

29 See in particular Leach and Mearns (eds.) (1996).

30 Scoones (1998) says in an endnote: '[reflections on] the term sustainable rural livelihoods ... [are] largely rurally based. However, rural and urban livelihoods are clearly intertwined and the rural–urban distinction is somewhat artificial'. Evidence that ideas about livelihoods are very relevant in urban situations can also be found in Rakodi (1999); DFID commissioned some research in 1999 that appears to suggest that there is little particularly rural or urban in the framework – in different situations, different capitals are important to different livelihoods. Nevertheless, the framework has not been used much in analysis of urban problems or planning and review of urban poverty programmes.

31 Based on Brock (1999); see also Neefjes (1998a,b); see also chapter 4 and literature on PRA and other methodology, for example Chambers (1997) and Thomas, Chataway and Wuyts (1998).

32 Neefjes (1999c); Neefjes and Woldegiorgis (1999).

33 Adnan *et al.* (1992), p. 28.

34 From Rangan (1996), p. 206 (italics in original). The Chipko movement became widely known for its non-violent protest against tree logging in the Himalayan forests, in part through 'embracing' or hugging trees; see also Davidson and Myers. It is a common experience of NGOs working with poor people in participatory ways that they are first and foremost interested in moving out of poverty through economic improvements in productivity as well as sustainability – see for example Neefjes (1998a, 1998b).

35 Based on Nelson and Wright (1995).

36 Ibid.

37 Long (1992), p.21.

38 Alberto Arce and Norman Long, 'The dynamics of knowledge: interfaces between bureaucrats and peasants', in Long and Long (eds) (1992).

39 Neefjes *et al.* (1997), Oxfam (1999a).

40 See Chambers (1997), who gives a very large number of references; Pretty *et al.* (1995) for discussions of tools and training in particular; and Neefjes (1997c) for some specific Oxfam learning and advice for trainers.

41 See e.g. Chambers (1997).

42 As documented in training, project appraisal, and evaluation reports of Oxfam, for example in Neefjes (1993, 1995, 1998a, 1998b), Oxfam (1994).

43 This is based in part on the above and on Neefjes (1997c); see also chapter 5.

44 Action research can be understood as a form of research in which the researchers and local people work together for some kind of political, environmental, or socio-economic change. This happens mainly through experiential learning, i.e. trying things out. The situation or people that are described by researchers are influenced by them; this means that there is no longer a clear sense of objectivity, and one is considering not a static situation but a dynamic one.

45 This is based on Chambers (1997) and other publications by the same author.

46 See for example Chambers (1997); contributors to Guijt and Shah (eds) (1998); Feeney (1998); Mosse (1995).

47 See for example Neefjes (1998a).

48 This is from Guijt and Kaul Shah (1998), who list even more constraints. Mosse (1995) describes 'social constraints' in the context of women's culturally sanctioned access to certain public places, for example, and constraints inherent in PLA/PRA methods: certain diagrams can depict certain parts of realities and knowledges, but much remains untold. Since work with groups or individual women may produce less (and less diagrammatic) output than those with men, the representations of women may become marginalised in the later stages of learning processes, when information and analysis are summarised and retold by others.

49 Cornwall (1998), p.55.

50 Neefjes et al. (1997), Oxfam (1999).

51 Neefjes (1998b).

52 Neefjes (1998c).

53 See Neefjes and Sabri (1996); see also Neefjes, Hart and Dem (1996).

54 ITDG-Bangladesh / REMS (1999).

55 This 'negative' approach of governments in the North and also in the South to the environment may be best expressed by the setting of standards that limit pollution, and also by the requirement of doing Environmental Impact Assessment as an important part of planning procedures, which are exercises that usually produce a range of scenarios of (more or less negative) environmental impact from which decision makers choose, weighing their decisions in particular against projections of economic gains and also potential impacts on health – see also chapter 4.

Chapter 4

1   The quote is from Chambers' Dictionary; see also Oxfam (1997b).

2   It is important to note that when agencies such as Oxfam talk of 'appraisal' they usually mean something that takes place after the design (and planning) stage, and they see it as part of the process of approving a grant: 'the appraisal stage involves a critical assessment of the project, the counterpart's capacity, and how well the project and the counterpart fit each other' (Oxfam, 1997). In practical usage in projects and by local NGOs, however, 'appraisal' – as in PRA (participatory rural appraisal) – is most often part of earlier stages: needs and problem assessment, baseline-data gathering, and project identification. Appraisal may then 'spill over' into the design stage, but is essentially a process *with* project beneficiaries and other stakeholders and not an internal assessment exercise.

3   This section draws in particular on chapter 12 of Gupta and Asher (1998) and various chapters in Donnelly *et al.* (1998); see also ODA (1996) and DFID (1999b).

4   Several additional steps are distinguished in literature with regard to the EIA-project cycle, most of which are compressed in steps 1 and 2 in the figure.

5   From Modak and Biswas (1999).

6   Bryan Spooner, 'Review of the quality of EIA Guidelines, their use and circumnavigation', in Donnelly *et al.* (1998).

7   This is reported by Mwalyosi and Hughes (1998); see also Ross Hughes: 'Environmental Impact Assessment and stakeholder involvement', chapter 3 in Donnelly *et al.* (1998).

8   DFID (1999b).

9   This sub-section draws heavily on Hughes in Donnelly *et al.* (1998); see also Mwalyosi and Hughes (1998) and ODA (1996).

10   See Adnan *et al.* (1992).

11   See for example Shepherd (1998).

12   See for example Pallen (1996).

13   See for example Eade and Williams (1995), vol.1 section 4.3.4, in which a basic checklist is presented.

14   Maesson (1992), who produced these guidelines for the CCIC, Canadian Council for International Co-operation.

15   The manual was developed by consultants (Mouchel & Partners, 1996) and funded by the UK Overseas Development Administration, now DFID.

16   Particularly useful are: IUCN (1997), Borrini-Feyerabend (ed.) (1997), Guijt (1996), and Defoer *et al.* (1998).

17   See for example Pretty *et al.* (1995); also sections 3.3.2 and 4.3.

18   See for example Conway (1985; 1997) and Conway, McCracken and Pretty (1987).

19 Moorehead (1992) analysed some NGO approaches and case studies, in particular those of Oxfam. On the basis of early experiences, Arrowsmith (1996) developed a proposal for guidelines with particular reference to ITDG work in Asia, and making use of some Oxfam work in Asia too.

20 David and Neefjes (1995); this was later incorporated in the Oxfam Procedures Manual (appendix PM7-A) (Oxfam, 1997b) and is based on Guijt (1996).

21 Oxfam (1999b): 'Exchanging Livelihoods' – natural-resources edition.

22 UNDP (1992) (available in English, French and Spanish).

23 Neefjes (1998a).

24 Neefjes (1996).

25 This sub-section is based in particular on Scott (1998).

26 ITDG-Bangladesh / REMS (1999).

27 See UNHCR (1996) and UNHCR (1998a,b,c,d). Black (1998) includes an interesting chapter entitled 'Towards an environmental toolkit', and Kelly (1999) presents a simple method for 'rapid assessment' of environmental impact associated with disasters, which is however not much tested in practice. See also Hoerz (1995).

28 See Black (1998) and Green Cross UK (1998), which reports discussions in a workshop about EIA and disasters.

29 Black (1998).

30 This is summarised from UNHCR (1996); Black (1998) presents more or less the same summary.

31 Summarised from UNHCR (1996); see further UNHCR (1998a,b, c); this table is also virtually the same summary as presented by Black (1998).

32 See in particular Neefjes (1999a); also Hallam (1998) and Black (1998).

33 Some literature also describes 'hybrids', for example in Shepherd (1998): a mix of sustainable agriculture, EIA, and PRA.

34 From: Sphere Project (1998) *Humanitarian Charter and Minimum Standards in Disaster Response,* first edition. See also: http://www.ifrc.org/pubs/sphere.

35 See for example Neefjes (1993a; 2000b); Eade and Williams (1995); and Arrowsmith (1996). The experience on which this section draws is mainly from Oxfam GB, and also ITDG, Novib, and other international NGOs and several of their national partner organisations.

36 Such processes have been conducted with Oxfam staff and partners in project appraisals and reviews in (for example) Cambodia, Sudan, Vietnam, Mozambique, Angola, and Rwanda, which are all well documented. Similar work in Uganda was done with counterparts of Novib: Neefjes and Nakacwa (1996). In all those cases an earlier incarnation of the sustainable livelihoods framework was used: see Chambers and Conway (1992).

37 Chambers (1997) summarises some of this debate and gives many references.

38 See for example Estrella and Gaventa (1997), and Abbot and Guijt (1998); *PLA-Notes* no. 31 on Participatory Monitoring and Learning, IIED (1998).

39   Smith (1997);Neefjes (1997c).

40   See Long and Long (1992) for some of the theory; also section 3.3; and CRDT/DFID (1998) for a practical training exercise about participation and stakeholder analysis.

41   Pretty (1994); Thomas *et al.* (1998).

42   Mosse (1995); Guijt (1996).

43   See in particular Abbot and Guijt (1998).

44   Roche (1999).

45   Compare Roche (1999), pp. 45-8.

46   Oxfam UK&I (1998).

47   Neefjes *et al.* (1997); Oxfam (1999); Neefjes (1999a); Neefjes (1999b).

48   Adnan *et al.* (1992); Nelson and Wright (1995); Chambers (1997); Abbot and Guijt (1998); Long and Long (1992).

49   See also discussion on 'ecological footprints' in Watkins (1995a).

50   From: Oxfam-PDT (1995): 'Cambodia: Programmes In Transition, An Oxfam Workshop, May 23, 1995'.

51   PREDES received funding from Oxfam and the ODA (now DFID) for several years from 1984. Local NGOs and others addressed the problem of river pollution with support from CIIR/ICD. See Maskrey (1989) and also Davidson and Myers (1992) on floods. A very interesting initiative is also ITDG-Peru's network on disaster prevention and its sustainable-development information centre, called SIG-DES: http://www.itdg.org.pe.

52   Johnson (1998).

53   See Neefjes (1998a).

54   In the literature on restocking, Oxby (1994) is very practical, Markakis (ed.) presents several case studies of pastoralism in decline as a result of war (in Africa), Prior (1994) outlines strategic choices in pastoral development, and Scoones (ed.) (1995) gives several papers on new ways and paradigms in range management and pastoral development.

Chapter 5

1   See Appendix 2 for details of several of those organisations, including their websites.

2   This draws on Barry Dalal-Clayton and Barry Sadler (1998): 'Strategic Environmental Assessment: a rapidly evolving approach', in Donnelly *et al.* (1998).

3   From Eade and Williams (1995).

4   Based on Dalal-Clayton and Sadler, in Donnelly *et al.* (1998).

5   From Dalal-Clayton and Sadler, in Donnelly *et al.* (1998).

6   This includes NGOs who contributed in some way to the project that led to the writing of this book, i.e. Oxfam GB, ITDG, and also Novib and ActionAid. ITDG's general policy is strongly rooted in the thinking of Schumacher, whose work is briefly touched upon in section 2.2.4. ActionAid promotes working *with* poor people to understand how they care for their environments, and addresses environmental issues for example through education, community-based land reform, and the development of low-external-input farming. Novib has sustainable development at the core of its mission statement, and it aims to increase the capacity of local organisations to raise living standards sustainably and to empower them to overcome social and economic oppression. Novib sees environmental degradation as a cause of poverty and also as a result of it, i.e. it believes that there is a vicious circle that needs to be broken by, for example, improving land rights and promoting sustainable land-use practices. It also believes that environmental degradation has strong implications for North–South relations, because much of it is caused by Northern lifestyles.

7   This is true for Oxfam GB, and also for the other members of Oxfam International, which include Novib in The Netherlands.

8   See in particular Ashley and Carney (1999), who show the various ways of using 'sustainable livelihoods', i.e. as an analytical tool, for setting organisational or operational objectives, and also as an approach to development that combines various tools and principles.

9   This is witnessed by a range of 'case histories', for example those published in Oxfam UK&I (1997a): 'Exchanging Livelihoods – food-security edition', and Oxfam GB (1999b) 'Exchanging Livelihoods – natural-resources edition'.

10   By Caroline LeQuesne, in Watkins (1995a). This report was developed by Oxfam GB in collaboration with a number of other members of the Oxfam International family, notably Oxfam America, Oxfam Canada, and Oxfam New Zealand. The campaign alluded to in the text was popularly known as the Basic Rights Campaign. On ecological footprints, see also Wackernagel and Rees (1996).

11   In section 2.2.4, three broad courses of action to this effect are suggested, namely government regulation, market-based policies (including taxation), and 'persuasion' in order to change behaviour.

12   A programme is conceived of as a cluster of inter-related projects, campaigning, and emergency responses, most of which happen with or are done by counterparts, working towards a common aim in a country or in a region consisting of several countries.

13   Based on Oxfam (1995b); the sustainable-livelihoods contribution to those guidelines obviously concerns an earlier incarnation of the framework, but the features are not essentially different from what is presented in this book. Earlier advice has been interpreted and adapted here in the light of more recent language expressing what 'sustainable livelihoods' are all about – see also chapter 3.

14   From Oxfam (1999c).

15 See also Pye-Smith and Borrini-Feyerabend, with Sandbrook (1994).

16 See Neefjes (1998a) on Vietnam; Neefjes *et al.* (1997) and Oxfam GB (1999) on Kenya.

17 See UNDP (1992); also Gupta and Asher (1998), who describe the environmental overview of the country programme not as EOC but as EOP.

18 The framework shows links and flow, for example increased income can lead to investments in maintaining or regenerating natural capital, but only if the investor expects to have long-term access to the resource (which depends strongly on policies and regulations). Whether an indicator in the table is listed with *outcomes, capitals,* or *policies* is often debatable.

19 Based on Holmberg *et al.* (1992); IUCN (1991); Scoones (1998); and *Human Development Reports* including UNDP (1998).

20 Various forms of environmentalism can be related to campaigns on issues such as those discussed here. Excellent, discursive books that analyse environmentalisms and ecological movements in developing countries include Guha and Martinez-Alier (1997) and Peet and Watts (1996). See also chapter 2.

21 Oxfam GB, Novib, and Oxfam Hong Kong.

22 See Hansungule, Feeney and Palmer (1998), and Cynthia Mwase and Sophie Bond, 'Land tenure insecurity in the Zambian Copperbelt', in Oxfam (1999b): 'Exchanging Livelihoods – natural-resources edition'.

23 This is taken mainly from an excellent case history reported by Böge (1999); see also Gillespie (1998).

24 Gaspar *et al.* (1998); SEAMEO (1997); Linda Stephen, 'Treading on ancestral domains', in: Oxfam UK&I (1997a): 'Exchanging Livelihoods – food-security edition'.

25 MST began in 1982 as a land-rights campaign and now claims to have supported up to 400,000 families all over Brazil in their successful efforts to acquire land through squatting and demonstrations, and more generally through demanding their rights to a livelihood, in particular through land titles and other support for small-scale agriculture. Brazil is vast; it has millions of dispossessed and a small minority of elite landowners who own most of the country's productive land. The latter often leave it fallow and own land for speculative purposes, or they use it for ranching or for large-scale plantations.

26 Feeney (1998), p. 45.

27 Feeney (1998), p. 54.

28 See for example Borrini-Feyerabend (1997); see also IIED (1994) and Panos (1997a) for discussion of community-based wildlife conservation and a large number of case studies.

29 See for example Oxfam UK&I (1996a); and Ric Goodman, 'Pastoral livelihoods in Tanzania: can the Maasai benefit from community based tourism?', in Oxfam GB (1999b): 'Exchanging Livelihoods – natural-resources edition'.

30 See for example Oxfam(UK&I) (1996a); Silas Likasi, 'Minority land rights in Tanzania', in Oxfam (1999b): 'Exchanging Livelihoods – natural-resources edition'; and various sources summarised in Palmer (1997).

31 There is a vast literature on the Green Revolution and alternatives to it. See Bull (1982) and Conway & Pretty (1991) on pesticides; Shepherd (1998), Moore Lappé *et al.* (1998) and Conway (1997) for general critiques.

32 See Sen (1981), Drèze, Sen and Hussain (eds) (1995), and also Hubbard (1995) and Moore Lappé (1998).

33 See for example Altieri (1987), Reijntjes *et al.* (1992), Shepherd (1998), Conway (1997), and Pretty (1995).

34 According to a genetic scientist, Dr Ricarda Steinbrecher (1998).

35 FAO data, autumn 1999, available through the FAO website.

36 See, for example, GRAIN (1998), Kelly (1999a,b), Spinney (1998), Steinbrecher (1998), Mae-Wan Ho (1998), Berlan and Lewontin (1999); Nuffield Council on Bioethics (1999).

37 Alternatives with regard to sustainable agriculture and permaculture have been documented in Altieri (1987), Reijntjes *et al.* (1992), Shepherd (1998), Conway (1997), Pretty (1995), Pretty (1999), and most recently in CIIFAD (1999). See also Oxfam UK&I (1997a), Oxfam GB (1999b), Bunch (1982); Conway and Pretty (1991).

38 See for example Bunch (1990) and Holt Gimenez (1999).

39 Rosset (1994).

40 Majlinda Priku and Teofik Fugarini (1997): 'Permaculture in Albania: securing livelihoods through innovations in agriculture techniques', in 'Exchanging Livelihoods – food-security edition', Oxford: Oxfam GB.

41 See Neefjes, Mafongoya and Mwangi with Ngunjiri and Mugure (1997) and Oxfam GB (1999a).

42 Francis McDonagh (1997): 'The Brazil Hunger Campaign', in Oxfam UK&I (1997a).

43 This is confirmed by the Kenya and Vietnam case studies referred to in several parts of this book and in Neefjes *et al.* (1997), Oxfam GB (1999a), Neefjes (1998b).

44 From John Gittings, 'Great Yangtze Dam in trouble: Beijing has finally admitted that the Three Gorges project poses a risk to people and the environment', *The Guardian*, 25 May 1999.

45 From Arundhati Roy, 'Lies, dam lies and statistics', *The Guardian*, 5 June 1999. Regarding the Narmada scheme much has been published; see for example Guha and Martinez-Alier (1997) and also Davidson and Myers (1992).

46 Smyth (1997).

47 See several contributors to Williams (ed.) 1998; see also Panos (1997b), which gives a more global or Northern outlook on industrial 'greening'.

48 Williams (1998), p. 13.

49 See Gupta and Asher (1998) and especially Sarangi (1998).

50 Satterthwaite (1996).

51 See for example several contributions to Oxfam UK&I (1994b): 'Exchanging Livelihoods – pilot edition', Oxfam UK&I (1995a): 'Exchanging Livelihoods – urban edition', and Oxfam GB (1999b): 'Exchanging Livelihoods – natural-resources edition'.

52 From Caccia Bava (1999); see also section 3.1.1. Oxfam GB is an important source of funds for SCJF.

53 See Davidson and Myers (1992); Neefjes, Hart and Dem (1996); Neefjes and Sabri (1996).

54 For some details on the history of environmental treaties and conferences, see section 2.1.2 and Appendix 1. For more on the UNCED and its sequels, see for example Gupta and Asher (1997), Sachs (1993); NGLS (1997); Keating (1993); Osborn and Bigg (1998); and the websites of UNEP and UNDP.

55 An important actor and source of information in this field is ICLEI, the International Council for Local Environmental Initiatives – see Appendix 2 for website address.

56 This is taken in particular from Gupta and Asher (1998), and Pickering and Owen (1994); it is also based on information from several Internet searches.

57 From Stephan Singer (WWF), in *ECO Newsletter on Climate Negotiations*, June 2, 1999, issue no. 2

58 See for example Kennedy (1998).

59 As explained by Kennedy (1998).

60 See Wackernagel and Rees (1996); Watkins (1995).

61 From Rayner and Malone (1998).

62 The 'Uruguay Round' or GATT, the General Agreement on Tariffs and Trade, was concluded in 1994 and incorporated in the WTO, the World Trade Organisation, which came into effect on 1 January 1995.

63 See Ahmed and Lipton (1997); also Reed (1992) for the possible effects of SAPs.

64 They were a number of policy-oriented Nicaraguan NGOs, Oxfam GB, and SNV, a Dutch development organisation. From GNC/Oxfam/SNV (1996).

65 Coote (1992).

66 Stillwell and Arden-Clark (1998).

67 From GRAIN (1998), Kelly (1999a,b), and Spinney (1998); important international NGOs who collect much information on these topics and play a key role in the lobby are RAFI and GRAIN, and also the UK Food Group – see Appendix 2 for website addresses.

68 For more on the IU and CBD, see for example the website of UK-ABC: http://dspace.dial.pipex.com/ukfg/ukabc.htm.

69 These negotiations are difficult, mainly because of the objections of the so-called Miami group of agro-exporting countries, which includes Argentina, Australia,

Canada, Chile, Uruguay, and the USA. Even though the USA is not a signatory of the CBD, it plays a dominant role in the Bio-safety Protocol negotiations; the USA, Argentina, and Canada are the largest producers of GM crops.

70   CGIAR stands for the Consultative Group of International Agricultural Research.

71   See for example Kelly (ed.) (1999a).

72   Kevin Watkins and Michael Windfuhr in 'The effect of the Uruguay Round on food security', in *Third World Resurgence*, no.67 (1995), argued that in the Uruguay Round tariff restrictions were far more severe than subsidy limitations, effectively putting greater limits on the policy options of developing countries than on those of developed countries.

73   This paragraph is based on Konandreas, Sharma, and Greenfield (1999); see also the regular updates of world market prices on the FAO website.

74   See for example Watkins and Windfuhr (1995).

75   Neefjes (1998b).

76   Watkins (1995b).

77   On bananas and coffee, and Oxfam GB's role, see contributions to Oxfam UK&I (1997a): 'Exchanging Livelihoods – food-security edition', and Oxfam GB (1999b): 'Exchanging Livelihoods – natural-resources edition'.

Appendix 1

1   The information in Appendix 1 was obtained from Tolba and El-Kholy *et al.* (1992). A comprehensive list of multilateral agreements is also given at http://www.tufts/fletcher/multilaterals.htm.

Bibliography

Abbot, Joanne and Irene Guijt (1998) *Changing Views on Change: Participatory Approaches to Monitoring the Environment*, SARL Discussion Paper 2, London: IIED

Adnan, Shapan, Alison Barrett, S.M. Nurul Alam, and Angelika Brustinow (1992) 'People's Participation, NGOs and the Flood Action Plan – an Independent Review', Dhaka: Research & Advisory Services (commissioned by Oxfam-Bangladesh)

Agarwal, Bina (1997) 'Environmental action, gender equity and women's participation', *Development and Change* Vol. 28, pp. 1-44

Agarwal, Bina (1998) 'The gender and environment debate', in Keil *et al.* (eds) (1998)

Ahmed, Ismael I, with Michael Lipton (1997) *Impact of Structural Adjustment on Sustainable Rural Livelihoods: a Review of the Literature*, Working Paper 62, Brighton: IDS

Altieri, M. A. (1987) *Agroecology: The Scientific Basis of Alternative Agriculture*, London: Intermediate Technology

André, Catherine and Jean-Philippe Platteau (1996) *Land Relations Under Unbearable Stress: Rwanda Caught in the Malthusian trap*, Namur, Belgium: CRED, University of Namur

Appleton, Helen (ed.) (1995) *Do It Herself: Women and Technical Innovation*, London: Intermediate Technology

Arrowsmith, Stephen R. (1996) 'Participatory EIA Guidelines for Small Community Based NGO Projects', unpublished MSc thesis, University of London

Ashley, C. and D. Carney (1999) *Sustainable Livelihoods: Lessons from Early Experience*, London: Department for International Development

Baechler, Günther (1999) 'Environmental degradation and violent conflict: hypotheses, research agendas and theory-building', in: Suliman (ed) (1999)

Bebbington, Anthony (1996), 'Movements, modernisations and markets: indigenous organisations and agrarian strategies in Ecuador', in Peet and Watts (eds) (1996)

Berlan, Jean-Pierre and Richard C. Lewontin (1999) 'Genetically modified food: it's business as usual', *The Guardian*, 12.2.99

Black, Richard (1998) *Refugees, Environment and Development*, Harlow (Essex): Longman

Blaikie, Piers and Harold Brookfield (1987) *Land Degradation and Society*, London/New York: Methuen

Böge, Völker (1999) 'Mining, environmental degradation and war: the Bougainville case', in: Suliman (ed.) (1999)

Borrini-Feyerabend, Grazia with Dianne Buchan (eds) (1997) *Beyond Fences: Seeking Social Sustainability in Conservation*, Volumes 1 and 2, Gland/Cambridge: IUCN

Braun, Bruce and Noel Castree (eds) (1998) *Remaking Reality: Nature at the Millennium*, London/New York: Routledge

Brazier, Chris (1992) *Vietnam: The Price of Peace*, Oxford: Oxfam

Brock, Karen (1999) *Implementing a Sustainable Livelihoods Framework for Policy-Directed Research: Reflections from Practice in Mali*, Brighton: Institute of Development Studies, University of Sussex

Brown, Lester R, Christopher Flavin, and Hilary F. French (with others) (1998) *State of the World: A Worldwatch Institute report on progress towards a sustainable society*, London: Earthscan

Bryant, Raymond L. and Sinéad Bailey (1997) *Third World Political Ecology*, London/New York: Routledge

Bull, David (1982) *A Growing Problem: Pesticides and the Third World Poor*, Oxford: Oxfam

Bunch, Roland (1982) *Two Ears of Corn*, World Neighbours

Bunch, Roland (1990) *Low Input Soil Restoration in Honduras: the Cantarranas Farmer-to-Farmer Extension Programme*, Gatekeeper series, London: IIED

Caccia Bava, Silvio (1999) *A Luta Pelo Direito a Moradia na Cidade do Recife e a Ação do Serviço Comunitário de Justiça e Paz*, Recife: SCJP and Oxfam GB

Carney, Diana (ed) (1998) *Sustainable Rural Livelihoods – What contribution can we make?* London: Department for International Development

Carney, Diana, with Michael Drinkwater and Tamara Rusinow (CARE), Koos Neefjes (Oxfam), Samir Wanmali, and Naresh Singh (UNDP) (1999) *Livelihood Approaches Compared: a brief comparison of the livelihood approaches of the UK Department for International Development (DFID), CARE, Oxfam and the United Nations Development Programme (UNDP)*, London: DFID

Chambers, Robert (1986) *Sustainable Livelihoods: An Opportunity for the World Commission on Environment and Development*, Brighton: Institute for Development Studies

Chambers, Robert (1992) *Rural Appraisal: Rapid, Relaxed and Participatory*, Discussion Paper 311, Brighton: Institute for Development Studies

Chambers, Robert (1995) *Poverty and Livelihoods: Whose Reality Counts?*, Discussion Paper 347, Brighton: Institute for Development Studies

Chambers, Robert (1997) *Whose Reality Counts? Putting the First Last*, London: Intermediate Technology

Chambers, R. and G. Conway (1992) *Sustainable Rural Livelihoods: Practical Concepts for the 21st Century*, Discussion Paper 296, Brighton: Institute for Development Studies

CIIFAD (1999) *Alternatives to Conventional Modern Agriculture for Meeting World Needs in the Next Century. Report of a conference on sustainable agriculture: evaluation of new paradigms and old practices, April 26-30, 1999, Bellagio, Italy.* Ithaca (NY): Cornell International Institute for Food, Agriculture and Development.

Clements, Frederick (1916) *Plant Succession: An Analysis of the Development of Vegetation*, Carnegy Institute

Conroy, Czech and Miles Litvinoff (eds) (1988) *The Greening of Aid: Sustainable Livelihoods in Practice*, London: Earthscan

Conway, Gordon R. (1985) 'Agroecosystem analysis', in *Agricultural Administration* vol. 20, pp.31-55, Elsevier

Conway, Gordon (1997) *The Doubly Green Revolution – Food for All in the Twenty-first Century*, London/New York/etc.: Penguin Books

Conway, G.R., J.A. McCracken, and J.N. Pretty (1987) *Training Notes for Agroecosystem Analysis and Rapid Rural Appraisal*, Sustainable Agriculture Programme, London: IIED

Conway, G., and J. Pretty (1991) *Unwelcome Harvest: Agriculture and Poluution*, London: Earthscan

Coote, Belinda (1992) *The Trade Trap: Poverty and the Global Commodity Markets*, Oxford: Oxfam

Cornwall, Andrea (1998) 'Gender, participation, and the politics of difference' in Guijt and Shah (eds) 1998

CRDT/DFID (1998) *Icitrap: Training exercise for examining participatory approaches to project management*, prepared for the Department for International Development by the Centre for Rural Development and Training, Walsall: University of Wolverhampton

David, Ros and Koos Neefjes (1995) 'A Note on the Environment Question in the PASF', Oxfam GB, internal memo

David, Ros, Mike Winter, and Mohamed Ould Mahmoud (1994) 'Projet Integré de L'Affolé: Republiques Islamique de la Mauritanie', mimeo, Oxford: Oxfam GB

Davidson, Joan and Dorothy Myers, with Manab Chakraborty (1992) *No Time to Waste*, Oxford: Oxfam

Defoer, T., A Budelman, C. Toulmin, S. Carter, and J. Ticheler (1998) 'Soil Fertility Management in Africa: Resource Guide for Participatory Learning and Action Research', draft for field testing (October 1998), Amsterdam: KIT/IIED/TSBF

DFID (1999a) *Sustainable Livelihoods Guidance Sheets*, Natural Resources Policy and Advisory Department, London: Department For International Development

DFID (1999b) *DFID Environmental Guide*, London: Department For International Development (Environment Policy Department)

Dinham, Barbara (1993) *The Pesticide Hazard: a Global Health and Environmental Audit*, London: Zed Books/The Pesticides Trust

Dobson, Andrew (1998) *Justice and the Environment: Conceptions of Environmental Sustainability and Dimensions of Social Justice*, Oxford: Oxford University Press

Dobson, Andrew (ed) (1999) *Fairness and Futurity*, Oxford: Oxford University Press

Donnelly, Annie, Barry Dalal-Clayton, and Ross Hughes (1998) *A Directory of Impact Assessment Guidelines – second edition*, London: IIED (with WRI and IUCN under the INTERAISE project)

Douthwaite, Richard (1996) *Short Circuit - Strengthening local economies for security in an unstable world*, Totnes (UK): Green Books

Drèze, Jean, Amartya Sen, and Athar Hussain (eds) (1995) *The Political Economy of Hunger*, Oxford: Clarendon Press

Eade, Deborah (1997) *Capacity-Building: an Approach to People-centred Development*, Oxford: Oxfam

Eade, Deborah and Suzanne Williams (1995) *Oxfam Handbook for Development and Relief*, Oxford: Oxfam

Ekins, Paul (1992) *A New World Order: Grassroots Movements for Global Change*, London and New York: Routledge

Estrella, Marisol and John Gaventa (1997), *Who Counts Reality? – Participatory Monitoring and Evaluation: a Literature Review*, Brighton, Sussex: Institute for Development Studies.

Fairhead, James and Melissa Leach (1996), 'Rethinking the forest-savannah mosaic – colonial science and its relics in West Africa', in Leach and Mearns (eds) (1996)

Feeney, Patricia (1998) *Accountable Aid: Local Participation in Major Projects*, Oxford: Oxfam

Fernandes, Edesio (ed) (1998) *Environmental Strategies for Sustainable Development in Urban Areas: Lessons from Africa and Latin America*, Aldershot (UK): Ashgate Publishing

Finger, Matthias (1993), 'Politics of the UNCED process', in Sachs (ed), *Global Ecology*, London: Zed Books

Gandhi, Mahatma K. (1980) *The Bhagavadgita,* (Gandhi's lectures from 1926), New Delhi: Orient Paperbacks

Gaspar, Carlos, Norma Javellana, and Koos Neefjes (1998) 'Kaliwat Theatre Collective (KTC) – Program Evaluation Report', unpublished mimeo, Manila/Davao: Oxfam/KTC

Gasana, James K. (1995) *Factors of Ethnic Conflict in Rwanda and Instruments for a Durable Peace. International Conference of Experts on Federalism against Ethnicity? Institutional, Legal and Democratic Instruments to Prevent or Resolve Minority Conflicts*, Basle

Geertz, Clifford (1963) *Agricultural Involution: the process of ecological change in Indonesia*, University of California.

George, Susan (1996) *Questionable Compatibility: Trade Liberalisation and Food Security*, Manila: ISIS

Gibson, Tony (1996) *The Power In Our Hands: Neighbourhood-Based, World-Shaking*, Charlbury (UK): Jon Carpenter Publishing

Gillespie, Rosemarie (1998) 'Ecocide, industrial chemical contamination, and the corporate profit imperative: the case of Bougainville', in: Williams (ed) (1998)

GNC/Oxfam/SNV (1996) *Food Security in Nicaragua: Implications of Structural Adjustment and Stabilisation Policies. A Discussion Paper.* Managua: Grupo Propositivo de Cabildeo/Oxfam/SNV

Goudie, Andrew (ed.) (1997) *The Human Impact Reader: Readings and Case Studies*, Oxford/Malden: Blackwell

GRAIN (1998) *Patenting, Piracy and Perverted Promises: Patenting Life, the Last Assault on the Commons*, Barcelona: Genetic Resources Action International

Green Cross (1998) *Environmental Responses in Emergency Situations: Workshop Proceedings, 19 March 1998*, Kingston-upon-Thames: Green Cross UK

Guha, Ramachandra and Juan Martinez-Alier (1997) *Varieties of Environmentalism: Essays North and South*, London: Earthscan

Guijt, Irene (1996) *Questions of Difference – PRA, Gender and Environment, a Training Video,* London: IIED

Guijt, Irene and Meera Kaul Shah (1998) *The Myth of Community: Gender Issues in Participatory Development*, London: Intermediary Technology

Gupta, Avijit and Mukul G. Asher (1998) *Environment and the Developing World: Principles, Policies and Management*, Chichester/New York/etc: John Wiley

Hall, Nicolas, Rob Hart, and Diana Mitlin (eds) (1996) *The Urban Opportunity – The Work of NGOs in Cities of the South,* London: Intermediate Technology

Hallam, Alistair (1998) *Evaluating Humanitarian Assistance Programmes in Complex Emergencies*, London: Overseas Development Institute, Relief and Rehabilitation Network

Hansungule, Michelo, Patricia Feeney, and Robin Palmer (1998) 'Report on land Tenure Insecurity on the Zambian Copperbelt', Oxfam GB in Zambia, unpublished, Oxford: Oxfam

Harrison, Paul (1992) *Inside the Third World*, London: Penguin

Hayward, Tim (1994) *Ecological Thought: an Introduction*, Cambridge/Oxford: Polity Press/Blackwell

Heslop, Ray (1996), 'Community-led water and sanitation projects in the urban sector', in Hall *et al*. (1996)

Hoerz, Thomas (1995) *Refugees and Host Environments – a Review of Current and Related Literature,* Oxford: Refugee Studies Programme/GTZ

Holland, Alan (1999), 'Sustainability: should we start from here?', in Dobson (ed) (1999)

Holm, Jean with John Bowker (eds) (1994) *Attitudes to Nature*, London/New York: Pinter

Holmberg, Johan, Stephen Bass, and Lloyd Timberlake (1992) *Defending the Future: A Guide to Sustainable Development*, London: Earthscan

Holt Gimenez, Eric (1999) 'The Campesino a Campesino Movement: agroecological vulnerability, resistance and resilience to Hurricane Mitch', Managua: World Neighbours (distributed at the Green Cross UK seminar 'Environmental Issues in Disaster Prevention, Preparedness and Response', London, 18 March 1999)

Hombergh, Helen van den (1993) *Gender, Environment and Development - a guide to the literature*, International Books/INDRA: Utrecht/Amsterdam

Hubbard, Michael (1995) *Improving Food Security: A Guide for Rural Development Managers*, London: Intermediate Technology

Hughes, Ross and Barry Dalal-Clayton (1996) *Participation in Environmental Impact Assessment: a review of issues*, London: IIED, EPG Environmental Planning Issues series no.11

IIED (1994) *Whose Eden? An Overview of Community Approaches to Wildlife Management*, a report to the ODA of the British Government, London: IIED

IIED (1997) *PLA Notes 29: Performance and Participation*, London: IIED

ITDG-Bangladesh/REMS (1999) 'Environmental Impact Assessment of Dholai Khal project: Final report', unpublished mimeo, Bourton-on-Dunsmore: Intermediate Technology Development Group

IUCN (1980) *World Conservation Strategy*, Gland: IUCN

IUCN (1991) *Caring for the Earth*, Gland: IUCN

IUCN (1997) *An Approach to Assessing Progress Toward Sustainability*, Tools and Training Series, the International Assessment Team, Gland/Cambridge: IUCN

Jackson, C. (1994), 'Gender analysis and environmentalisms', in M. Redclift and T. Benton (1994) *Social Theory and the Global Environment*, London: Routledge

Jackson, T. with D. Eade (1982) *Against the Grain: The Dilemma of Project Food Aid*, Oxford: Oxfam

Joekes, Susan, Melissa Leach, and Cathy Green (eds) (1995) 'Gender relations and environmental change', *IDS Bulletin*, vol. 26 no. 1, Brighton: Institute for Development Studies

Johnson, Douglas (1998) *Distributing Seeds and Tools in Emergencies*, Oxford: Oxfam GB

Keating, Michael (1993) *The Earth Summit's Agenda for Change: A Plain Language Version of Agenda 21 and the other Rio Agreements*, Geneva: Centre for Our Common Future

Keil, Roger, David V.J. Bell, Peter Penz and Leesa Fawcett (eds) (1998) *Political Ecology: Global and Local*, London/New York: Routledge

Kelly, Charles (1999) 'Disasters and the Environmental Impact: A Framework for Rapid Assessment and Planning by Response Personnel', paper presented at the Green Cross UK seminar 'Environmental Issues in Disaster Prevention, Preparedness and Response', London, 18 March 1999

Kelly, Laura (ed.) (1999a) *WTO and Food Security: Opportunities for Action*, London: ActionAid

Kelly, Laura (ed.) (1999b) *Patents and Food Security: Options for Research and Action*, London: ActionAid

Kennedy, Donald (1998) *Environmental Quality and Regional Conflict: A Report to the Carnegie Commission on Preventing Deadly Conflict*, New York: Carnegie Corporation

Ketel, Hermen (1998) 'Workshop discussion paper: Environmental responses in emergency situations', in: Green Cross (1998)

Khan, Akhter Hameed (1994) *Orangi Pilot Project Programs*, Karachi: OPP Research and Training Institute (third edition)

Konandreas, Panos, Ramesh Sharma, and Jim Greenfield (1999) 'The Agreement on Agriculture: Some Preliminary Assessment from the Experience So Far', paper presented on the CIIR/UKFG conference 'The Uruguay Round Agreement on Agriculture: Taking Stock', 28.1.99, London

Lal, P. (1965) *The Bhagavadgita*, ('transcreated' into English) New Delhi: Orient Paperbacks

Leach, Melissa and Robin Mearns (eds.) (1996) *The Lie of the Land – Challenging Received Wisdom on the African Environment*, London/Oxford/Portsmouth(NH): The International African Institute/James Currey/Heinemann

Leach, M., R. Mearns, and I. Scoones (1997a) *Environmental Entitlements: A Framework for Understanding the Institutional Dynamics of Environmental Change*, Discussion paper 359, Brighton: IDS

Leach, M., R. Mearnsm and I. Scoones (eds) (1997b) '*Community based sustainable development: consensus or conflict?*', *IDS Bulletin* vol. 28, no. 4

Long, Norman (1992) 'From paradigm lost to paradigm regained? The case for an actor-oriented sociology in development' in Long and Long (eds) (1992)

Long, Norman and Ann Long (eds) (1992) *Battlefields of Knowledge: the Interlocking of Theory and Practice in Social Research and Development*, London and New York: Routledge

LeQuesne, Caroline (1996) *Reforming World Trade: The Social and Environmental Priorities*, Oxford: Oxfam

Lovelock, James (1979) *Gaia: A New Look at Life on Earth*, Oxford and New York: Oxford University Press

Macrae, Joanna and Anthony Zwi, with Mark Duffield and Hugo Slim (1994) *War and Hunger – Rethinking International Responses to Complex Emergencies*, London: Zed Books

Maesson, O. (1992) *Environmental Screening of NGO Development Projects*, Ottawa: CCIC

Mae-Wan Ho (1998) *Genetic Engineering, Dream or Nightmare? – The brave new world of bad science and big business*, Bath (UK): Gateway Books

Magsanoc Ferrer, Elmer, Lenore Polotan dela Cruz, and Marife Agoncillo Domingo (eds) (1996) *Seeds of Hope: a collection of case studies on community based coastal resources management in the Philippines*, Quezon City: University of the Philippines

Markakis, John (ed.) (1993) *Conflict and the Decline of Pastoralism in the Horn of Africa*, London: Macmillan, with ISS

Maskrey, Andrew (1989) *Disaster Mitigation: A Community-Based Approach*, Oxford: Oxfam

McDowell, Christopher and Arjan de Haan (1997) *Migration and Sustainable Livelihoods: A Critical Review o the Literature*, Brighton: IDS

McIntosh, D.H. and A.S. Thom (1978) *Essentials of Meteorology*, London: Wykeham

Meadows, D.H., D.L. Meadows, J. Randers, and W.W Behrens (1972) *The Limits to Growth*, London: Earth Island

Mies, Maria (1996) *A Breakdown in Relations: Women, Food Security and Trade*, Manila: ISIS

Modak, Prasad and Asit K. Biswas (1999) *Conducting Environmental Impact Assessment for Developing Countries*, Tokyo: United Nations University Press

Moorehead, Anne (1992) 'NGO Development Projects and Environmental Assessment', unpublished MSc thesis, School of Planning, Oxford Brookes University

Moore-Lappé, Frances, Joseph Collins, and Peter Rosset with Luis Esparza (1998) *World Hunger – 12 Myths* (second revised and updated edition), London: Earthscan

Mosse, David (1995), 'Authority, gender and knowledge – theoretical reflections on Participatory Rural Appraisal', *Economic and Political Weekly*, March 18, 1995

Mouchel & Partners (1996) 'Independent Development Trust: Environmental Manual', funded by the UK ODA, unpublished mimeo

Murton, John (1997) 'Sustainable Livelihoods in Marginal African Environments? The social and economic impacts of agricultural intensification in Makueni District, Kenya', paper presented to the ESRC Conference on Sustainable Livelihoods in Marginal African Environments, Sheffield University, 10-11 April 1997

Mwalyosi, Raphael and Ross Hughes (1998) *The Performance of EIA in Tanzania*, IRA Research Paper no. 41 and IIED Environmental Planning Issues no.14, London: IIED

Myers, Norman (ed.) (1994) *The Gaia Atlas of Planet Management* (revised and extended, with an extra chapter by Oxfam), London: Gaia Books

Myers, Norman (1996) 'Environmentally Induced Displacements: the State of the Art', paper presented to the International Symposium on Environmentally Induced Population Displacements and Environmental Impacts Resulting from Mass Migrations, Geneva: IOM/UNHCR/RPG

Naess, Arne (1973) 'The shallow and the deep, long-range ecology movement', in *Inquiry*, 16 pp. 95-100

Naess, Arne (1989) *Ecology, Community and Life Style: Outline of an Ecosophy*, Cambridge: Cambridge University Press

Neefjes, Koos (1993a) 'Participatory Environmental Assessment and Planning for Development: report on a workshop in Cambodia', mimeo, Oxford: Oxfam

Neefjes, Koos (1993b) 'Sustainable Resource Management in Asia/ME – report of an Oxfam workshop', mimeo, Oxford: Oxfam

Neefjes, Koos (1993c) 'South-South Exchange "Campesino a Campesino", Managua, 2-9.9.93', mimeo, Oxford: Oxfam

Neefjes, Koos (1994) 'Workshop on Sustainable Livelihoods, Agriculture and Environment, Oxfam - Bangladesh, 11-15 May 1994', mimeo, Oxford: Oxfam

Neefjes, Koos (1995a) 'Resettlement in Northern Mutara – a Report of a Participatory Planning Exercise', mimeo, Kigali: Oxfam

Neefjes, Koos (1995b) 'Oxfam (UK&I) in Vietnam and Sustainable Livelihoods, a report on an advisory mission (15.4-10.5.1995)', mimeo, Oxford: Oxfam

Neefjes, Koos (1995c) 'Trip Report Namibia, 16.11-4.12.95', mimeo, Oxford: Oxfam

Neefjes, Koos (1996a) 'A Short Report on a Workshop on PRA and Land Issues in Ololosokwan village, Ngorongoro District, Tanzania', mimeo, Oxford: Oxfam

Neefjes, Koos (1996) 'Sustainable livelihoods: What's in it for AT?', *Appropriate Technology* vol.23 no.3, Rugby: ITDG

Neefjes, Koos (1997a) 'Displacement and Environmental Change in the Great Lakes Region – Do we need to respond? A Discussion Paper for Novib and Oxfam (UK&I)', April 1997, mimeo, Oxford/The Hague: Oxfam/Novib

Neefjes, Koos (1997b) 'Report of a Workshop on Food Security in Southern Africa', mimeo, Oxford: Oxfam

Neefjes, Koos (*et al.*) (1997c) 'Training of PLA Trainers: the scope of participation in extension, monitoring and evaluation – report of an international workshop by & for Oxfam in Southern Africa, Mulanje, Malawi', mimeo, Oxford: Oxfam

Neefjes, Koos (1998a) 'Food Security in Southern Niassa – A mid-term review of the impact of Oxfam's programme in Nipepe, Metarica and Maua districts', mimeo, Cuamba/Nipepe/Oxford: Oxfam

Neefjes, Koos (1998b) 'Oxfam's Impact on Livelihoods in Lung Vai – a study of change in a commune in Lao Cai Province, Vietnam', mimeo, Hanoi/Oxford: Oxfam

Neefjes, Koos (1998c) 'Ecological needs of communities during and after dryland crises', in H.D.V. Prendergast, N.L. Etkin, D.R. Harris and P.J. Houghton (eds), *Plants for Food and Medicine*, Kew: Royal Botanic Gardens

Neefjes, Koos (1999a) *Participatory Review in Chronic Instability – the Experience of the 'Ikafe' Refugee Settlement Programme, Uganda*, London: ODI

Neefjes, Koos (1999b), 'Ecological degradation: a cause for conflict, a concern for survival' in Dobson (ed) (1999)

Neefjes, Koos (1999c) 'Oxfam GB and Sustainable Livelihoods: lessons from learning', paper presented at the Natural Resources Advisors Conference (NARC) 12-15 July 1999, Sparsholt Agricultural College, Winchester, Oxford: Oxfam

Neefjes, Koos (2000a) 'People defining their environments: a future of change', in Alan Holland, Keekok Lee, and Desmond McNeill (eds) (2000) *Global Sustainable Development: An Ethical and Practical Challenge to the 21ˢᵗ Century*, Edinburgh: Edinburgh University Press

Neefjes, Koos (2000b) 'Learning from participatory Environmental Impact Assessment of community centred development: the Oxfam experience', in: Bhaskar Vira and Roger Jeffrey (eds) (2000) *Participatory Natural Resource Management: Analytical Perspectives*, London: Macmillan

Neefjes, Koos and Rosalind David (1996) 'A Participatory Review of the Ikafe Refugee Programme', mimeo, Oxford: Oxfam

Neefjes, Koos, Rob Hart, and Mariam Dem (1996) 'Examples of urban development work from Senegal and Egypt', in Nicolas Hall, Rob Hart, and Diana Mitlin (eds) (1996) *The Urban Opportunity – The work of NGOs in Cities of the South*, London: Intermediate Technology

Neefjes, Koos, Paramu Mafongoya, and Muthoni Mwangi, with Eliud Ngunjiri and Esther Mugure (1997) 'Conservation Farming, Food Security and Social Justice – A sectoral review of agricultural work with small NGOs and national networking by Oxfam-Kenya', mimeo, Nairobi/Oxford: Oxfam

Neefjes, Koos and Beatrice Nakacwa (1996) *To PEA or not to PEA? Assessment of Learning Needs on Environment & Development of some Ugandan NGOs*, Oxfam/Novib/SNV & Environmental Alert

Neefjes, Koos and John Rowley (1994) 'Report On a PRA Workshop in North Tokar, Sudan, April 1993', mimeo, Oxford: Oxfam

Neefjes, Koos and Amal Sabri (1996) 'Community and Environmental Health in the Moqattam – Report on training in Participatory Learning and Action, and assessment of environmental health and project impact', mimeo, Cairo/Oxford: Oxfam

Neefjes, Koos and Abraham Woldegiorgis (1999) 'Environments, Livelihoods and Staff Capacity: An assessment of impacts of training', mimeo, Oxford: Oxfam

Nelson, Nici and Susan Wright (eds) (1995) *Power and Participatory Development: Theory and Practice*, London: Intermediate Technology

NGLS (1997) *Implementing Agenda 21: NGO Experiences from Around the World*, Geneva: UN Non-Governmental Liaison Service/UNCTAD

Nuffield Council on Bioethics (1999) *Genetically Modified Crops: the Ethical and Social Issues*, London: The Nuffield Foundation

ODA (1996) *The Manual of Environmental Appraisal*, London: Department for International Development (DFID)

OPP Research and Training Institute (1996) *The Orangi Pilot Project, Pakistan*, London: IIED

Osborn, D. and T. Bigg (1998) *Earth Summit II – Outcomes and Analysis*, London: Earthscan

Oxby, Clare (1994) *Restocking: A Guide. Herd Reconstitution for African Livestock-Keepers as Part of a Strategy for Disaster Rehabilitation*, Roslin (UK): VETAID

Oxfam UK & Ireland (1993) *Women and the Environment,* special edition of *Focus on Gender,* edited by Geraldine Reardon, Oxford: Oxfam

Oxfam UK & Ireland (1994a) 'PRA and Planning for Sustainable Development: report on a workshop in Muong Kuong District, Vietnam', mimeo, Oxford/Hanoi: Oxfam

Oxfam UK & Ireland (1994b) 'Exchanging Livelihoods – pilot edition', unpublished collection of case studies, Oxford: Oxfam

Oxfam UK & Ireland (1994c) 'Report of a Workshop on Sustainable Livelihoods for Some Oxfam Staff and Partners, Manchester June 30 & July 1 1994', mimeo, Oxford: Oxfam

Oxfam UK & Ireland (1994d) 'Discussion Paper on Sustainable Livelihoods', internal memorandum, Policy Department, 18.2.1994

Oxfam UK & Ireland (1995a) 'Exchanging Livelihoods – Urban Eition', unpublished collection of case studies, Oxford: Oxfam

Oxfam UK & Ireland (1995b) 'Guidelines for Strategic Planning, Action Planning and Reporting', mimeo, Oxford: Oxfam

Oxfam UK & Ireland (1996a) 'Land Tenure and Claims in Ololosokwan, Ngorongoro District in Tanzania', mimeo, Arusha: Oxfam/KIPOC

Oxfam UK & Ireland (1996b) 'Supporting Communities to Withstand Shocks and Stresses: a Developmental Approach (A study of 5 ODA/Oxfam(UK&I)-funded projects in Peru)', mimeo, Oxford: Oxfam

Oxfam UK & Ireland (1997a) 'Exchanging Livelihoods – Food Security Edition', unpublished collection of case studies, Oxford: Oxfam

Oxfam UK & Ireland (1997b) 'Programme and Project Management and Support Guidelines', draft March 1997, Oxford: Oxfam

Oxfam UK & Ireland (1998) 'Reporte del trabajo sobre evaluación de impacto con las contrapartes de Oxfam UK/I en Copán, Honduras, del 3 al 7 de febrero de 1998', mimeo, Oxford: Oxfam

Oxfam GB (1999a) 'Oxfam (GB)'s Work With Agricultural Communities in Kenya: Promoting Food Security and Social Justice Through Conservation Framing, A Review of Project Impact', Report for DFID, Oxford: Oxfam

Oxfam GB (1999b) 'Exchanging Livelihoods – Natural Resources Edition', unpublished collection of case studies, Oxford: Oxfam

Oxfam GB (1999c) 'Draft Proposal: Revised SCOs as of 7 May 1999', internal mimeo, Oxford: Oxfam

Owen, Dan (1996) 'The Mozambique Participatory Poverty Assessment: Lessons from the Process', paper presented at the PRA and Policy Workshop, 13-14 May 1996, Brighton: IDS

Pallen, Dean (1996) 'Environmental Assessment Manual for Community Development Projects' (draft version), CIDA-Asia Branch

Palmer, Robin (1997) *Contested Lands in Southern and Eastern Africa: A Literature Survey,* Oxford: Oxfam

Panos (1997a) *People and Parks: Wildlife, Conservation and Communities*, media briefing, London: Panos

Panos (1997b) *Green or Mean: Environment and Industry Five Years on from the Earth Summit*, media briefing, London: Panos

Pasteur, Katherine (1994) 'Environmental Appraisal of Development Projects: the Opinions and Practices of Non-governmental Organisations', unpublished dissertation, Department of Geography, University of Strathclyde

Paul, Bardolf (1996) 'Scaling-up PRA: Lessons from Vietnam', paper for the PRA and Policy Workshop 13-14 May, Brighton: IDS

Payne, Lina (1998) *Rebuilding Communities in a Refugee Settlement – a Casebook from Uganda*, Oxford: Oxfam

Payutto, P.A. (1993) *Good, Evil and Beyond: Kamma in the Buddha's Teaching*, Bangkok: Buddhadhamma Foundation

Payutto, P.A. (1994a) *Buddhist Solutions for the Twenty-first Century*, Bangkok: Buddhadhamma Foundation

Payutto, P.A. (1994b) *Buddhist Economics: A Middle Way for the Market Place*, Bangkok: Buddhadhamma Foundation

Pearce, David, Anil Markandya, and Edward B. Barbier (1989) *Blueprint for a Green Economy*, London: Earthscan

Pearce, David (ed.) (1991) *Blueprint 2: Greening the World Economy*, London: Earthscan

Peet, Richard and Michael Watts (eds) (1996) *Liberation Ecologies: Environment, Development, Social Movements*, London & New York: Routledge

Penning-Rowsell, Edmund (1998) 'The floods in Poland and Germany in 1997: report of a visit on the 25th-30th January 1998', in: Green Cross (1998)

Pepper, David (1984) *The roots of Modern Environmentalism*, London: Routledge

Periperi (1999) *Risk, Sustainable Development and Disasters: Southern Perspectives*, Rondebosch: Periperi Publications (University of Capetown)

Pickering, Kevin T. and Lewis A. Owen (1994) *An Introduction to Global Environmental Issues*, London and New York: Routledge

Pigou, A.C. (1920) *The Economics of Welfare*, London: Macmillan

Ponting, Clive (1991) *A Green History of the World*, London: Penguin

Pretty, Jules (1994), 'Alternative systems of inquiry for a sustainable agriculture', *IDS Bulletin* vol.25 no.2, Brighton: IDS

Pretty, Jules (1995) *Regenerating Agriculture: Policies and Practice for Sustainability and Self-reliance*, London: Earthscan

Pretty, Jules (1999), 'Genetic modification of crops: partner or pariah for sustainable development?', *The Biochemist*, October 1999, pp 19-25, The Biochemical Society

Pretty, Jules N. and Irene Guijt (1992) 'Primary Environmental Care: an alternative paradigm for development assistance', *Environment and Urbanization*, Vol. 4, No. 1, April 1992

Pretty, Jules N., Irene Guijt, John Thompson, Ian Scoones (1995) *A Trainer's Guide for Participatory Learning and Action*, London: IIED

Prior, Julian (1994) *Pastoral Development Planning*, Oxford: Oxfam

Pye-Smith, Charlie and Grazia Borrini-Feyerabend, with Richard Sandbrook (1994) *The Wealth of Communities: Stories of Success in Local Environmental Management*, London: Earthscan

Rabinovitch, Jonas (1998) 'Global, regional and local perspectives towards sustainable urban and rural development', in Fernandes (1998)

Rangan, Haripriya (1996), 'From Chipko to Uttaranchal – development, environment, and social protest in the Garhwal Himalayas, India', in: Peet and Watts (eds) (1996)

Rahnema, Majid (1992), 'Poverty', in Wolfgang Sachs (1992) *The Development Dictionary: A guide to knowledge as power*, London/New Jersey: Zed Books

Rahnema, Majid with Victoria Bawtree (eds) (1997) *The Post-development Reader*, London: Zed Books

Rayner, Steve and Elizabeth L. Malone (1998) *Ten Suggestions for Policy Makers: Guidelines from an International Social Science Assessment of Human Choice and Climate Change*, Columbus: Batelle Press

Rakodi, Carole (1999) 'Tackling Urban Poverty: Principles and Practice in Project and Programme Design', (paper presented at a seminar at Oxford Brookes University, 1999), Department of City and Regional Planning, Cardiff University

Redclift, Michael (1987) *Sustainable Development – Exploring the Contradictions*, London and New York: Routledge

Reed, David (ed) (1992) *Structural Adjustment and the Environment*, London: Earthscan (with WWF International)

Reijntjes, C, B Haverkort, and A Waters-Bayer (1992) *Farming for the Future, an Introduction to Low-external-input and Sustainable Agriculture*, London/Leusden: MacMillan/ILEIA

Renner, Michael (1996) *Fighting for Survival – Environmental Decline, Social Conflict, and the New Age of Insecurity* (The Worldwatch Environmental Alert Series) New York/London: W.W. Norton

Richards, Paul (1996) *Fighting for the Rain Forest: War, Youth and Resources in Sierra Leone*, Oxford/Portsmouth (NH): James Currey/Heinemann/with the International African Institute

Roche, Chris (1999) *Impact Assessment for Development Agencies: Learning to Value Change*, Oxford: Oxfam

Rocheleau (1995) 'Gender and biodiversity: a feminist political ecology perspective', in Joekes *et al.* (1995)

Roe, Dalal-Clayton and Hughes (1995) *A Directory of Impact Assessment Guidelines*, London: IIED

Rosset, Peter (1994) *Two Steps Back, One Step Forward: Cuba's National Policy for Alternative Agriculture*, London: IIED

Sachs, Wolfgang (ed) (1992) *The Development Dictionary: A Guide to Knowledge as Power*, London / New Jersey: Zed Books

Sachs, Wolfgang (ed) (1993) *Global Ecology: A New Arena of Political Conflict*, London/New Jersey: Zed Books

Sandilands, Catriona (1998) 'The good-natured feminist: ecofeminism and democracy', in Keil *et al.* (eds) (1998)

Sarangi, Satinath (1998) 'The Movement in Bhopal and its lessons', in Williams (ed.) (1998)

Sarupria, Shantilal (1994) 'Paradigms of an integrated technology policy for development', *Science, Technology and Development*, Vol. 12 no 1, London: Frank Cass

Satterthwaite, David (1996) 'Urban poverty: reconsidering its scale and nature', in Arjan de Haan (ed) (1997) 'Urban Poverty: A New Research Agenda', *IDS Bulletin* Vol. 28, no 2, April 1997

Schumacher, E.F. (1973) *Small is Beautiful: a study of economics as if people mattered*, London: Sphere Books (Abacus edition, first published in 1974)

Scoones, Ian (ed) (1995) *Living with Uncertainty – New Directions in Pastoral Development in Africa*, London: Intermediate Technology

Scoones, Ian (1998) *Sustainable Rural Livelihoods: a framework for analysis*, IDS working paper no. 72

Scoones, I., M. Melnyk, and J. N. Pretty (1992) *The Hidden Harvest: Wild Foods and Agricultural Systems – a Literature Review and Annotated Bibliography*. London: IIED

Scott, Andrew (1998) *The Environmental Impact of Small Scale Industries in the Third Word*, Global Environmental Change Programme Briefing May 1998, Brighton: GEC

SEAMEO (1997) 'Policy Consultation -Workshop of Oxfam (UK&I) and Partners on Sustainable Resource Management of Indigenous People's Ancestral Domain – summary documentation', mimeo, 15-18 January 1997, SEAMEO Innotech, Diliman, Quezon City, Philippines

Sen, Amartya (1981) *Poverty and Famines: An Essay on Entitlements and Deprivation* Oxford: Clarendon Press

Shepherd, Andrew (1998) *Sustainable Rural Development*, Basingstoke / London: Macmillan

Shestakov, Alexander (1998) 'Pipeline oil spill in Komi Republic, Russia', in: Green Cross (1998)

Shiva, Vandana (1988) *Staying Alive: Women, Ecology and Development*, London/New Delhi: Zed Books/Kali for Women

Shiva, Vandana (1996) *Caliber of Destruction: Globalisation, Food Security and Women's Livelihoods*, Manila: ISIS

Smith, Richard (1997) 'Greater Horn of Africa Workshop Report – Advancing PLA', mimeo, Oxford: Oxfam

Smyth, Ines (1997) *Industrialisation and Natural Resources: Household Adaptive Strategies in Java, Indonesia*, Bandung: Akatiga

Smyth, Ines and Koos Neefjes (1997) 'Gender and Natural Resources Management in East Asia: A Natural Link?', Report of the AGRA-East workshop 24-28 September, Yogyakarta, mimeo, Oxford: Oxfam

Sphere Project (1998*) Humanitarian Charter and Minimum Standards in Disaster Response,* First edition, Geneva: IFRC

Spinney, Laura (1998) 'Biotechnology in Crops: Issues for the Developing World', mimeo, Oxford: Oxfam

Spooner, Bryan and Nigel Walsh (1991) 'Fighting for Survival: Insecurity, People and the Environment in the Horn of Africa, IUCN Sahel programme study report'; edited and published separately as Robert A. Hutchison (ed) (1991) *Fighting for Survival: Insecurity, People and the Environment in the Horn of Africa*, Gland: IUCN

Steinbrecher, Ricarda (1998) 'Gene-ecology: more than one reason to protect food and environment from genetic engineering', *Resurgence*, April 1998

Stillwell, Matthew and Charles Arden-Clark (1998) 'The WTO shrimp-turtle ruling: international trade versus the global environment', in *Dispute Settlement in the WTO: a crisis for sustainable development*, WWF/Oxfam/CNI/CIEL

Störig, Hans Joachim (1972) *Geschiedenis van de filosofie*, (volumes I and II) Utrecht/Antwerpen: Het Spectrum

Suliman, Mohamed (ed) (1999) *Ecology, Politics and Violent Conflict*, London/New York: Zed Books

Satterthwaite, David and Cecilia Tacoli (2000) *Seeking an Understanding of Poverty that Recognises Rural-Urban Differences and Rural-Urban Linkages*, IIED Working Paper, London: IIED

Thomas, Alan, Joanna Chataway, and Marc Wuyts (eds) (1998) *Finding Out Fast: Investigative Skills for Policy and Development*, London/Thousand Oaks/New Delhi: Sage Publications (in association with The Open University)

Tiffen, Mary, Michael Mortimore, and Francis Gichuki (1994) *More People, Less Erosion – Environmental Recovery in Kenya*, Chichester/New York/etc.: John Wiley

Tolba, M. and O. El-Kholy *et al.* (eds) (1992) *The World Environment 1972-1992. Two Decades of Challenge,* Chapman & Hall on behalf of UNEP

Ullrich, Otto (1992) 'Technology' in Sachs (ed) (1992)

UNDP (1992) *Handbook and Guidelines for Environmental Management and Sustainable Development*, Environment and Natural Resources Group, New York: UNDP

UNDP (1998) *Human Development Report 1998*, New York/Oxford: Oxford University Press

UNDP (1999) *Human Development Report 1999*, New York/Oxford: Oxford University Press

UNHCR (1996) *Environmental Guidelines*, Geneva: UNHCR

UNHCR (1998a) *Environmental Guidelines: Forestry in Refugee Situations*, Geneva: UNHCR

UNHCR (1998b) *Environmental Guidelines: Domestic Energy in Refugee Situations*, Geneva: UNHCR

UNHCR (1998c) *Environmental Guidelines: Livestock in Refugee Situations*, Geneva: UNHCR

UNHCR (1998d) *Environmental Management within Refugee Operations: Training Module*, Geneva: UNHCR

Wackernagel, Mathis and William Rees (1996) *Our Ecological Footprint: Reducing Human Impact on the Earth*, Gabriola Island, BC: New Society

Walker, P. (1989) *Famine Early Warning Systems: Victims and Destitution*, London: Earthscan

Warren, D. Michael, L. Jan Slikkerveer, and David Brokensha (eds) (1995) *The Cultural Dimension of Development: Indigenous Knowledge Systems*, London: Intermediate Technology

Watkins, Kevin (1995a) *The Oxfam Poverty Report*, Oxford: Oxfam

Watkins, Kevin (1995b) *Agricultural Trade and Food Security*, Quezon City: Oxfam UK & Ireland (Philippines)

Watkins, Kevin (1998) *Economic Growth with Equity: Lessons from East Asia,* Oxford: Oxfam

Watts, Michael (1998), 'Nature as artifice and artifact', in Braun and Castree (eds) (1998)

WCED (World Commission on Environment and Development) (1987) *Our Common Future,* Oxford/New York: Oxford University Press

WFP (1999) 'An Overview of Vulnerability Analysis and Mapping', draft March 1999, Rome: WFP

Williams, Christopher (1997) *Terminus Brain: The Environmental Threats to Human Intelligence*, London and Washington: Cassell

Williams, Christopher (ed.) (1998) *Environmental Victims: New Risks, New Injustice*, London: Earthscan

Williams, Suzanne with Janet Seed and Adelina Mwau (1995) *The Oxfam Gender Training Manual*, Oxford: Oxfam

Wilson, Gordon (1995) 'Technological capability, NGOs, and small-scale development projects', *Development in Practice* 5/4: 128-42

World Bank (1991) *Environmental Assessment Sourcebook*, 2 volumes, Washington: IBRD

World Bank (1992) *World Development Report 1992: Development and the Environment*, Washington/Oxford: IBRD/Oxford University Press

World Bank (1995) *World Bank Participation Sourcebook*, Washington: IBRD

Worster, Donald (1993), 'The shaky ground of sustainability', in Sachs (ed) (1993)

Index

activism 99–100, 213
Africa
    Horn of Africa, livelihood and survival
        strategies 41
    nature conservation and tourism
        groups 181
    nature parks 17
    rational actions of pastoralists 54,158
    see also Congo, Democratic Republic
        of; Guinée (West Africa); Kenya;
        Liberia; Mozambique; South Africa;
        Tanzania; Uganda
Agarwal, Bina 25–6
Agenda 21 14, 15, 163, 185, 196–7
Agent Orange 38
Agreement on Agriculture (AoA) 211–13
agriculture
    and biodiversity 183–91
    effects of intensification 207
    Lung Vai, Vietnam 71–9
    recovery of production 156–9
    and refugees 138, 151–2
    southern Niassa, Mozambique 63–4,
        69–9, 79, 150
    subsidies and support for in rich
        countries 211
    and trade 211–14
    see also conservation farming; Green
        Revolution; sustainable agriculture
agro-ecological systems 37, 185
agro-ecological zones, shifts of 199
agro-forestry, Lung Vai 76, 150
aid money 207
Albania, permaculture and sustainable
    agriculture techniques 189–90

analytical processes, in PLA 104–5, 105
appraisal 240n
assets see capitals
atmosphere 20–1, 82

Bangladesh 46
    floods 26, 36, 123, 199
    small workshops 194
        EIA 131–2
        health and safety risks 111, 131, 133–4
        review of environmental impact of 62
'behaviour', ways of understanding 145
benefit-cost ratios and projections
    118–19, 135
biocentrism, of deep ecology 16
biodiversity 41, 81, 185
    and agriculture 183–91
    dependency of poor people on 4
    ecological diversity 47
    and GM crops 186–8
    of rainforests 180
Biosafety Protocol 15, 211
biotechnology 81–2, 186–8, 209
Blaikie and Brookfield, on political
    ecology 21–3
Bolivia, patenting problems 209
Boserup, Ester, challenged Malthusianism
    13, 22
Brazil
    Curitaba, 19, 57
    dam, São Francisco river 192
    extractive reserves 18
    Hunger Campaign 190–1
    MST (Movimento Sem Terra)181, 189,
        244n

Polo Petrolândia, and the Itaparica dam 124

protests about GM crops 55,188

rainforests, deforestation by colonisers 180–1

Recife, democratisation in 59–61,110, 149–50, 195

rubber tappers 18

Brundtland Commission
Our Common Future 14, 45, 50, 196
sustainable development defined 27, 45

Buddhism 11, 26, 27

Cairo, Egypt, and the Zabaleen 19, 62, 110–11, 195–6

Cambodia, Phnom Penh water-supply system 154–5

campaigns, by civil-society groups 177

Canadian Council for International Co-operation (CCIC), practical guidelines for rural community-based projects 125–6

capacity building 91

capital 87, 237n

capitals *83*, 86, 94, *96*, 147, 169
flows and substitutions 87
Honduras 148
livelihood capitals 86–7, *88–90*
represent an endowment 90
ultimate sources of 87
see also types of capital

carbon dioxide (CO$_2$) 199, 201, 202

Caribbean banana trade 214

carrying-capacity 53, *137, 138,* 158

Carson, Rachel, *Silent Spring* 13

cash-crops 64, 207

CCIC *see* Canadian Council for International Co-operation (CCIC)

change
attribution of 149–52
indicators of 146–9
negotiation of 98–112

checklists 7, 144, 81–2, 135

China
religions 12
Yangtse River, Three Gorges Dam 192–3

Chipko movement 25, 100, 238n

chlorofluorocarbons (CFCs) 199

Christianity 13

cities 56–7

citizens, participation in EIA and rights to information 122–4

citizens' groups 91

Clean Development Mechanism (CDM) 203

climate change 31, 81, 198–205

Climate Change Convention (1992) 14, 202

Club of Rome, *Limits to Growth* 14

clustering 95

Commission on Sustainable Development (CSD) 14, 15, 163

community development projects 124–40
EIA guidelines for 125–30
mass displacement and environmental quality 134–40
small enterprises, environmental impact of 130–4

complex emergencies 38, 39, 92

conditionality 208

conflict 35–6, 38–41, 43, 152
see also war

conflicts of interest, between North and South 36

Congo, Democratic Republic of, environmental impact of Rwandan refugees 42–3

conservation, community-based 181

conservation farming, Kenya 103, 110, 151, 190

conservationism, and the Third World 17–18

consumption
by the affluent drives environmental degradation 46
climate change and campaigning 203–5
high, environmental effects of 204
in modern economics 27
and technology 50–1
see also ecological footprints

Conventions
on Biodiversity 14, 210–11
on Climate Change 14, 202
on Plant Breeders' Rights 210
to Combat Desertification 14
see also Appendix 1

cost-benefit ratios, *see* benefit-cost ratios and projections

cotton industry, southern Niassa 66, 67

critical capital 29–30, 49
CSD *see* Commission on Sustainable
    Development (CSD)
Cuba, development of low-external-input
    agriculture 189
cyclones 31, *33*, 36, 154, 199

dams 192–3
debt 270
decision-making 152–3
deep ecology 16–17
defoliants 38
deforestation 18
    in the Brazilian Amazon 180–1
    enhances greenhouse effect 204
    Ikafe refugee camp, mitigated by
        afforestation 152
    Rimac valley, Peru 155
democratisation, Recife, Brazil 59–61
devaluation, impact of 206
developing countries
    Agreement on Agriculture (AoA)
    environmental management in 197
    legislation, effectiveness of and
        enforcement problems 120
    need for import protection 189
    needs, environments, and livelihoods
        208
    positive environmental effects of
        poorer people 52
    should be allowed to protect their food
        systems 213
    urban growth mainly of the low-
        consuming poor 56
    valuation of environmental resources 30
    see also Third World
development
    effects of dominance of male
        professionals 108–9
    gender and environment *see* gender,
        environment and development
    rights-based approaches to 85
development agencies 58,103
    aims of 80
    desired outcomes of livelihood
        strategies 85
    environmental policies and strategic
        plans 167–74

focus support in cities 61–2
    response to human disasters *32–4*, 35
    as stakeholders 101–2
    strategic plans 4–5
    and technological development 51
Dholai Khal project *see* Bangladesh, small
    workshops
diagrams, use of in environmental
    analysis 117
dialogues, semi-structured 107–8
disasters 8, 81, 153–4
    environmental and human causes 197
    more or less natural 31–7, 215
    people-induced 31–2
    potential impact increased for many 46
    slow-onset *34*, 35, 38
    vulnerability depends on income 46–7
diseases, tropical, potential spread to
    temperate zones 199
displaced people 42–4
    see also mass displacement; refugees
drinking water 66, 182, 192
drought 31, *33*, 36, 37, 47, 154, 199, 201
dryland degradation, reassessment of 54
dualism, in Western thought 13, 16, 24–5

early warning systems 37
Earth Summits
    II and III 15
    Rio (1992) 15,196
earthquakes 36, 154, 197–8
    and tsunamis *32*
eco-logical systems 20–1
ecofeminism 24–6
ecological diversity 47
ecological footprints 50
    of high consumers 46, 167–8, 203–4
ecology
    changes in 54
    deep ecology, an environmentalism
        16–17
    meaning questioned 20
    permissive ecology 54
    political 21–4
    shaping of 13
economic growth 17, 28
economic systems, sustainability of
    29–30, 48
economic-change processes 206

economics, modern 26–7
education
    Lung Vai 71
    in refugee settlements *139*
    southern Niassa 64, 69
EIA *see* environmental impact assessment
    (EIA)
El Niño 201–2
El Niño-Southern Oscillation effect
    (ENSO) 201
electricity generation 192–3
emergencies, 35, 43–4
emissions trading 203
EMP *see* Environmental Management Plan
    (EMP)
employment
    by small enterprises 130
    effects of stabilisation and structural
        adjustment 207
empowering/empowerment 99, 100
    dialogue and behaviour shifts 107–8
energy consumption 50
energy policies 15
environment
    definitions 1–2
    gender and development 24–6, 53
    global, management of 196–8
environment-conflict causal links 39
environmental analysis 115–21, 117, 125–6
    Dholai Khal project, Bangladesh 131
    Strategic Environmental Assessment 165
'environmental audit' 122
environmental change
    class-gender effects of 25–6
    and conflict 39
    local 81
    management of 4
    and political ecology 21–4
    theories of and environmentalism 16
environmental conservation 3
environmental data, access to 129–30
environmental degradation 8, 17, 177, 184
    by large enterprises and poor
        entrepreneurs 46
    campaigns to reduce 204
    caused by poverty and population
        growth, myth 52
    linked to poverty creation 3
    Papua New Guinea 179

and poverty 45–7
    reduces productivity 30
    through war 38
environmental economics 26–30
environmental factors, importance of 4
environmental health 59
Environmental Impact Assessment (EIA)
    8, 113–14, 161
    of community development projects
        124–40
    comparison with SEA *166*
    constraints on involvement of
        stakeholders 123–4
    consultative not participatory 123
    criticism of use in NGO-type projects
        124
    guidelines, use of 119–20
    Harrison's model (1992) 50
    improvements 120
    'informal' engineering workshops,
        Bangladesh 131–2
    limitation in transference to NGO-type
        projects 132
    large scale projects 115–24
        screening, scoping and full EIA
            115–21
    mitigation of negative impacts 119, 122
    a multidisciplinary study 117–19
    not fully relevant for refugee situations
        134–5
Environmental Impact Statement (EIS) 119
environmental impact(s)
    by refugees, 43, 134
    reduced by sectoral activities *137–9*
    cumulative impact of small-scale
        projects 5–6
    of EMPs, auditing of 121–2
    and livelihood outcomes 146–53
    and livelihood recovery, various
        disaster types *32–4*
    of small enterprises 130–4
    UNHCR guidelines 135–9
    of war 38
environmental issues, checklists of 81–2,
    135
Environmental Management Plan (EMP),
    implementation of 121–2, 197
environmental measures, in refugee
    responses (UNHCR) *136*

environmental myths 52–7
environmental policies
    anticipatory or reactive 28
    and strategic plans of development
        organisations 167–74
    and strategies of government 161–7
environmental policy, global, and
    campaigning 196–214
environmental policy documents,
    national 162–3
Environmental Profiles 163, *164*
environmental regeneration 5
environmental regulations 208
environmental resources
    and conflict 38–40
    as critical capital 29–30
    dependence on 2
    desired changes in 174–5
    and externalities 27
    future prospects for sustaining 112
    home-made 81
    local, social actors and interfaces
        causing pressure 111
    local management of and local
        participation 41
    present and future economic values 112
    valuation of in developing countries 30
environmental risk 47, 61–2
    from production improvements, Lung
        Vai 75
    southern Niassa 80
environmental screening 115–17
    CCIC guidelines for in NGO projects
        125–6
environmental and social changes,
    analysis of 111–12
environmental standards 166–7, 208–9
environmental sustainability 3, 6, 48, 49,
    52–3, 85, 148
environmental theory 20
environmental threats
    urbanisation and urban consumption 56
    related to climate 197–8
environmental treaties and conventions,
    international 14–16
    see also Appendix 1
environmentalism 8, 10–13, 25, 14–19, 44
equity 29, 52–3, 85
ethnic minorities, Lung Vai 72, 78

ethnicity, Rwanda 40
externalities 27, 112
extractive industries 4, 15
extractive reserves, Brazil 18

facilitators 106, 144
fair-trade organisations 214
famine 37, 92
farmer-to-farmer extension 77
    campesino a campesino movement 37,
        189
feedback mechanisms, and rise in Earth's
    temperature 199–200
finance and trade 207
financial capital 21, 87, *90*
    Lung Vai 73
    southern Niassa 66
flexibility mechanisms 203
floods/flooding 32, *33*, 36, 154
    Bangladesh 26, 36, 199
    Rimac river and valley, Peru 155–6
focus groups 106,110
Food and Agriculture Organisation (FAO)
    211
food aid 212
food crisis, global 54–6
food security 5,156
    effects of environmental degradation 30
    and genetic modification of crops *186–8*
    and the Hunger Campaign, Brazil 190
    southern Niassa 63–70
    and sustainable agriculture 184–5
food surpluses, dumping of 211–12, 213
forest degradation, by refugees *138*
forest fires *33*, 199, 201
forest foods 47, 63, 71
forests, Lung Vai 76
    see also rainforests
fossil fuels 51, 203–4

Gaia hypothesis 20–1, 200
gender
    environment and development 24–6, 53
    and gender relations, misconceptions
        109
    and knowledge 111
gender naivety, in PLA-based processes
    108–9
gender roles 156, 193–4
gene-banks 211

genetic modification 19
genetic resources 15, 172
  see also patenting; Trade Related
    Intellectual Property Rights (TRIPS)
    agreement
genetically modified (GM) crops 55,
  186–8, 211
global climate negotiations 202–3
Global Environment Facility (GEF) 14, 205
Global Forum, Rio (1992) 15
global warming 20–1, 199–200, 201
governments, environmental policies and
  strategies 161–7
grassroots movements 11, 181
  see also Chipko movement
green conditionality 208
Green Cross International 35
green manure 191
Green Revolution 19, 54–5, 183–4
greenhouse effect 198, 199, 201, 203–4
greenhouse gases 180, 199, 200, 293
guidelines
  on environmental impact, UNHCR 135–9
  internal, for NGO project appraisal 127–9
  and NGO staff capacities 6–7
  use of EIA guidelines 119–20
Guinée (West Africa), creation of forest
  patches by the poor 52, 94

hazard-prone areas 35
health 154
  Lung Vai 72, 75
  of poor urban people 47
  of refugees *137*
  southern Niassa 64
health problems
  from the Green Revolution 184
  from industrialisation 194
  from war destructiveness 38
health and safety, in small enterprises
  111, 131, 133–4
Hinduism 11
Honduras, developing impact indicators
  with NGOs 148–9
housing tenure, security of 195
human activity, and the global
  environment 20–1
human capital 21, 86, 87, *88*, 170, 184,
  215–16

Lung Vai 71–2
  southern Niassa 64
human development index (HDI) 48
human disasters 31, 154
human displacement *34*, 154
human security, described by UNDP 48
humanitarian agencies 135
humanitarian relief, minimum standards
  in 140
  Sphere Project 140, *141–2*
hurricanes 37, 46–7, 198–9, 233n

ice caps and glaciers, melting 202
impact assessment 5
import restrictions (GATT) 209
income generation, refugee settlements *139*
India 199
  Bhopal disaster 35, 194
  grassroots movements 11, 214
  Narmada River project 11, 193
  Trade Related Intellectual Property
    Rights agreement 210
  protests about GM crops 55, 188
  social movements 100
  see also Chipko movement
indigenous peoples 12, 25, 180
industrial areas, effects of exposure to
  toxic substances 194
industrial disasters *33*, 35, 36, 154, 194
industrial sites, auditing environmental
  impacts 122
industrialisation, and urbanisation 192–6
inequality 15, 19, 207
  due to the Green Revolution 55, 184
infrastructure damage 38
institutional development 91
interface encounters 103
interfaces 103, 107–9
intergenerational equity 85
Intergovernmental Panel on Climate
  Change (IPCC) 205
internally displaced people (IDPs) 42
international agreements on the
  environment (selected) 14–16, 217–20,
  Appendix 1
international aid agencies 168
International Institute for Environment
  and Development (IIED) 126
International Monetary Fund 198

International Undertaking on Plant
Genetic Resources 211
International Union for the Conservation
of Nature (IUCN) 27, 162, 231n
see also World Conservation Union
(IUCN)
intragenerational equity 29
investment capital 184
irreversible nature, type of environmental
sustainability 49
irrigation 192
Lung Vai 74
Islam 12

Java, industry affects livelihoods and
environments 193
Joint Implementation and Emissions
Trading 203

Kenya 173
conservation farming 101, 103, 151
impacts of NGOs and grassroots
groups 103, 190
increased tree densities 52
organic farming programme 151
Kosovo war, toxic pollution from
bombing raids 38
Kyoto Conference 202, 203, 205
Kyoto Mechanisms 203
Kyoto Protocol 203

labelling, mandatory 209
land 184
land degradation, discussed, Blaikie and
Brookfield (1987) 21–3
land and livelihoods 177–83
mining and traditional land rights
178–80
pastoralism and wildlife in Tanzania
181–3
rainforests in Brazil 180–1
land managers 21, 22–3, 53
land problem, and violence in Rwanda 40
land rights, traditional, Papua New
Guinea and Zambia 178–9
land tenure 5, 130, 173, 185
landesque capital 21
legislation
Lung Vai, Vietnam 74, 75, 177

Tanzania 183
Zambia 178
Leopold matrix 117, *118*, 135
Liberia, survival strategies 40–1
livelihood assets *see* capitals
livelihood capitals *176*
livelihood diversity 147
livelihood outcomes 82, *83*, 94–5, *96*
and environmental impacts 146–53
indicators of sustainable development
174, 175, *175*
overall aims of certain social actors 84–5
and strategies 84–6
livelihood strategies *83*, 84, 86, 93, 94–5,
96, 98, 147, 160
and hazard impact 36–7
Lung Vai 71
and public policies 215
southern Niassa, Mozambique 63–4
livelihoods
alternative, sought by the Maasai 182
analysis of 93–5, *96*
and environments
affected by industrialisation 193–4
Lung Vai, impacts on 74–7
southern Niassa, impact of Oxfam
programme 67–70
impact of small NGOs and grassroot
groups on, Kenya 103
and the policy process 3, 9
recovery and rehabilitation of 153–9
see also rural livelihoods
livelihoods improvement programme,
Zambia 178
livestock *89*
Lung Vai 71, 74, 77
patterns of herding 159
in refugee settlements *138*
small, southern Niassa 64, 157
see also pastoralism/pastoralists
Local Exchange and Trade Systems
(LETS) 19
log-frame (logical framework) 148, 174
logging 180
Lung Vai 71, 73
Lovelock, James, and the Gaia hypothesis
20–1
Lung Vai *see* Vietnam, Lung Vai,
improved livelihoods in

macro-economic policies 4, 171, 205–14, 215
Malaysia 208
Malthusianism 13
maps, combining data 135
marginality, of resources and people 22
market-based instruments 29–30, 162
markets
    Lung Vai 71
    southern Niassa 70
    and true values of environmental resources 27–8
Marxism/neo-Marxism 21–2, 24
mass displacement 38, 134–40
    see also displaced people; refugees
Mendes, Chico 18
methane (CH$_4$) 199, 204
micro-enterprises, southern Niassa 64, 68–9
migration, a survival strategy 41
mining and traditional land rights
    Papua New Guinea 178–9
    Zambia 178
mitigation measures, response to negative impacts 119, 122, 124, *138*
modernisation and globalisation 205–6
monitoring, of the Environmental Management Plan 121
motorways, effects of 204
Mozambique
    southern Niassa, food security 63–70, 109–10, 150
    effects of peace accords 66–7
    farmers' groups and capacities 68
    goods-for-work schemes 157
    impacts of Oxfam programme 67–70
    interface between traditional leadership and administration 78
    monitoring visits 97
    political wrangling, effects of 79
    rural communities defined 108
    sunflower oil and micro-enterprises 68–9
    support by Oxfam 157
    use of basic rainfall data 130

National Conservation Strategies (NCSs) 162
National Environmental Management Plans (NEMAPs) 162
National Strategies for Sustainable Development (NSSDs) 162, 163

natural capital 21, 7, 5, 7, *9*, 70
    Lung Vai 72–3
    maintenance of 29
    southern Niassa 65
    substitution to infrastructure 139
natural disasters *32*, 33, 154, 198–9
natural resources
    conflicting rights to manage 123
    and conflicts 38–41
    control over, central issue for poor and disadvantaged 5
    environmentally sustainable management of 41
    Indian, Gandhian view of 11
    management mainly by women 44
    protection and regeneration, Lung Vai 80
natural value, type of environmental sustainability 49
nature 2, 13, 16, 81
negotiation, to improve poor people's surroundings 109–12
NEMAPs *see* National Environmental Management Plans (NEMAPs)
neo-Malthusianism 13, 55
Net Food Importing Countries (NFIDCs), effects of Agreement on Agriculture (AoA) on 212–13
network diagrams 117, 35
NGOs 5
    influence on legislation and project-management procedures 180–1
    developing impact indicators in Honduras 148–9
    development
        empowerment as an aim 100
        lack detailed policies on environmental sustainability 167
        support low-external-input agriculture 167
    and development agencies, mandates of 3
    and environmental data 129–30
    and environmental sustainability in development programmes 127–8
    indirect support to livelihoods in the informal economy 61–2
    internal EIA processes and guidelines of and for 124–40
    internal guidelines for project appraisal 127–9

limited conceptual understanding of
poverty links 4
national and international, shift in
areas of work 6–7
opportunities offered by EIA 114
Polo Petrolândia, Brazil, mitigation
achievements 124
in Recife, Brazil 59–61
SCJP (Serviço Communitário de
Justiça e Paz) 59, 60,195
response to human disasters *32–4*, 35
Rio+5 15
role in development of low-external-
input agriculture 184–5
study of local participation in World
Bank Brazilian project 181
see also Oxfam GB
Nicaragua, effects of adjustment and
stabilisation 207
Nigeria, Ogoniland 18
NSSDs *see* National Strategies for
Sustainable Development (NSSDs)
nuclear disaster, Chernobyl 197

'optimal ignorance' 95
optimum yield 53
outcomes 86
over-grazing 158–9
Oxfam GB
Caribbean banana trade 214
grant-application procedure 5, 127
livelihoods and environments
impacts of Lung Vai programme on
74–7
impacts of southern Niassa
programme on 67–70
monitoring/assessment visits by 97–8
organic farming programme, Kenya 151
overall strategic aims 167
Strategic (Business) Plans 168
strategic planning guide 170–2
rehabilitation of Phnom Penh's water-
supply 154–5
sustainable livelihoods framework 7
ozone layer 15, 204

Papua New Guinea (PNG) copper mining
and growth of independence
movement 179
participation 58, 99, 100, 101, 152
in EIA and citizens' rights to
information 122–4
participatory analysis, and gender
relations 109
participatory approaches 104–9, 146
in Lung Vai 76–7, 78
to project management 7
to technology development 19
participatory environmental assessment
58, 142–6, *143*
Participatory Learning and Action (PLA)
104–5,142
advantages and productive uses of
tools 106–7, 126, 144
dialogues at the interface 107–9
weaknesses 145
see also Participatory Rural Appraisal
(PRA)
participatory methodologies 9, 96, 97, 153
Participatory Monitoring and Evaluation
(PM&E), application of PLA 145
participatory processes 84
can be exclusionary 108–9
local people central to 153
must involve women 140
Participatory Rural Appraisal (PRA) 70,
104, 144
Participatory Technology Development
232n
pastoralism/pastoralists 54, 158
patenting 55, 209
people–environment relations, theories of
20–30
people-power 102
Peru, Rimac river and valley 19, 155
156
pesticides 64, 80, 184
Philippines, the
environmental screening criteria 116
recognition of rights over 'ancestral
domains' 180
strategic plans, support poor
fisherfolks' livelihoods 172
support for campaigns against
industrial fishing 19

physical capital 87, *89*, 170
  Lung Vai 73
  southern Niassa 65–6
PLA *see* Participatory Learning and Action
  (PLA)
plants/plant-breeding processes 209
policies for consumption and technology
  50–1
  for focusing development programmes
    3–4
  management tools for formulation and
    implementation of 161
policies, processes and structures *83*, 84,
  90–2, 147, 152, 160, 170
  indicators of sustainable development
    176
  interaction between stakeholders 102
  in livelihoods analysis *96*
  Lung Vai 74
  southern Niassa 66–7
policy instruments 161–2
policy options, for humanitarian
  emergencies 44
policy processes 91, 160
political ecology 21–4, 25–6, 45, 53
political economy 24, 39, 102–3
'polluter pays' principle 162
pollution *33*, 122, 208
  by toxic substances 38, 194, 197
  cross-border 15, 82
  from fossil fuels 50
  industrial 193–4
  Rimac river and valley, Peru 156
poor people
  basis of urban livelihoods 62
  disaster risks greater for 37
  and improvement of livelihoods and
    environments 215
  and marginalised people, changing
    environments 111
  negotiation to improve surroundings of
    109–12
  positive environmental effects of 52
  positive valuation of the environment
    110,153
  urban 47
  very poorest 191
  and vulnerable people 90, 193
  see also rural poor
population growth 13, 50, 52

poverty
  and the environment 3, 7
  and environmental degradation 45–7
  urban, reduction of 195
  see also poor people
poverty alleviation 3, 4
power
  and action 99–103
  decentred and subjectless 101, 108
price and trade liberalisation 206
primary environmental care (PEC) 3, 52–3
problem trees 117
productivity increases 51
project achievements 147
project appraisal, by NGOs, internal
  guidelines for 127–9
project cycle (spiral) 113, *114*
  and EIA 115, *116*
  and environmental sustainability 8
  weak management, effect of 123
project management 98
projects 113–14
property rights, and sustainable
  development 53
public campaigns 162
public-expenditure cuts, results of 206
public policies, and livelihood strategies
  215

rainforests 180–1, 201
ranching 181
Rapid Rural Appraisal (RRA) 104, 144
refugee camps/settlements 4
  economic and environmental
    sustainability 43
  physical planning of *137*
  Tanzania and D.R. Congo 42–3
refugees 44, *137–9*
  see also displaced people
regulation, a policy instrument 50, 161
regulations, for minimising environmental
  impacts 111
resilience 22, 38–9, 93
resource taxes 162
resources
  and capitals, acess to 95
  depletion of 82
  pressure on 23
  see also environmental resources;
    genetic resources; natural resources

review processes, short-term 151
rice production, Lung Vai 71
rights
    of citizens to information 122–4
    policies and processes 90–1
    to environmental resources 172
    see also land rights; property rights;
        Trade Related Intellectual Property
        Rights (TRIPS) agreement
Rio Declaration 196, 120
    see also Agenda 21
risk analysis 118
risk mapping 37
risk and uncertainty 28
river development 192–3
rivers 15, 192–3
rural livelihoods 63–77, 154
    food security, southern Niassa,
        Mozambique 63–70
    lessons from Niassa and Lung Vai 77–80
    Lung Vai, Vietnam, improved 70–7
rural poor, and food security 184
rural–urban differences 59
Rwanda, causes of extreme violence 40

sanitation, for refugees *137*
Saro-Wiwa, Ken 18
savings *90*
scenarios, use of in EIA 118
Schumacher, E.F., *Small is Beautiful* 26–7
scoping *see* environmental analysis
SEA *see* Strategic Environmental
    Assessment (SEA)
sea-level rise 202
seasonality 92
seeds and tools projects 156, 157–8
Senegal–Mauritania border conflict 39
sequencing 95
shifting cultivation, Lung Vai 72, 76, 150
shocks 92
Sierra Leone, civil war 40
small enterprises, environmental impact
    of 130–4
SMART indicators, environmental impact
    147
social actors 86, 91, 97, 101, 102, 106,
    109, 111, 149
social capital 21, 48–9, 87, *88*, 102, 170
    Lung Vai 72
    southern Niassa 65

social change 101–2
social difference, consideration of 94
social groups 103, 106, 111
social oppression 18, 19
social sustainability 48
social-impact assessments 122
soil erosion 184, 192
    Lung Vai 72, 76
soil fertility 184, *187*
South Africa, Independent Development
    Trust 126
southern Niassa *see* Mozambique,
    southern Niassa, food security
Soviet Union (former), legacy of disaster
    threats 35
Sphere Project 140, *141–2*
SPICED properties, of indicator
    development 147
spiritual values 29
stakeholders 7, 8, 101, 122–4, 139–40,
    144–6
standards 129, 140, *141–2*
    see also environmental standards;
        patenting
Stockholm Conference (UNCHE: 1972) 14
Strategic Environmental Assessment (SEA)
    9, 163, 165–7
strategic planning 9, 168–72, *169*
    external context 169, 170–1
    internal resources, strengths and
        weaknesses 169, 171
    mandate and scope 168, 170
    and stakeholders 172
    strategies 170, 171–2
    use of sustainable livelihoods
        framework in 98
    vision and strategic aims 169, 171
structural adjustment 198, 206–7
subsidies 162, 211–13
substitutability 30
substitution 95
    capital substitution *88–90*
Sudan
    biodiversity reduced by mesquite tree
        41, 110
    civil war and internally displaced
        people 42
sui generis systems 210
sunflower oil, southern Niassa 68–9
survival strategies 41

sustainability 98, 44–57
  strong 56, 85
  weak or strong 28–9
sustainable agriculture 6, 19, 56
  an alternative to GM crops 188
  examples 189–91
  and food security 184–5
  sustainable farming techniques 103
  techniques and approaches 185
sustainable development 3, 8, 9, 14
  core aspects (Pearce *et al*) 27
  defined by Brundtland Commission 27,
    45
  equated with sustainable utility (Pearce
    et al) 28–9
  indicators of 174–5, *175–6*
  national policies and campaigns for
    177–96
    biodiversity and agriculture 183–91
    industrialisation and urbanisation
      192–6
    land and livelihoods 177–83
  planning for 161–76
  'strong' view 29
  what should be sustained? until when?
    48, 93
sustainable human development 48, 148,
  167, 243n
sustainable land-use 3
sustainable livelihoods 3, 8, 82–4, 94, 144
sustainable livelihoods analysis 127
sustainable livelihoods framework 7,
  80–98, 142, 215
  analysis of livelihoods 92, 93–5, *96*
  checklists of environmental issues
    81–2, 135
  environmental sustainability a key
    livelihood outcome 152
  generalised and ultimate
    changes/improvements 146–7
  hybrid approach 114–15, 140, 142–59
  lessons from practice 96–8
  livelihood capitals 86–7, *88–90*
  livelihood outcomes 174,175
    and strategies 84–6
  policies, processes and structures *83*,
    84, 90–2, 147, 152, 160
  some aims not articulated in the
    framework 85
  too abstract for field-level staff 98
  use of analytical framework remains
    weak 97
  vulnerability context 92–3
sustainable natural resource management
  (SNRM) 98
systems diagrams 117

Tanzania
  groundwater depletion by refugees 43
  NGOs fight for legislation serving land-
    users 183
  northern, data for assessment of land-
    tenure and ownership disputes 130
  pastoralism and wildlife 181–3
  Rwandan refugees 42
  Serengeti wildlife park 17, 182
  Singida region, Barbaig people 183
tariffs 162
taxation 162
technological optimism 28
technology development 22, 50 185
technology(ies) 27, 50–1, 185
tensions, internal and international, and
  conflict 35–6
terminator genes 55, 236n
Third World
  and conservationism 17–18
  countries marginal to many
    discussions/negotiations 197
  uneven playing field 211–12
tornadoes, and La Niña 202
tourism 15,181, 182
toxic chemicals/substances 38, 188, 194,
  197
trade, and agriculture 211–14
trade negotiations 208
trade policies 209
Trade Related Intellectual Property Rights
  (TRIPS) agreement 210, 211
trade-offs 95
traditional belief systems 12
traditional land rights, abused by
  government and mining companies
  178–9
The Tragedy of the Commons, Garret
  Hardin 13
trends 92, 95
triangulation (of information) 106, 145,
  146, 153

trigger mechanisms 39
TRIPS *see* Trade Related Intellectual
    Property Rights (TRIPS) agreement

Uganda, Ikafe refugee settlement 110,
    151–2
UK, Country Strategy Papers 168
UN General Assembly, Special Session
    1997 (Earth Summit II) 15
UNCED (UN Conference on Environment
    and Development) 14, 15, 167, 196
    see also Earth Summits, Rio (1992); Rio
        Declaration
UNCHE (UN Conference on the Human
    Environment, Stockholm) 14
UNDP
    Capacity 21 programme 197
    Country Programmes 168
        environmental overview of 173–4
    Handbook and Guidelines for
        Environmental Management and
        Sustainable Development 128
    Human Development Report 1994
        concept of sustainable human
            development 48
        human security described 48
    summary of project management
        (environmental guidance) 128–9
UNEP (UN Environment Programme:
    1972) 205
UNHCR
    environmental guidelines 6
    guidelines on environmental impact
        135–9
    initiatives rarely refer to sustainable
        development 44
    and refugee settlements 134
    training to increase staff environmental
        awareness 139
UPOV Convention on Plant Breeders'
    Rights 210
urban environments, and livelihoods
    59–63
urban infrastructure, recovery and
    rehabilitation of 154–6
urban livelihood improvement, key
    questions for 62–3
urban livelihoods, important factors in 94
urban poverty, reduction of 195

urban settlements, unsustainable 56
urban–rural migration 207
    urbanisation 36, 56, 192–6
USA
    and the Caribbean banana trade 214
    the Dust Bowl 53
    import bans on ethical or
        environmental grounds 209
    standard patenting criteria not applied
        to USA *neem* products 209

vegetation, climax theory of 53
Vietnam
    Lung Vai, improved livelihoods in 70–7
        Agroforestry Project 70, 76, 173
        change in government approach to
            land allocation 75
        commune discussion groups 72
        further support programmes 70–1
        important impacts of development
            programmes 150
        Land Allocation Project 70
        land allocations stimulate soil and
            water conservation 75
        Land Use Certificates 72, 74, 78–9,
            150, 173
        monitoring visits 97
        poor farmers and 'environment' 110
        poorest do not suffer environmental
            degradation 52
        water for drinking and irrigation 73
        Women's Union 78
    poorest families increase productivity
        and income 213
    use of defoliants by USA 38
volcanic eruptions *32*, 36, 154, 197–8,
    200
voluntary compliance 134
vulnerability 36, *83*, 84
    decreased in southern Niassa 70
    defined by trends, shocks and
        seasonality 93
    questions of 31–44
    reduction of and sustaining
        environments 47–50
    to natural disasters, should be reduced
        159
vulnerability context 92–3, *96*
    strategic planning 169, 170

war, 38, 68
water
   groundwater depletion by refugees 43
   supplies for refugees *137*
   use of, Lung Vai 73
West Arctic Ice Sheet 202
Western behaviour and views re nature
   13, 16
wild foods, a means of survival 41
women
   constraints on time 109
   in Lung Vai 72, 73, 74, 76, 78–9, 150,
      173,
   Maasai, increased burden 182
   and minority groups, participation and
      empowerment 108
   participation and influence, Niassa and
      Lung Vai 78–9
   the Philippines, indirect benefit of
      improved household security 172
   southern Niassa 65, 69–70, 110, 150
   special relationship with nature 24
   suffering during Bangladeshi floods 26
   voices often unheard during EIA 123
   Zambia, can have legal title to land 178
World Bank 205
   challenged by NGOs over Brazilian
      project 181
   PLANAFLORO, new approach to
      Brazilian Project 181

   supports NEMAPs 162
   withdrawal from Narmada River project
      193
World Commission on Environment and
   Development (WCED) 14
   see also Brundtland Commission
World Conservation Union (IUCN) 126
World Meteorological Office (WMO) 199
World Trade Organisation (WTO)
   Agreement on Agriculture (AoA) 211,
      212–13
   agreement on Trade Related
      Intellectual Property Rights (TRIPS)
      210, 211
   amendments and additions to 213
   and environmental matters 209
   and GM crops 188
   trade restrictions on environmental
      grounds not allowed 198, 209
World Wide Fund for Nature (WWF) 231n

Zaire *see* Congo, Democratic Republic of
Zambia, copper mining and traditional
   land rights 178
Zimbabwe
   Campfire programme 17, 181–2
   impacts of brick-making enterprises
      133
   promotion of organic farming 190